The World according to God

F. X. Cronin

The World according to God

The Whole Truth about Life and Living

SOPHIA INSTITUTE PRESS
Manchester, New Hampshire

Cover design by LUCAS Art & Design, Jenison, MI.

On the cover: detail from the Sistine Chapel.

Sophia Institute Press
Box 5284, Manchester, NH 03108
1-800-888-9344

www.SophiaInstitute.com

Sophia Institute Press® is a registered trademark of Sophia Institute.

ISBN 978-1-64413-235-7

ebook ISBN 978-1-64413-236-4

Library of Congress Control Number: 2020933964

First printing

To my wife, Annie, and my three daughters:
Kristine, Micki, and Molly.
Thank you for being who you are.
You are each a gift of God to me. God bless.

And to Dr. Ronda Chervin for her expertise,
her encouragement and her generosity,
for which I am ever grateful. God bless you, Ronda.

Contents

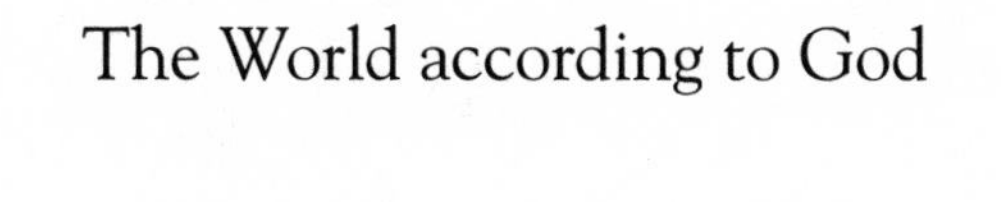

The World according to God

1

A Matter of Truth

When I became Catholic, it seemed everyone I knew, and even those I didn't, had some trouble with my decision. Whether people heard the news from me or through the grapevine, whether they knew me or just knew of me, they all seemed to have an undue amount of concern about my decision.

It wasn't as if I had decided to get divorced or to leave my job after years of commitment and work. It wasn't as if I had a midlife crisis or had abruptly changed my political affiliation or even my sexual orientation. Anyone who knows me knows I'm too stable for radical change, unless it's well founded and rational. But this change, or at least my reason for making it, seemed odd to most.

You see, I was born an Irish Catholic in the Bronx. Later, my parents moved to upstate New York. They raised my seven brothers and sisters and me as nominal Catholics, just as many are today. But by my late teens, I had cast off the routines of faith, because the reasons for having faith and believing in God no longer seemed remotely real.

A decade later, I began to be curious about God's existence, and I gradually left behind my professed atheism and found my way back to Him. Along the way, after working with troubled children and adolescents in residential, psychiatric, and group home settings, I picked up a master's degree at the University of Connecticut. With my master's, I began teaching troubled adolescents in the public schools. During my early teaching years, my wife and I had three daughters, and I found Jesus.

As I pursued my Christian faith and explored God's calling for my life, I found myself at a Protestant seminary and then at Harvard and Columbia, the two top graduate schools of education in the country. Pretty weird for a conservative Evangelical and former atheist.

I remained a Protestant for almost two decades. But when my secretary at the high school where I was an administrator asked me to read a book about a Presbyterian's conversion to Catholicism, my entire view of my faith changed within a few short months.

My conversion from Protestantism to Catholicism was a challenge for many of my friends and acquaintances and many members of my community, but at least I was still a Christian. After all, a Catholic is a Christian, right? Well, not necessarily, as I found out.

To many of my evangelical Protestant friends and acquaintances, converting to the Catholic faith was like contracting a diabolical, doctrinal disease, the theological equivalent of the bubonic plague. Others thought my conversion was the result of pride or sin (probably both) and would only lead me into further error, eventual idolatry, and ultimately spiritual death and damnation.

Even some of the Catholics I knew saw my move to Catholicism as a change based merely on personal preference, a decision arising from my desire for spiritual comfort and my need for philosophical certainty and practical closure. Many of my unreligious and irreligious friends and acquaintances saw this change in a similar vein, as a change in my personal preference, a matter of opinion and nothing more.

But whether they were Protestants or Catholics, atheists or agnostics, they all had trouble when I explained why I was becoming a Catholic: They did not think my reasons for converting were true or valid, except maybe for me. Most of my atheistic and agnostic friends and acquaintances generally did not believe there existed any actual objective and factual truth about life and how to live, let alone any such truth about God. Or they may have thought there was some truth about life, but not all that much.

Even for my Christian friends, truth was in short supply. Beyond some core ideas about God, Jesus Christ, the Trinity, the Scriptures, miracles, the virgin birth of Christ, and everlasting life, there was not much more to be had or to be certain of, no matter what your denominational affiliation.

And there I was, explaining my conversion in a language both unfamiliar and inflammatory to Christians and Catholics alike. For I explained to them that my decision was based on truth, on the truth of our factual existence and experience, on the truth of reason, the truth of history, the truth of our common sense.

I told them I was becoming a Catholic because the Catholics were right—the Catholic Church is where the fullness of truth is found. That's why I was becoming a Catholic. And while there is some small shadow of doubt that faith must dispel or disperse, the Catholic Church is the right church and the rightest church.

While there are sometimes shadows of doubt, shadows come in intensities, in degrees. And these shadows are not of such intensity as to be confusing. They are just the shadows of ambiguity and complexity, the shadows that require another level of analysis and sophistication to explore.

But no matter how I sought to explain and elaborate why I was becoming a Catholic, people resisted for one of two reasons:

1. Either they believed that there are no right answers about life in the ultimate sense or about living in the practical sense. They did not believe in truth as an idea or truth of any type or kind.

2. Or they believed that truth exists, but it must not be very extensive or particularly detailed beyond the fundamental doctrines of Protestantism.

Almost without fail, whether they were atheist or Protestant, Catholic or agnostic, they were either incredulous or incensed —and sometimes both. Because I maintained the existence of truth, I angered or befuddled my secular acquaintances. Because I maintained the certainty of the Catholic faith, many of my Protestant and Catholic friends and acquaintances became angry or perplexed too.

But were their reactions justified? Were they right to be angry or annoyed with me because I asserted that the Catholic faith is true? Were they right to be incredulous or patronizing or condescending to me when I asserted the truth of the faith?

For me, the answer is no—but their reactions are certainly understandable. My assertions about truth challenged some basic and pivotal beliefs they held dear. I directly challenged their belief in the complete absence of truth or in the amount and type of truth that can be known.

When these ideas, so crucial to life in the ultimate sense and living in the practical sense, are challenged in such a direct and flagrant manner, such reactions are more than understandable: they are almost inevitable.

Since all but the most courageous or curious avoid this discomfort and potential instability, it's not surprising that people prefer to blame the messenger rather than deal with the message directly.

And it is to this critical message of truth that we will now turn as we explore the world according to God. I will examine atheism and agnosticism, as well as science and reason, as I address the crucial question of God's existence. Then, I'll spend some time looking at who God is, according to the other major world religions. Next, I'll discuss Jesus and who He is, as well as the Church He instituted, and I'll compare the Protestant and Catholic faiths to determine which Christian faith is truly the right Christian faith, the truest faith.

Sound a bit arrogant, a bit narrow-minded? Well, it is, unless truth actually exists. But, if truth about God exists, then such a statement is not arrogant, but accurate, not narrow-minded, but clearheaded.

Remember, I told you this stuff is going to challenge the way we think nowadays. So, buckle up.

Let's begin without prejudice and predispositions. Let's take on the first real challenge—the idea of truth and how it can be known. Try to meet this idea with an open and active mind, eager to explore this bold and preposterous assertion. Try not to harden your heart or defend it too strongly. Try to keep your heart supple and receptive and your mind open and rationally curious.

Open yourself to the truth as it comes to you. For you are about to enter a reality both familiar and foreign, a reality that is rational and real, a reality that may seem preposterous, yet oddly predictable and more than possible—a world more than vaguely familiar.

2

Matters of Knowing

Truth is a provocative topic in the modern world and in our modern moment, particularly when the truth in question is about something as seemingly ambiguous and arbitrary as religion, religious philosophy, or morality. That is why my explanation for my conversion was so disconcerting or foolish to most people.

And so it should be, unless I could prove that my belief is true. For truth is always a matter of proof.

Now, for most of us in our modern world, science is the primary and singular source for factual truth. Science stresses methods and procedures designed to make sure that how we think our world works is how it does, in fact, work. This is why scientific studies are subjected to rigorous review, including replication, so we can all be sure that what we learn from science is certain and applied properly in keeping with the actual and factual scientific truth of things.

Biology, chemistry, and physics all generate truths that guide and inform the many applied sciences, such as engineering and medicine. This is why a continual process of research and experimental and applied verification exists in both the pure and applied sciences. And, all of this scientific-technological process yields a vast and expanding body of truth about the physical world in which we live.

But, when it comes to philosophical, religious, and moral truths, claiming that beliefs in these areas are actually and factually true can seem more than a bit arrogant, naïve, or ignorant. For the modern mind, such truth claims are matters of mere opinion or preference.

Science gives us facts that we can know for certain and apply and verify practically. But philosophy, religion, and morality give us ideas, theories cast in the light of divine imperatives, above analysis and question. These are matters of willful belief, not actual fact; matters that entail a blind leap of faith, not a rational and real response to reality.

Or are they? Are they simply matters of subjective opinion that are believed to be factual by the adherents of any and every faith? Or are they provable and demonstrable matters of fact?

Surprisingly, and shockingly to our modern minds, religious, moral, and philosophical truths are indeed provable and demonstrable with both science and reason.

And that is what this book is all about. For the remainder of this book, I will prove and demonstrate philosophical, religious, and moral truths. Science and reason will be my primary tools where appropriate. For instance, I will use science when addressing questions rooted in the physical world, such as the origin and order of the universe.

But reason and common sense, augmented by scientific fact where appropriate, will provide the method for the rest of the questions I address. For the remainder of this chapter, I will explore and refute the modern conclusion that science is the only way to know actual and factual truth.

Together, we will look at what science is and what its practical limits are. And we will look at the role reason plays in the scientific method and the dissemination and use of scientific findings. We will also examine reason's rules, its rigor, its reach, and its real power. Along the way, we will point out the flagrant and fatal contradictions of our modern view about what and how we can know anything, even the very idea of real truth.

The remainder of this chapter and each of its sections are crucial to the later chapters. So take your time with this material. When necessary, close the book and think deeply and critically about what is being said. For the purpose of the book is not to persuade you. It is to invite you to look deeply at reality and to see clearly the truth right in front of you.

Remember, let the truth persuade you. Don't just believe; be convinced. Be convinced by scientific facts and by rational proof. Be convinced by the harmonic certainty of science and reason. Be convinced, and then believe. And when you do believe, open yourself to God.

Knowing

According to the modern mindset, the best way to know anything is through science. In fact, most moderns believe that science is the only way to know anything. Most moderns believe that to know truly the facts about anything, those facts must be tested in a lab or in a rigorously and reliably controlled manner, following the scientific method.

Let's look closely at the scientific method to see just how it acquires such importance and power. And let's take time to analyze the basic premises guiding the scientific method, its practical applications, the tools guiding its use and its implicit assumptions. For pure science and applied science have discovered and developed the many modern marvels to which we attribute such veracity and certainty.

Probably the essential aim of the scientific method is rational and careful observation of the physical world. A rigorous observer will generate some educated guesses, some hypotheses, about the nature of the interesting phenomenon he is considering. In the fields of pure and applied science, scientific inquiry usually begins with some previously proved knowledge and some observations of the physical phenomenon under investigation.

Scientists and engineers typically make such observations through the senses directly or with the aid of some type of instrument. These observations prompt the observers to begin to develop some ideas about the behavior and nature of the observed phenomenon.

Such ideas are "hypotheses"—educated guesses about how and why such phenomena exist, about their structure and function, about their purpose and response to manipulation, and about what is known already about the phenomena under investigation.

Through this rigorous process, with its careful and rational observation, along with thorough documentation, critical analysis, and thoughtful review, our collective knowledge of the physical realm expands, growing more detailed and sophisticated with each passing year.

But the underlying crucial component guiding the entire process relies on principles that have little to do with observation and data and everything to do with logic, reason, and even common sense.

For observation in itself is inherently rational. Reason guides sound observation. Reason is the critical component in deciding what to observe, how to observe most effectively, how to understand what has been observed, and how to know the implications and meanings of the observed data.

In short, the scientific method cannot be scientific or accurate without an implicit rational basis. Reason must be infused all along the way, from the selection of the initial phenomena right through to the conclusions generated by the investigative method.

The scientific method is shot through with reason.

Imagine trying to do science without our rational minds, without the rules of reason, without our critical rational capacities, without the ability to distinguish a rightly reasoned scientific study or case from a fallacious one. Thankfully, this reasonless science doesn't really exist in the real world of the pure and applied sciences.

Science, when properly deployed, is the sole pathway to the facts about the physical world, which is the purview of the pioneering field of research science, and the proper application of those facts, which falls to the practical fields of engineering and medicine, for example.

In a word, science is *the* way to know the facts about the physical world, its nature, its behavior, its order, its immediate purpose.

But science and the scientific method offer not a singular but a composite way of knowing things. Science and its method rely on reason from the beginning to the end of the empirical process. They also rely on the accuracy of our senses and the order and predictability of the physical world. Finally, they rely on the certainty of the link between causes and effects.

Most scientists rightly assume that certain actions or causes on the part of the researcher could have effects related to these experimental actions, these experimental causes. That is why they conduct experiments. But good scientists conduct critical reviews to ensure that the observed effects are related to their deliberate, intentional causes and to determine the degree to which this cause-effect link is present.

Reason is essential to any scientific endeavor. So are the inherent order and predictability of the physical world, the reliability of our sensory perceptions, and the law of cause and effect. Without any of these, science would not be possible. It could tell us nothing. It would be a meaningless and fruitless waste of time.

By teasing out science's basic, yet crucial assumptions, we have unveiled science's composite nature. Science is truly built on three crucial facts about the physical world and one crucial fact about the intangible, yet equally real, mental world. Scientific knowledge is possible only if there is order to observe, if our senses are reliable, if the law of cause and effect holds true, and if our rational capacities and powers to know all these are, in fact, real.

But without our rational abilities to make sense of sensory data, without our rational abilities to see the order of things and the links between causes and effects, science would not exist. Our rational abilities are truly the keys to attaining knowledge through the scientific process.

Reason's role in scientific and technological advancement is crucial. Reason allows us to investigate our physical world and its many manifestations. This foundational reality and the preeminent role of reason in the scientific process are indisputable and unassailable. If someone were to dispute reason's crucial, foundational role in the scientific process, he would have to use reason to dispute this premise. In doing so, he would contradict his very point rationally, logically, and fatally.

To prove any case, even a case against reason, requires that we use reason properly and fully. Yet our inevitable use of reason contradicts the idea of reason's weakness or impotence.

But what about reason's capacities in and of itself? What can reason show us when applied to intangible things, not just physical things? Is it possible for us to know things that are not bound to the physical realm explicitly or implicitly?

We don't have to go too far from science to find a field that offers the same pure and applied uses of reason yet belongs to a more mental realm of inquiry, with its focus on the use of logic and reasoned proof to effect crucial certainties impacting even our scientific knowledge. This field is mathematics.

Mathematics is an innately logical field of study based on proofs derived through a logical process, which yields correct answers. Mathematics is often part of scientific investigations, from the social sciences and their use of statistics and probability, to physics and its use of calculus and other complex mathematical fields.

A typical way to understand the relationship of mathematics to science is to look at the various scientific fields hierarchically. A cellular view of biology reveals it is mostly chemistry, the interplay of chemicals beneath the structure and function of biological organs and systems. The closer we examine chemistry, the more we see that it is mostly physics, the mathematical descriptions of motion and dynamics of substances at the molecular level. Finally and most basically, physics is mostly mathematics, wherein reality is reduced to mathematical formulae and equations. A shorter version says simply, "Biology is all chemistry, chemistry is all physics, and physics is all mathematics."

So what is the point here regarding how we gain knowledge? Well, we know through science, but this is not the only way we know. Science is a composite way of knowing, and the scientific method is based on reason and proper reasoning, upon logic and rationality. Even in the different scientific fields, with their particular uses of mathematics, reason and its rules are present every step of the way. You simply can do neither science nor mathematics without reason.

Reasoning

But can reason get to truth all by itself? Can it demonstrate factual information or knowledge on the same level of certainty as the sciences can? Well, the dominant modern attitude about the explanatory ability of reason ranges from a deeply skeptical opinion of reason's capability and power to outright certainty that reason, on its own, is impotent when it comes to discovering truth.

To most moderns, reason and logic are really just manipulative means of persuasion, not proof, not actual and factual proof about reality or truth. In other words, reason on its own, without any connection to science, is a form of manipulative persuasion behind a mask of rationality and logic. Reason, for most moderns, is just a head game and nothing more without the verification inherent in the physical sciences. Corroboration through science is reason's only validation, the only way to prove that reason's guesses are actually true.

Such is our modern mindset about reason and the mind of man. And while this may seem a bit esoteric, an argument only for philosophers and academics, you can hear this same belief at your local coffee shop and in the many ways we express ourselves in modern times. This view of reason as merely persuasive and manipulative is ubiquitous in our modern world, though it is often implicit or inferentially explicit. It is almost an unconscious assumption of our culture. You can hear it in many of our common aphorisms, such as "Beauty is in the eye of the beholder" and "That's intolerant," or "Who are you to judge?" and "That's just your opinion."

This view of reason as valid only when linked to some form of physical verification is the source of modern relativism. Relativism's primary conclusion is that all of life, in its many facets and features, is merely a matter of personal perception or cultural belief, based on tradition and consensus.

But relativism is a natural and necessary consequence of the loss of reason's innate explanatory power when physical verification is the only standard for truth. And while physical verification is a necessary and essential feature of science, what is the standard for verification in the intangible realms of life's bigger questions, such as the nature and meaning of existence? What about the question of the origin of the rational abilities we all possess, experience, and use, or the truth about our human mind, personality, and such intangible things as love, goodness, and reasoning?

To put it another way, if reason is the guiding standard for research in science and application in engineering, why is reason's explanatory power lost when it is used in other ways? Why is reason not valid when it comes to questions and issues not connected to the physical domain of the sciences? What makes reason so impotent in matters of ideas, when it is so important to the advance of the sciences?

And just to add an odd twist to this case against reason's use and explanatory power in the realm of the mind and ideas, how can you prove that reason is limited to science and its physical uses? Wouldn't you have to make a reasoned case against reason's validity beyond its scientific and physical uses? And in making such a case against reason's inability to prove things about the mind and ideas, wouldn't you be contradicting yourself?

To use reason to prove that reason is incapable of proving anything about the intangible world of the mind and ideas is a fatal contradiction, by definition. To use reason to prove that reason is incapable of proving that truth exists and is knowable is flagrantly false, even to an untrained mind. Case closed. Game over.

Using reason to prove that reason doesn't work is not just a contradiction. It's downright stupid. Yet it is so commonplace today, it seems like a given.

So the obvious conclusion is that reason can prove things in the realm of science, as well as about things of the mind and the validity and certainty of ideas. This conclusion is not only obvious; it is inevitable. But not every reasoned case is properly reasoned: sometimes its rational validity is compromised because of how reason is used. And sometimes its premises, its initial observations, its starting points, are in error, are incomplete, are not soundly grounded in reality or reason.

So let's look at a couple of examples for clarity and practicality. Let's look at how reason, using sound observations about the physical world, points to some necessary conditions and conclusions about the origin and order of the physical world.

For instance, in science and in the scientific method, there is an inherent and observable truth about reality. Simply stated, every observed effect must have a cause. This law of cause and effect is a scientific certainty, a rational principle of observation and logical thought.

Effects don't just happen. Something or someone must cause them to exist. Be they a seed and flower in biology, the chemical elements hydrogen and oxygen combining to make water, or the forces of physics, realities of the observable universe must come to exist by some external cause, by some cause outside their discrete existence. For something does not and cannot come from nothing.

In a rational and logical sense, if something exists as an effect, it must have a cause. An effect with no cause is sheer nonsense, an irrational, illogical, and impossible conclusion. Causes necessarily and absolutely create effects, but no effect creates itself.

Well, if an effect must always be preceded by a cause, all of reality—space, time, matter, energy—must trace its ultimate origin back to some initial cause. Yet this initial cause must necessarily be uncaused. All of observed reality must be derivative of an uncaused cause. And as Thomas Aquinas said centuries ago, we call this uncaused cause "God."[1]

God is *the* uncaused cause of every effect we observe, and His existence is not a matter of faith, but a matter of logical and scientific fact. His existence is factually and physically necessary, scientifically and rationally necessary, inevitably and indisputably necessary.

For a string of effects is like a string of dominoes: the toppling of all the dominoes depends on the toppling of the first in a specific way. That first domino must be toppled by an outside cause.

Similarly, when we observe reality, we see movement all around us. We see things go from having the potential to do or to be something to actualizing this potential. Things have the capacity,

[1] Thomas Aquinas, *Summa Theologica* (*ST*), I, Q. 2, art. 3.

the potential, to be or do things, and they move to actualize that potential. Well, if you drill down on that movement, you will see that underlying everything in reality, there must be some fully actualized thing that is not moving from potentiality to actuality, but that is fully actualized. Like the necessary uncaused cause, there is the necessary "unmoved mover" or the "necessary and fully actualized actualizer," which, Aquinas tells us, we call "God."

Now, both of these quick examples prove the existence of God, which we will examine in detail later. For now, let it suffice that an "uncaused cause" and an "unmoved mover" are absolutely necessary. They are inevitable realities of our physical universe, indisputable facts of reality. They are facts about the whole of existence, with both scientific and rational credibility and certainty.

Through observation and reason, we can know the unmoved mover and the uncaused cause exist for certain. To reach this conclusion, our senses and our minds must work together in a realm that is not merely mental but is also grounded in the physical realities of our universe and the rational necessities predicated on the lawfulness of the physical and mental dimensions of existence.

Proving

Science can prove things to be actually and factually true. When done properly and replicated accurately, science gives us facts, truths about the physical reality we observe. There is no question: science tells us the truth. That is why we are so cautious and careful when we conduct scientific research. It is why we are so thorough and thoughtful when we apply scientific knowledge in the real, practical world.

It is important that we conduct research correctly so we truly know the facts, the truth about reality. It is important that we get these facts right, so we can properly apply the knowledge, the truth we have scientifically discovered, to the practical, real world.

But how can we prove things with reason? Science is the primary way we prove things about the physical world. What about intangible or mental things? Are there truths in this intangible realm, as there are in the physical plane? Can we know such truths? And is it possible to prove things in the realm of ideas and mental truths? Is it possible to discover the truth about life's overarching and most essential questions? And are these answers as bulletproof as the factual truths and basic laws of the sciences?

Despite our modern sensitivities and our ambiguous certainties, including relativism, the answers to those questions are a resounding and resolute yes. Yes, intangible and mental truths exist. Yes, such truths are indeed knowable. Yes, these assertions of truth are provable at a level of certainty that science can only shadow. Yes, the majority of life's most prominent and most fundamental questions have true answers.

And despite our modern intellectual and cultural proclivity for skepticism and the solitary role of science when it comes to truth, reason can not only elucidate these answers but also prove them beyond a shadow of doubt. By virtue of reason alone, such truths have a certainty that allows no alternative, no variation, no ambiguity, no compromise, no possibility, no error.

Just look at the two examples regarding origin and motion described briefly earlier in this chapter. The necessary conclusions we drew tell us of the absolute certainty of an uncaused cause and an unmoved mover. Their absolute necessity proves the certainty of God, for these two aspects of cause and effect regarding the universe's origin and the movement from potentiality to actuality demonstrate the necessity and existence of a noncontingent, all-powerful, eternal, wholly immaterial being. And this being we call "God."

Lest we miss the inevitable certainty here, the law of cause and effect is an essential element of the scientific method. Not only does science rely on this dynamic quality of the physical universe, but it also uses this law in its experimental methods and conditions, including its use of experimental and control groups as a formal means of separating specific causes and their incident effects.

But let's take this emphasis on reason a step further, a step beyond the specifics of the cause and the mover. Let's look at some practical and unavoidable aspects of truth. For the truth arising from the proper use of reason yields some obvious, crucial, and unavoidable truths about truth itself.

Let's take a brief, step-by-step look at the process by which we can know the truth and simultaneously dismantle our scientific and relativistic biases. This is a straightforward, transparent, elementary, and almost obvious means for making clear both the existence of actual truth and some specific truths about truth too. This is all accomplished by applying reason to the particular case at hand, by taking the content of beliefs seriously as they are articulated and justified, and by making sure all real possibilities are considered. Let's look at three simple questions, whose answers have profound effects on our daily lives and life's ultimate nature and purpose.

Let's start with a fun one: death. What happens at death? On the most basic level, death is the end of life. One moment you exist, the next you don't. And this applies to death however you define it. Not breathing—dead. Heart stopped—dead. No brain activity—dead. When you're dead, you're dead, no matter how death is defined or determined.

But what about beliefs about life after death, eternal life? Well, those are at least alternative ways of looking at what happens at death. For those who believe in life after death, death isn't the end of life: death is a point of transition to another form of life. So the moment of death is either the end of life or a transition to another way of being, another world, or another existence. That's it. Either death is an end, or death is a transition, a change.

And it should be clear that you can't be actually and factually dead and still have some form of transition at the same time. If at death you undergo some form of transition, then that is the reality of death. For death is a transition, not a final end. But if you die and cease to exist in any form of consciousness, then you are dead.

Reality requires that only one of these two possibilities can be real, correct, true, right, a fact. The other must be unreal, incorrect, false, wrong, an illusion. Only one way is real, despite your personal beliefs, religious teaching or scientific inclinations. Regardless of the evidence for each perspective, one answer must be true. The other must be false. So we can be absolutely certain that we can know the absolute truth about death because the positions on this issue are absolutely different from each other. The possibilities about death are mutually exclusive and irreconcilable by nature and substance. So when it comes to truth, we can know with absolute certainty that we can have absolute truth about the nature of death.

Clearly, the answer about whether death is the end of life or a transition in life is a function of evidence: scientific and rational evidence, inductive and deductive evidence. But it is certain there is truth about death, because on this basic level, there are two fundamental, mutually exclusive possibilities that constitute the full range of actual possibility. One way or another, we know there is truth about the nature of death. And it *is* one way or another. It can't be both.

This process for ascertaining truth is simple, yet profound: Begin with a crucial and profound question. Generate a comprehensive list of possible answers that reflect the complete range of actual possibilities. Make certain these possible answers are representative of reality. Be sure the options are discrete, mutually exclusive answers. With all possible answers enumerated and clarified, the right answer must exist and be on the list. As a result, truth is knowable one way or another.

Not convinced yet? Let's apply this process to another profound question to make it a bit clearer. Let's consider the question of human nature. What is our basic nature? What are human beings? The first thing that springs to mind is our bodies. We are physical beings; we have biological bodies of immense complexity and sophistication. From our brains to our toenails, we are truly amazing biological specimens.

But what about our minds? The human mind is a big part of our nature, and it is the single component that most distinguishes us from all other organic life forms. We all know the mind is connected to the brain and its functioning. But what about our souls, our spirits, our personality? Are they all just the result of biochemical interactions, just a string of related and simultaneous neural events? If so, what about our will, our decision-making? And what about the laws that govern reason? Are they just sensations that give us the illusion of having rationality and existence? And what about love and the many human virtues? Are these, too, mere sensations arising from neural events and biochemical activity?

Once again, as when we considered death, we face a choice that leads directly to the truth about human nature. Either human nature is wholly and completely biological, as evidenced by our bodies and brains, or it consists in the integration of our tangible bodies with our intangible minds and the unity of what we often refer to as the soul, mind, spirit, will, and consciousness—which are more than simple biochemical, biologically bound illusions, and truly give an intangible quality to our being.

At the most basic level, this is the full range of choices when it comes to human nature: it must be one way or the other. These two fundamental possibilities cannot be merged. One must be right. The other must be wrong. And so again, we can know with absolute certainty the truth about human nature.

Can you see how, if we address crucial, foundational questions and examine the limited number of possible answers to these questions, we can discover the right answers with absolute certainty? In this way, the existence of truth is easily demonstrated, though the nature of such truths is a function of evidence—scientific evidence and inductive evidence, as well as rational, deductive evidence.

Let's take a look at another huge question we all must face as we live and think about our lives, our world, our universe: the question of God. This question begins first and fundamentally with the existence of God. Does He exist? Well, this question can be answered in only one of two ways: either God exists or He doesn't. This cannot be a matter of personal perception. It can and must be a matter of fact. God can't exist for me and not exist for you. If I think there is a God and you think there isn't, we can't both be right. For it is a logical and practical, scientific and realistic absurdity to think God can both exist and not exist, that both of these mutually exclusive answers are right.

Just as there are definitive answers to the questions of death and human nature, so, too, is there definitive truth about the existence of God. That is why we can know, with absolute certainty, that we can uncover the factual and actual truth about God, just as we can discover the truth about death and human nature. When we look at such things on the most fundamental level, we can know that the truth about the basic issue at hand must be on the list of real possibilities. If we have all the real possibilities and their differences are mutually exclusive, we can know the truth is somewhere on that list.

This process will be crucial to understanding the questions and the evidence and justifications that follow in later chapters. So remember: if the list of possibilities is comprehensive and such possibilities are mutually exclusive, the truth is on that list. This is a logical and practical certainty, an unavoidable and inevitable consequence of proper analysis.

And such an analysis yields us all possible truths. But determining specific truth requires evidence—evidence of a scientific nature and of a logical, rational nature. And along with a review of this evidence, our analysis requires an explicit and deliberate decision. For uncertainty in the face of definitive evidence often masks our implicit commitments to alternative viewpoints, despite the presence of clear evidence. In the face of insufficient evidence or a lack of time to examine the evidence properly and fully, it is important to adopt a working hypothesis guided by prudence, until we have sufficient time for a thorough review of the evidence.

When we understand the inevitable and necessary truth resulting from our proper and incisive use of reason, we can know two things for certain. We can know our conclusions are absolutely true beyond any doubt, and we can know reason is our primary pathway to life's crucial truths. For the truths of origin and order, meaning and purpose, ethics and morality are much more accessible to us with the right use of reason, whether that reason is employed within the scientific method or through deductive processes.

But for now, be content with the basic knowledge that we can know truths beyond the core truths of science and its methods. Be excited by the prospect of entirely new degrees of truth in the realms of the metaphysical and theological, the philosophical and logical, the ethical and aesthetic, the political and cultural. Be intrigued by the sheer possibility of truth beyond the mere physical plane. But be careful not to rush headlong into this heady prospect of an abundance of truth.

Be cautious and circumspect, lest in your haste you move too quickly beyond the deliberate nature of reflection, reason, and rational analysis and argument. Be brave enough to consider objectively and dispassionately the errors and omissions inherent in the modern world's scientism. And be brave enough to pursue the resurrection of reason as a long-lost and misapprehended route to truth.

Also, be willing to consider the maker of reason. For reason's ability and power are effects, too, meaning they must have a cause, which is ultimately the same uncaused cause underlying everything tangible and intangible in our cosmos.

3

Matters of Truth

Let's begin by applying our reason and common sense to some basic questions. Let's look at the different answers to see whether they are logical and reasonable. By using our reason, we can actually evaluate whether truth is real and knowable.

If "true truths" really exist, then what are they? And if there are truly "true truths," how many of them can we know? How detailed and accurate are they? How practical and useful are they in the here and now, in the mundane practicalities of everyday life? And how accurate and important are they to the big picture of life and existence in the ultimate and final sense, in the timeless and eternal sense?

Does this sound a bit complicated, a bit philosophical, a bit obscure? If it does, it is mostly because we are in new, unfamiliar territory right now. But be patient. While it feels foreign now, as we go along, you will see it is more familiar than you may think at this moment.

After all, if there is actual truth about life and living, discovering it must be worth your time and effort. Otherwise, life in general and your life in particular really are just pointless confusions, experiences without any meaning or purpose other than the demands of staying alive and the satisfactions derived from comfort and distraction, sensory stimulation, and worldly success. Life without truth, without an ultimate purpose and end is really "a tale told by an idiot, full of sound and fury, signifying nothing," as Shakespeare tells us.[2]

So let's look at the possibility of real, actual, and factual truth. Does it exist? That will be the primary focus of this chapter and the next.

Once we can know with certainty that truth exists and that it can be known and proved, we can move on to how much truth we can know, as well as what some of these knowable truths are and just how much we can know about them individually and collectively.

All this will be accomplished implicitly as we turn from the question of knowable truth to the question of the existence and nature of God. For the purpose of this book is to make clear and certain the truth about truth: the truth that truth does, in fact, exist and that we can know truth as certainly as we know any facts about the physical world, such as the big bang, gravity, and planetary movement.

But as we go through the process of making the case for truth clear and certain, it may seem a bit heady, a bit conceptual, a bit elusive to grasp. That's normal, because making the case for truth in modern times is difficult for two reasons. First, it requires a strong rational approach and relies on applying the rigors of reason and rationality to some of life's biggest questions, particularly how we can know anything for certain. Secondly, making the case for truth with reason goes against the implicit modern bias about how we can know anything, how we can know everything. For in modern times, we have come to accept that the only way to know anything is with science and the experimental method—if, indeed, we accept that we can know anything at all.

[2] *Macbeth*, act V, scene 5, 26–28.

Overall, in modern times, we have collectively assumed that, unless we can demonstrate something in a lab, it isn't a fact; it's just an opinion, nothing more. That's it. And this is our modern prejudice, our biased assumption, often implicit in many of our beliefs and assumptions about what we can know and what we believe about real truth.

As we discussed in the previous chapter, this same prejudicial assumption about knowledge adds another layer of difficulty to our attempts to grasp the rational arguments that prove the certainty of truth beyond mere scientific truths. Under such assumptions, we struggle to see how such rationally proved conclusions can have the same force and power of scientific and mathematical certainties.

Now, this idea about truth is crucial to everything else in this book and to the big questions beyond it, even to life itself. So stick with it as we make our case about truth itself and the nature and content of some particular truths over the ensuing chapters. Know that you will need to stop and reflect on these ideas. You may even wish to revisit this and the next few chapters in order to grow in your understanding and facility with this level of reasoning, as well as the confidence inherent in the right use and application of reason.

Be assured that conceptual thinking and rigorous reasoning are inherently difficult. Know, too, that the difficulty you may experience in treading these deep and unfamiliar waters arises from modern assumptions about the power of reason to prove things, and to prove them as certainly and as solidly as science can.

Now, let's turn to our case for the existence of truth and its importance to everything we do, think, and believe. And let's do so with an open yet active and rationally critical mind. For truth, if it is indeed "real truth," will prove itself true when examined within the confines of rigorous reason and science. It will be vindicated through this rational process. And its findings will resonate and harmonize with your heart as well as with your mind.

Real Truth

The only reason you or anyone else should believe anything at all is because it is true. And that is a true statement. If a statement isn't true, we shouldn't believe it, because if we believe a statement that isn't true, we are believing an error, a mistake, a false notion, a wrong idea.

We should believe something only because it is true, not because we want it to be true, not because it feels good, not because significant others or authority figures believe it. We should believe something is true because it passes the tests of reason and science, when those tests are appropriately applied.

So how can we know what is true? This depends first of all on what truth we want to know. When it comes to physical things, we typically apply the scientific method. If the truth in question concerns something intangible, we must investigate it with reason, logic, and common sense.

Now, as seen through the modern lens of "science alone," this reliance on reason can seem weaker than the scientific method. No doubt, science is a very powerful tool. But most of its power derives from its use of reason. Diminishing the power of reason, as the modern paradigm does, diminishes the power of science, for the two are intimately and inextricably linked. In fact, there can be no science without reason, because reason is the foundation of the scientific method and the guiding light for scientific investigation.

In contrast, properly applied, reason can tell us many things simply on its own, by properly applying the laws of reason. As we discussed earlier, we need look no further than the field of mathematics to see this. Though mathematics has many applications and connections to the physical world, its reasoned truths hold true whether we apply them directly to the physical realm or not.

Just like science, mathematics is a form of applied reason. As an example, think of geometry and geometric proofs. Both focus on real relationships and require reason to derive their truths. Similarly, science and mathematics share a core reliance on and use of reason within their every endeavor and throughout their every process.

Think about this for just a moment. Think about some scientific fact that strikes you as odd or some mathematical process that concerns you. Think about being even a bit critical of a scientific fact or a mathematical conclusion. If you had a critical concern or question about the findings of any scientific study or experiment, you would have to work out your question and justify it based on some reasonable grounds, upon some rational concern, wouldn't you?

Do you recognize this need to justify your concern or question? Can you see how your questions or criticisms themselves rely implicitly on the correct use of reason and, therefore, how doing, questioning, and criticizing science and mathematics all require the use of reason?

Can you see that if science and mathematics cannot meet their own standards or follow the principles of proper reasoning, we don't have to accept their professed facts and conclusions as true? In fact, we must dismiss them as wrong, flawed, false.

And what's the opposite of falsehood? That's right—truth. So the truths demonstrated by science and math are, in fact, true, not because of science or mathematics themselves, but because of their methods, which are implicitly reasonable and rational.

To make things even clearer: if we were to conclude that reason couldn't prove anything for certain, then we would have to prove this conclusion demonstrably. And we would have to use reason itself in order to meet the demands of reasoned proof. And that is an irrational conclusion. It doesn't make sense to use reason to prove that reason can't prove things.

Get it?

It's an inescapable fact that we need reason to prove anything rationally. We must use reason implicitly when we use science or mathematics and explicitly when we argue with reason, with formal logic, with common sense. Anything and everything we hope to know as factual, as actual, as practical, as conceptual relies on the nature and power of reason, either explicitly or implicitly.

This unavoidable and indisputable fact about reason's nature and power, as well as its presence in virtually everything we know or hope to know, has been lost to the modern world. But reason can't be dismissed as mere manipulation, as a means of unprincipled persuasion, as simple sophistry or relativistic rhetoric, for such criticism would require rational, practical, and scientific justification in order to be accepted as true. This would require that the case made for these points of view to meet the demands of evidence and rational explanation. And, in that very moment, reason's nature and power would be vindicated by their use.

This goes for science, mathematics, reasoned proofs, and many practical things in life too. It certainly goes for many of life's big questions: questions about God and the nature of God, about life's overriding purpose and ultimate destination, about the nature of life and human existence, about beauty and goodness, about ethics and morality, about social and political life, and about all the many other derivative questions we face when we think about life in the ultimate sense or in the immediate sense.

The God Question

Reason is very helpful when addressing such questions. As important as it is to establish reason's role and its use in science and mathematics, it is even more important to understand reason's essential power and usefulness in addressing the big-picture questions listed above.

As most philosophers and thinkers, scientists and theoreticians will tell you, the biggest of all of life's questions is the question of God's existence and nature. This question involves both the most important questions about life itself and the most important questions for practical, daily living, both the most timeless and the most timely questions. In other words, contained within these questions about the existence of God and His nature are other crucial questions about the purpose and meaning of life, about what is right and what is wrong, about what is important and what is trivial. Even questions about beauty, law, politics, and economics are wrapped up in the questions about God and His nature.

Oddly, the answers to these questions draw on much that we already know. It may seem a weird twist to think of God, His nature, and all the implications of His existence as familiar. But how else could we determine that He exists? How else could we recognize His nature? Somehow, He must be familiar—familiar to our minds, our hearts, our senses.

And we will find much evidence of His existence and His nature all around us, in our nature and all its many facets and faculties, in our physical world, and in reason and beauty and love.

The Bible and the dogmas of our faith testify that we are all "image bearers" of God, that our very nature reflects His being, though we are imperfect reflections of His true perfection. Through our many faculties and facets, we can see Him. We can see Him in others, just as we can see Him in His vast and complex creation, in the nature that surrounds us with its breathtaking beauty, variety, and abundance.

And through these many means, we can know God exists, and we can comprehend His very character. What's more, we can come to know Him personally as our beloved Father, as our "Abba," our "Daddy." For He promises us that what we seek, we most certainly will find.

Personal Truth

Nowadays, we encounter many obstacles that keep us from knowing what truth is, even when it is right before our eyes, right before our minds, right before our hearts. To begin with, our culture and our world have led us to think that truth doesn't exist. Most of us, when we hear the word "truth," don't take it to mean objective truth or factual truth, absolute truth or irrefutable truth. Rather, we hear it the way our culture has taught us to hear it and understand it: as "personal truth" or "collective truth" or as "cultural truth." We think, even unconsciously, that truth is some form of tradition or social convention, or an informed opinion that someone may hold as if it were true.

Ultimately, our modern world tells us that truth is nothing more than an opinion or a good guess. For as modern, educated people, we tend to see truth and truth claims, almost universally, as nothing more than working hypotheses, as temporary theories, as tentative conclusions, or as personal truths, at best. As citizens of the modern world, we are absolutely certain of very little, except perhaps the basic laws of science, such as the law of gravity. Any other claims about real truth or about particular truths beyond these basic laws are simply seen as personal opinions, subjective theories, or arbitrary, working hypotheses.

Cloaking these opinions, theories, and hypotheses in the rhetoric of real truth, in the semantics of certainty, does nothing to prove such assertions of absolute truth. To the modern mind, such claims of real truth are merely masquerades by which we deceive ourselves into believing we actually have the truth.

Ultimately, one of our most fundamental and crucial modern beliefs is that there is no truth. The single, solitary certainty we have is that there is no certainty beyond the laws of the physical universe.

In other words, to the modern mind, when Catholics declare their truths, they are really just offering opinions. Cloaking Catholic "opinions" in the rhetoric of certainty does nothing to convince anyone of how such opinions may be made certain, how these "truths" may be defended as facts. Such is the modern mind when it listens to and observes religious people. But is the modern mind right? Well, let's just see.

The First Contradiction

It is an odd way of thinking not to believe in any real truth. It is an even odder twist of reason that to believe in the total absence of truth beyond the physical laws of science is a truth claim in itself.

To say that there is no truth beyond the physical truths that science reveals is a definitive declaration about truth. But, it is also a statement that the modern mind believes to be true—actually, factually true, not just an opinion. But this is a fatal contradiction in logic, an irrational conclusion from a contradictory premise.

It is a logical and practical fallacy because it contradicts its basic premise about the total absence of truth by insisting that the absence of truth is itself a factual truth.

Now, this contradiction is logically inevitable when you claim that truth doesn't exist and yet believe and insist this is true for everyone, everywhere, at every moment. Such a contradiction is more than a minor problem that can be overlooked or minimized; it is more than an inevitable failure of logic itself. In fact, the failure of this fatal contradiction isn't due to logic, but to the assertion that there is no truth, no right answers.

The truth that there is no truth is really irrational, outside of the realm of reason, a conclusion as nonsensical as any fantasized or concocted belief taken as truth. Because this assertion that there is no truth is illogical, irrational, nonsensical, there is no way we should accept this idea or conclusion.

But what about the practical world, in which real, everyday life takes place? Maybe the modern view of truth is illogical in a strictly logical sense, but is it practically true, according to common sense and practical living? Let's take a look at some simple, practical moral examples.

Are first-degree murder or systematic racial genocide morally neutral events? How about torture or brutality inflicted on innocent people? You may think these are obvious moral transgressions. Well, if you do, you just found some truths about life in the practical world. There goes the idea that there is no truth. Case closed.

But you may think these are extremes, cases and situations far removed from practical life for most people. I mean, murder, torture, and genocide don't really affect most of us personally.

Well, that's not a valid objection, because the modern truth claim is that there is no truth whatsoever. It takes a single exception to defeat this claim. We just found three with almost no reflection or subtlety whatsoever.

But for the sake of debate, let's look at smaller, more commonplace truths by which we live every day of our small, local lives. Is it right to give your word and then withdraw it for no reason? Is it right to be rude and inconsiderate? Is it right to be wasteful or lazy or irresponsible? No. These things are wrong. Just as wrong as the brief list of more grievous and heinous truths above.

Again, these are additional exceptions to the modern claim that there is no truth at all. But you may still think these smaller truths could have exceptions, circumstances in which you would be right to withdraw a promise, for example.

Well, in such circumstances, as might well exist, the burden would fall on you to outline how those circumstances would affect the morality of your actions. And in doing so, you would have to rely on other moral principles that bear on the case in point.

Such appeals to moral principles demonstrate, once again, an even greater number of practical moral truths that exist, that are inherent truths, and that are inherently practical and necessary.

Let's take it from the angle of goodness, as well, just to drive the point home. Aren't altruism and generosity and love virtues we all should aspire to? Don't we all admire such virtues? Wouldn't we all admit these are important character traits to have? And wouldn't we all be better people if we could more richly embody these virtues?

Again, these are all truths, actual and practical truths. If there are circumstances that modify them in a more sophisticated and more perfect way, then those modifications arise from other truths too, as do the circumstances surrounding the world's many moral evils, including those mentioned above.

Can you see and hear the contradiction? Could it possibly be true that there is no truth? Isn't it a truth claim to say there is no truth, since to say there is any truth about anything, even the truth that there isn't any, is a truth statement?

In sum, this modern maxim of the truth that there is no truth contradicts itself and is therefore false. It is false because it is self-refuting and self-contradictory in both a logical and a practical sense.

Now, many moderns often act amused by this clear contradiction, because they believe that this fatal flaw in logic is simply a laughable matter of language, with no real basis in determining truth.

In addition, when moderns want to believe something, their will is able to disregard all of the compelling counterarguments we might present. This will can affect us unconsciously. So we must be rigorous, even ruthless, in our honesty and introspection, lest we become subject to our will's implicit influence.

For the same will that denies the ability of reason to prove anything leads the modern mind into another contradiction, a deeper, more profound contradiction. It leads to the utter rejection of reason, as we discussed earlier.

The Second Contradiction

The role of reason is radically reduced in the modern mind's view of life and living. For many moderns, reason is limited conceptually and has little or no practical usefulness. Many philosophically informed moderns think reason cannot provide them with answers about the universe and its purpose, or with any practical moral applications. They think logical reason is unreliable. Reason is a rhetorical tool that persuades and offers potential explanations, rather than a means of proving things in a real and practical sense.

And even if reason is reliable to any degree, as some moderns believe, it is certainly not as reliable as science and scientific reasoning in discovering truth. To moderns, reason applied to things such as life's purpose, its meaning, or the existence of God and His nature has no real meaning or usefulness. Modern reason is only a path to personal opinions that we may call "truths." Such is the claim, however implicit, of many moderns, just as it was with those who thought my conversion was based only on my personal truth.

Yet, to moderns, when used in science, reason is a real, viable, and powerful tool. So reason has an important role in scientific matters, yet it has virtually no practical use for matters of the ultimate questions of life, for matters of what philosophers and theologians refer to as "metaphysics." Rather, when applied to metaphysical concerns, logical reasoning is a semantic sleight of hand, a form of rhetorical manipulation, and certainly not a rigorous regimen for discovering and determining truth.

For them, reason has a real role only when tied to science and the world of the senses, according to moderns. Any other use of reason outside of science is generally thought to be persuasion, rhetoric, not real, rational facts, facts as rigorous as scientific ones.

You can see this sometimes tacit, sometimes explicit modern bias against reason by comparing scientists with philosophers. Which group is more credible, more knowledgeable, more powerful in our modern world? To whom are you apt to turn for truth? To whom would our culture turn for truth, for factual truth? Think about it for a minute, and you will see the modern bias toward scientific knowledge and against reason.

Yet the very idea that all reason is sophistry means that their claim that all reason is sophistry must be sophistry itself, because it, too, relies on reasoned proof.

In short, both of the conclusions we have examined—that there is no truth and that reason applies only to physical things—cannot be proved without using reason. Thus, they are fundamentally self-contradictory, with false premises and nonsensical conclusions.

But to one degree or another, many educated, modern people still hold these fallacious beliefs, which undergird our culture, our morality, our values, our laws, and our politics. They influence our relationships with each other and our perceptions of ourselves. They influence our practical actions, our philosophical perceptions, our religious convictions. And most importantly, they influence how we look at God and His very nature.

Contradictions Applied to Content

This is why, when most modern people look at the world's religions, they see many options and conclude that there is no truth in any of them, or that God is behind all of them, meaning it doesn't matter what we believe or which God we follow. Or they don't believe in God at all.

This is why my religious, irreligious, and unreligious friends and acquaintances objected so strenuously to the reasons I gave for my conversion. Because I was so insistent on the truth of the Catholic faith, I trampled on their assumptions about the existence of truth and our ability to know it. And I trampled on their convictions about reason's laws and their implicit theories of knowledge.

As we close this chapter, I ask you to ponder the idea of reason and logic and how self-contradiction is fatal to any logical, rational case. Think about how these critical contradictions break down modern ideas and distorted exaggerations about the absence of truth and the weaknesses of reason outside of the scientific method. Think about how these critical contradictions remand so many modern principles to the realm of the irrational, the ridiculous. Try to see the contradictions for what they are: irreversibly false, unjustifiable conclusions—in other words, blind beliefs without rational foundations or substantiation.

Think about truth and the many truths you already know. Think about the virtues and vices you see exhibited every day. Think about love, beauty, romance, courage, kindness, and all the many noble and base behaviors you witness and perform each day as you go about your life.

Think honestly and fairly about this. Do you still believe there are no real truths about life? When you begin to see the truth of even a few basic moral principles, you discover that the universe and human nature and society contains at least some truths. And these truths must have come from somewhere, for they inherently belong to human life and experience. "Inherent" means "intentional, created"; or it strongly suggests that they were meant to be an intentional and inherent part of our existence.

So, take your time to think and digest the meaning of that startling and signal fact of a small set of truths and what that means. It's obvious but odd, vaguely familiar but surprisingly novel all at once. That's because our modern perspective doesn't account for these facts other than to ascribe them to some kind of personal opinion. But this perspective just doesn't hold up under simple scrutiny and rational reflection.

So think again. Think long and hard. But most of all, think well, think rightly, think logically. If you do, the faint light of reason will begin to shine, though dimly at first. But its light will grow as you think better and reflect further.

And for those fortunate enough to find a piercing burst of insight, the light of truth will burst forth as a blazing insight, illuminating everything in an instant, though time will be necessary to scan and understand the broad landscape of truth now illumined for you by reason and common sense.

Either way, stay the course. But keep thinking. For your mind must be liberated from the confines of a narrow theory of knowledge, a theory you have imbibed through culture and its many assumptions and presuppositions. The keys to escaping your confinement are in your hands, in your mind, in your heart. And those very keys are reason and logic and common sense and love and beauty. So keep thinking and reflecting. Don't just accept what our modern culture says about reality.

4

Matters of Fact

As we've already seen, when it comes to the truth, reason is crucial. If we don't follow reason and common sense, we have no way of knowing much of anything. Everything becomes a matter of pure conjecture, personal opinion, random thought. If reason is left out, all anyone can say is, "This is what I believe," and nothing more. There is nothing to debate, nothing to discuss, nothing to prove, nothing to disprove.

When we hold reasonless and groundless beliefs, they are just that—mere beliefs. If any such beliefs contradict the laws of reason, they are irrational beliefs. If they are mere assertions about life and reality that we must accept without scrutiny, explanation, or defense, they are only assumptions, blind beliefs.

So without reason, we are left with irrational claims, groundless assumptions, and blind beliefs. Not the kind of certainty that comprises truth. All this certainly emphasizes the necessity of thinking—specifically, thinking clearly and correctly. So the question is: Do you think? And how well do you think? And how often? Do you think about important and ultimate things or just temporal and trivial ones?

We all must consider the crucial matters of God and religion, which lie at the root of all our individual practical lives and the ultimate things in life across all time and space. When we discover that our assumptions about God are illogical, we cannot rationally hold on to them.

Irrational Faith

In religious matters, we often label our beliefs in irrational things as acts of faith. Yet this is not the case when it comes to the Catholic Church. The Church recognizes the role of faith, but never to the exclusion of reason where appropriately applied.

For Catholics, faith and reason are integrated, so there is no real conflict between them. So, too, with science and faith and with science and reason. While some aspects of the faith are difficult to describe, adequate explanations are available to us through our capacity for and use of reason. Sometimes we must rely on deep, sophisticated explanations that arise from applying and blending our different ways of knowing.

So having to think hard shouldn't surprise us or put us off. Such complexities are to be expected, for we are trying to understand and explain God and His revelation, even though we are just human beings. We are trying to explain the infinite, even though we are finite and limited—limited by our language and intelligence and limited in our capacity to juggle ideas simultaneously, to comprehend the physical, the mental, and the spiritual dimensions of life and living all at once.

And despite some apparent conflicts between science, reason, and faith, in the end, these ways of knowing affirm one another. Though integrated, they retain their inherent usefulness in their customary and appropriate domains as well. For the Catholic faith is neither a faith of the blind, nor a mindless leap, nor a kind of willful hope, nor a form of knowing based solely on a personal revelation or experience of God. Every personal experience of God must be consistent with the whole of God's revelation, with Holy

Scripture, with the deposit of faith, with the Church's teaching down through the ages, and with the natural revelation available to us through science and reason.

Informed Faith

Our faith uses and integrates all of our God-given means of knowing. We are called to apply these gifts rigorously and relentlessly to their fullest. And though we may encounter some small element of uncertainty in a philosophical proof or a piece of scientific evidence for God's existence, as we grapple to understand these proofs fully, we see that any uncertainty is a question of degree, a very small degree.

It is in this small degree of uncertainty that faith finds its rightful place within our growing understanding, not as blind faith, but as informed faith; not as a leap, but as a bridge. Faith doesn't rest on irrationality or mindlessness or sheer will, but on reason, science, and revelation; it doesn't come from confusion, but from the gift of faith that God bestows on each person who sincerely seeks Him.

You may have raised reasonable and rigorous questions in your quest to find God, and He will respect your honest and sincere questions. He will reveal Himself in the answers and explanations to your questions and in your personal experience of Him.

God invites and asks you to be curious. He exhorts you to seek Him. And He promises each and every one of us that He will be found. For those who seek find. And an important means by which we seek and find Him is through reason.

Now, reason is not the only way you may seek and find God, but it is an important method, particularly as you begin to explore the Catholic faith and as your personal faith grows and develops. God expects and encourages us to use all of our faculties, including the reason He bestows on us, as we seek and follow Him.

We must abandon any beliefs based on mere opinions, without any roots in reason, science, or faith, especially when these beliefs demand our acceptance without offering us any logical reason to do so. For such beliefs and assumptions that demand acceptance simply as they are, without any appeal to reason, common sense, science, or the Church, must be rejected. Such arbitrary beliefs are false, and we should cast them aside as meaningless and deceptive.

Imagine asking someone why you should do or believe something. Now imagine that person answering, "Because." (This will be familiar to parents and children alike.) What can you say to such an answer? "Because" is no explanation for anything. We may not always know exactly or completely why we believe something, but we usually have some reason, some experience, some authority to which we may appeal to explain our faith.

For when it comes to the big questions of life, it is ridiculous to hide behind blind faith as an explanation, particularly when God exhorts us to seek Him and eventually to love Him with all our mind, our heart, and our strength (see Deut. 6:5). That is why He teaches us through Scripture and directly through the teaching ministry of Jesus Christ. That is why Jesus appeals to our reason.

Our opinions must be grounded in reason and reasonable ways of knowing to the best of our abilities and with the best of our experience and learning. If we appeal to reason and common sense, then we must follow the rules of reason. That is why we use reason and common sense whenever we seek to explain something. When we debate philosophy or morality, law or politics, we use reason and common sense. When we discuss science or economics, we use reason routinely. We even use it when we think about or discuss what we will wear, what we will eat, and what we will do.

Almost every aspect of life and living is subject to reasonable analysis and scrutiny. That is why when we critique or object to something, we give reasons for our objections. That is also why we must use reason and common sense to prove things or to show why one viewpoint or alternative or choice is better than another. That is why we use it to persuade people or to influence them or to criticize them.

In the end, reason assists and articulates our faith. In turn, our faith is grounded in reason and science, in the doctrines and the teaching authority of the Catholic Church.

God—A Matter of Fact

So let's use our reason to look at one of the most critical and profound questions there is in life: the question of God. Now, there are many questions to ask about God, but the most profound and the most basic of these is whether such a being exists in an actual, factual sense, not merely in the minds of believers. Other questions about the nature of God, His abilities, His intentions, and how He communicates all rest on whether He exists. So let's begin with the existence of God.

Now, many of us modern people have come to think God's existence depends only on belief, on faith. But it is just here that we make a grievous and fatal error in thinking and thereby tacitly rule out the truth. God's existence is not, nor can it ever be, solely a matter of faith. As we saw earlier, either God exists, or He doesn't exist. Only one answer can be right. The other must be wrong. That is an absolute fact of reason and common sense.

So we can and must conclude that the existence of God is not a matter of belief. It must be a matter of fact. Let me say it again: the question of God's existence is a matter of fact. It is not, nor can it ever be, a matter of belief.

Our beliefs may be our beliefs, but our beliefs cannot create God. God is, or God is not. Our beliefs have nothing to do with God's actual, factual existence. If we think our beliefs create God's existence, then we ourselves become the makers, the creators of God.

When God is a matter of our personal opinion, of our faith, without any factual evidence for His existence, we create an imaginary God, a God of our will, our desire, our delusion. So God's existence can never be a product of our opinions; otherwise, we become God, because we have created Him by our beliefs.

So which answer is the truth? Does God exist? Well, the fact that you are reading this book proves you are at least curious about this question. Your curiosity indicates you may already be leaning in the direction of affirming God's existence. But you probably have questions and concerns about this pivotal theological, philosophical, moral question. That is how it is supposed to be.

Your questions are a function of reason. You know that any belief must be based on evidence, on right reasoning. You know your reason is a significant tool in answering the question of God's existence and other such questions, for reason is a tool through which we explore our world, our lives, our existence.

So let us think about God's existence and the implications of this within the light and limits of reason, common sense, and mutually exclusive answers. Let's look at the real and limited range of potential answers to this crucial question. Let's examine the factual choices and the evidence from which we may determine the truth about God's existence.

And let us do so in the fair light of reason and common sense; in the light of our sensory experience and science; in the light of our moral and aesthetic sensibilities; in the light of our intuitions and His revelation; and in the light of history and culture, politics and economics, practicalities and personality. For we may be surprised by how much we already know, how much truth we already have.

Atheism and Agnosticism

Let's begin with the existence of God. This question separates the answers into two possibilities, as we discussed above. On one side there are atheists, those who believe God does not exist. Related to atheists are certain people who believe we cannot know that God exists. They are generally called agnostics, though they are often organized into subdivisions based on their level of commitment to the possibility of knowing anything about God.

The kind of agnosticism aligned most closely with atheism firmly concludes that knowledge about God's existence is not possible. These people are sometimes referred to as "hard agnostics." They have determined that knowledge of God is inaccessible to us or simply absent altogether. In contrast, "soft agnostics" aren't certain about the absence of evidence for God's existence. They wonder if there is a God and, if so, how He might be known to us.

You may be this type of agnostic, or perhaps you once were. At one time or another, many of us—including me—have held soft-agnostic beliefs. Like me, you may be asking important questions and feeling a bit torn, a bit lost. I was interested, but perplexed; skeptical, but reasonable; confused, but curious.

God encourages us to be curious in these and other ways. He wants us to be curious enough to seek out answers to our questions, to find out if He exists, to come to know Him personally, and to know Him well enough to love Him.

Though you may be a soft agnostic at the moment, this doesn't mean you don't have some hard questions about God, hard questions about the nature of the universe, hard questions about the meaning and purpose to life. So let's start with the existence of God and dispense with atheism and hard agnosticism first. From there, we can move on to the nature of God and deal with the other world religions in subsequent chapters.

Atheism

Let's take a look at the definition of "atheism" for starters. The *Shorter Oxford English Dictionary* defines "atheism" as a "disbelief in, or denial of, the existence of God or gods." That seems pretty straightforward. But it may be helpful to know, too, what the Catholic Church means by "God." Though complicated, this question is crucial, even at this early stage of our discussion.

The Catholic Church understands "God" to mean "the one absolutely and infinitely perfect spirit who is the creator of all," as defined in the *Oxford Dictionary*. Because God is the Creator of all, He is the one and only being who can't not exist. While there are many other things we can and must say about God, for now, suffice it to say that for Catholics, God must exist, and for atheists, He can't exist. So either Catholics are right and atheists are wrong, or Catholics are wrong and atheists are right.

Let's look at atheism in more detail. The challenge of atheism is rooted in the question of whether God exists. According to most atheists, there is no God of any sort. This is the one crucial premise of atheism — that there is no God or no gods whatsoever.

And most of these convinced atheists are virtually certain that the physical universe is all there is. These deliberate atheists are convinced that there is only the reality of our physical universe. While less deliberate atheists implicitly believe similarly, they are less aware of the implications of their belief and less sophisticated in their understanding of their own belief. And so they may be unaware of the implications of a godless, wholly physical universe.

Though a minority of atheists believe that hyperintelligent, highly developed aliens might exist within the far reaches of the universe and might appear to be gods, the traditional idea of God is totally implausible and irrational to them. They certainly believe there is no transcendent God, nor do they believe in any group of gods who are infinite, eternal, all-knowing, all-powerful, and ever present. For if they held to any of these descriptive traits, they would cease to be atheists. So in the end, they don't believe in God or in any gods at all. Period. End of story.

Moreover, many atheists think believing in God arises from some deep psychological need or issues related to authority and compliance. Many atheists often think that believing in God borders on the absurd, the laughable, the pitiful, the delusional.

Now, the reasons they give for these beliefs seem fairly plausible on the surface. Atheists often appeal to science explicitly and reason implicitly to explain their beliefs. Also, they demand evidence for the existence of God and given the absence of evidence—evidence as they define it—they conclude there is no God.

They frequently demand "demonstrable" evidence or proof. And, given that there is no "demonstrable" evidence or proof of sufficient quantity or quality, according to them, they conclude there is no god. That's why they don't capitalize the word "god," because God is not a being. God is merely a myth, a fantasy, a delusion.

Often, they claim it is unscientific to believe in God, for they believe science has disproved God. After all, if science hasn't discovered God, God can't be there. He must not exist. And, because believing in God is unscientific, it must be irrational. For them, reason cannot demonstrate the existence of God, just as science cannot show us God. Given the absence of "demonstrable" scientific and rational evidence—as they define it—atheists conclude that there is no God.

So they believe it is irrational from the standpoint of reason and primitive from the standpoint of science to believe in such a God or any god.

Well, let's take a look at three atheistic and agnostic perspectives. First, let's examine a universe without God and what that might look like. Let's see if an atheistic description of life, humanity, and the universe really makes sense. Second, let's see what scientific evidence there is for God. And third, let's see if reason can offer any proofs of God's existence.

Just remember that such atheists and agnostics are pretty confident about their beliefs. But their confidence is unearned, because it is based on a shallow analysis of the question of God's existence and on deep distortions of both science and reason. As a result of these distortions, the universe they believe in is incoherent and nonsensical, consummately irrational and ridiculously erroneous.

In the end, atheists are wrong—utterly and completely wrong; wrong beyond a shadow of real doubt.

Now, I'm not speaking merely rhetorically, nor do I intend to ridicule atheists. I'm simply stating the facts. Remember, the existence of God is a matter of fact. It is not a matter of belief, no matter how insensitively this fact assaults the modern mind's sensibilities and confidence, no matter how seriously it challenges the current paradigm of relativism, political correctness, and interpersonal sensitivity.

The question of God's existence is and will always be a matter of absolute fact. If the atheists and hard agnostics are indeed wrong, then it is not by a certain degree or by a certain amount or up to a point. They are wrong in the old-fashioned sense—completely, thoroughly, profoundly wrong. Wrong about science. Wrong about thinking. Wrong about the universe. Wrong about anything and everything that matters. Period.

If you think all this a bit arrogant and prideful, remember the stakes we face when it comes to life and living. Remember, the existence of God has been the single most important question facing every man and woman since the beginning. It is also the most practical question, for it involves how we live our lives and why we live them. It involves eternity and immortality and our ultimate destination.

If there is indeed truth about life and about God, it is not the creation of an individual or the Catholic Church. If there is truth, it must be discovered, not invented. And if it is to be discovered, then it can't be ours or the Church's; it must be God's. So let's see who's right, the atheists and agnostics or God and His theists.

Keep in mind, these questions we will address and the answers they generate are not meant to persuade or manipulate you. You must be persuaded only by the facts, the evidence of reason, the evidence of science.

So try to read through the following case with a critical eye and an open mind. For the truth about God's existence on this most basic level is fairly straightforward, more straightforward than you may imagine. That may be what you find most jarring, for you may find the ease and obvious nature of the case for God the easy part, and you may find the ease through which the case is made more startling.

If you do, know that this is probably not a function of your intelligence. To one degree or another, the modern world has implicitly programmed most of us to believe that reason cannot show us truth and that the truth about God is not real truth. It is just opinion dressed up in the garments of reasoned truth.

So be kind to yourself as you review the case for God's existence. Some of your thinking surely comes from our cultural programming, which we receive inadvertently and deliberately, without an overt explanation of the rationale for these ideas, without any rationale for reason's diminished power, without any rationale for the exaggerations and distortions of science.

Most of all, take time to think clearly about the evidence and reasoned case for God's existence. Clear thinking and clear evidence should make the answer clear, certain, sure. And remember, the answer to the question of God's existence is knowable one way or another. For God exists or He doesn't. You can know for certain.

Commit to taking the time to think and to look into the facts and reasons for God. For no other question or issue has such an enormous impact on so many other questions and issues, on questions about how and why you live your life.

Just give this critical question the time and the thought it deserves. And don't be surprised if you find yourself at times vacillating, oscillating between the two possibilities before you. That is the nature of reasoned inquiry. That is the nature of the question and its gravity and enormity.

Just stay with it. Put in the time. And make it quality time, thoughtful time, rigorously reasoned time. Do the research and think long and rightly about the case. For the answer is there for the taking.

5

Matters of Materialism

As we now know, not everyone can be right about God. Either He is or He isn't. Someone is right. Someone is wrong. But the answer depends on the evidence available to us through our senses, through our minds, through our personal experience of being alive, and through our everyday experience of practical life.

The first question we must face is that of God's existence. And the first challenge we must meet is the argument raised by atheism, as we discussed in the previous chapter. We established the truth that only one point of view, only one belief, can be true. And as we know, truth is a function of evidence. So let's begin examining the evidence inherent in atheism.

Let's take some time to see how atheism looks at the universe. Let's see if its basic belief in a godless universe makes sense. I think you'll find it neither accurate nor coherent. It is neither a rational nor a scientific view of the universe. The atheistic concept of the universe rests on a deeply flawed philosophy and a distorted description of the world, mankind, and practical experience.

And remember, these views of atheism are merely rhetorical, a form of ridicule—unless they are true. And I think you'll discover that they are accurate descriptions of the atheistic view of our universe and of God.

The Universe according to Atheists

According to atheists, there is nothing beyond what is in the universe. For them, there is nothing beyond the matter and energy of the universe itself. No intangible being. No God. No cosmic consciousness. Nothing but the universe.

Even for some atheists who might venture to imagine some kind of spiritually immanent entity within the universe, this entity would have to arise from the universe itself. So everything that exists in the cosmos is matter, energy, or their derivatives.

This means the only thing that exists is the universe. There is nothing beyond this universe, except more universe. And over time, if we find there is something beyond the universe as we now know it, you know what we'll find. You guessed it—more universe, a physical universe, a universe of matter and energy. For most atheists, the physical universe is all there is, all there ever will be. It is all we can know, because we can perceive nothing else, whether with our senses, with the aid of technology or with the application of certain mathematical extrapolations. Atheists must have "demonstrable" evidence of God's existence to know He exists. By this, they mean sensory evidence only. Demonstrable evidence is a very narrow category, a limited type of evidence, as we will see.

Ultimately, when atheists look at the universe, they don't see God in any sense of the word. God is not directly visible, they reason. God cannot be observed or seen. Therefore, He is not there. He does not exist.

They looked. He's not there. There is no God. Case closed. Move on. Grow up. Get with the future. Leave the Dark Ages behind. Science has proved that God doesn't exist. Any god. Every god. God is nothing more than an artifact of primitive, ignorant, and naïve times, or the product of the weak-minded, the weak-willed, the weak period. Explicitly or implicitly, that's how atheists think.

But wait a minute. Let's just explore the universe as atheists see it before we begin to justify and describe the real universe, the universe as Catholics see it. Let's spend some time developing a description of the universe articulated by atheism in its most basic and deliberate form. For it is easy to state that there is no evidence of God, especially when atheists narrow the very idea of what evidence is. But it is another thing altogether to examine what the universe looks like without God. It is another matter entirely to examine *what* we can know about the universe without God; or *how* we can know about the universe without God; or *if* we can know about the universe without God.

Let's examine this atheistic description of the universe and see if it offers a thorough description of reality, of the physical universe, of our human faculties and experience, of our science, of our technology, and of reason and mathematics.

What do you want to bet they come up short? After all, I would not mention this stuff if I just wanted to persuade you. I'm not trying to sell you salvation or a membership in a church club. I want to inform you, so you can know the truth and live life to the fullest, so you can know what love and truth really are, so you can know and love God now and forever.

A Universe of One Thing

The universe is made of matter and energy. With the exception of gravity and the other fundamental forces, these are the two forms in which the universe manifests itself, the two things of which it is composed.

This means everything is one of two forms of the natural cosmos, the natural order.

This view of the universe is known as "naturalism" or "materialism" in philosophical and scientific discussions. "Materialism" means that everything in the universe is one thing. Everything is composed of the material of the universe, the naturally occurring "stuff" of the cosmos. Materialism seems to make sense. It even appears to be scientific, which is why it is so persuasive and pervasive nowadays. But appearances are often deceiving.

Let's take a closer look. If everything is matter and energy, the material of the universe, the natural substance of the cosmos, how can we explain thought? Take a minute to think about that idea.

What if thought is simply matter and energy? If the activity of our brain's neurons and the energy firing through them really constitute thought, then thinking may feel real, but it is not. Thinking is not a personal experience but merely an illusion arising from the biochemical activity of our brains and their patterns of matter and energy.

Think again, only this time, have a different thought. Now the pattern is different, because it involves a different pattern with a different sequence of neurons and a different intensity or speed of energy flow. These thoughts are by-products of biochemical activity, nothing more. Your patterns of thought are simply physical, neural patterns, even when you think about different ideas.

Now think about a truth, something you know is certain, some physical law or some mathematical proof or some moral certitude. This brings us to a conundrum. Could all the certainty of logical laws and rational proofs be nothing more than biochemical activity following some arbitrary and accidental neural pattern? Which is real, the pattern or the thought?

Well, in a material universe, the pattern is all there is, meaning that the law or the proof you were thinking about is just a biochemical by-product, a neural sensation, an illusion generated by biochemical activity. The pattern is the only truth, not the specific truth, the specific content of the thought or truth. Those things are just illusions of biochemical origin because the reality is the biochemical activity.

Let's imagine we can open the top of your skull and observe what is going on when you think about or feel something. When we look at your brain, there is nothing more than a pattern of neural activity. That's it. It's all we can see. Therefore, that is all there is.

Really? That can't be true.

Well, how do you know that you know what you saw? After all, what you saw and what you know are just patterns of biological activity, right? It's all just biochemical activity. So can you even know that what you saw was, in fact, what you saw?

Do you see how the materialist view makes every single thing unknowable? Do you see how materialism requires a relentless reduction and regression to biochemical patterning, leaving us without any real validity to the realities we experience? It reduces what we know to complete absurdity, even our knowledge of complete absurdity. Weird, huh?

Take love, for example. When we love someone, we believe our love is real. But if everything we experience is only biochemical, love no longer exists. How can this be true? Surely, at least love is real. Nope. The relentless, atheistic reality of materialism, the solitary and unitary biochemical assault, destroys everything in its path, including love, beauty, truth, and morality. It kills even our knowledge of any and every single thing, including the sciences. It destroys knowing itself. And it destroys human consciousness, leaving us estranged even from ourselves.

Given this absolute physical basis for all human experiences, how do we know whether any form of reasoning is correct or incorrect, when the only real difference in reasoning is only a different pattern of neural activity? When reason is simply biochemical patterns and activity, reason is destroyed. For reason's power comes from reasoning itself, from the absolute rules of logic, from common sense, not from biochemical patterns of neural activity.

The Illusion of Real Reason

If reason is simply biochemical, then reason doesn't exist at all. Only the neural patterns do. And they exist as mere patterns only. The truth of neural patterns is no real truth: it's just a pattern of biochemical activity. There's no truth there, no matter how you look at it.

I mean, faulty reasoning is a neural pattern, just as sound reasoning is. How do you tell them apart? The only way is in the patterns of activity. There is no way to say which is better, without an appeal to some intangible standard of logic originating beyond biochemistry. In a universe of matter and energy, that's not possible. So reason and its objective standards of logic are really just neural illusions, and, if they are illusions, biochemical illusions, then they don't actually exist.

If reason is undermined and destroyed, then so is science. Science can't exist without reason, without philosophically based presuppositions and assumptions. Think about that. Oh! Wait a minute. You can't think about that, because even thinking about thinking isn't possible. It is illusory and meaningless.

Can you see how reason and science are relentlessly and inevitably destroyed when we use a wholly material worldview to describe even this one facet of human experience? Science can't exist without reason and other philosophically based presuppositions and assumptions. And reason can't exist because it is all neural activity.

Can you see how this belief system creates limitless problems and launches a devastating assault on the very possibility of knowledge? How can we know anything about morality or justice or beauty or love? How can we know the purpose of anything in a universe where purpose, along with every other question and idea, is an illusion created by biochemistry and biochemical neural activity?

Matters of Materialism

It is an odd and insidious reality of atheism's materialist view that if everything is one thing—the material of the universe—then all we can know is the one thing—the material of the universe. And if everything is one thing, then everything immaterial becomes a mystery or, better yet, an illusion. Think about that.

We ourselves are not real: we are just a biochemical side effect. So we are even illusions ourselves—biochemical illusions. Even our very consciousness, our sense of self, is all just a by-product of the biochemistry of our brains, just atoms and molecules and energy. That's it. If we know this and yet act as if these illusions are real, we cross over from illusions to delusions. Illusions that we claim are real, despite all evidence to the contrary, are delusions, deliberate delusions. The illusions of our very being become delusions. Ponder this for a moment or two. It makes us all delusional. And that makes us all crazy. Whoa!

When these material implications of atheism are explored, even briefly, their inadequacy is glaringly obvious. For it is all too easy to say there is no God. But once God is cut out of the picture, what remains for the atheist? In the end, nothing but the stuff of the universe remains. That's it. No reason, no science, no knowledge, no consciousness, no meaning, no morality, no love, no friendship, no beauty. What's left is nothing but the one thing that's real: the material of the universe.

Even if you set aside the despair of such a world, do you really think this is correct? Is this truly what the universe is? Could it be such a place?

Factually Wrong

Well, the answer is no. The atheists are not right: not right about God, not right about the universe. And they're not right for sound and solid reasons. I don't say this just to avoid the despair of the depressing reality of materialism, naturalism, atheism. The atheists are wrong not because we reject the darkness and despair of the universe. They are wrong because they have the wrong answer, as we can show with the sound and solid logic of science and reason. We can say this with absolute certainty.

They are wrong because they are wrong, not because we don't like their answer. We can know this by two crucial ways of knowing—science and reason. And we can know they are wrong with certainty, absolute certainty. They are so wrong at a level so basic that to be an atheist in any reasonable and conscious way is impossible. And that's not hyperbole; it really is just that simple, just that clear.

Ultimately, the only avenue left for atheists is the blind leap of faith, the faith of believing without scrutiny, without examining the assumptions or the substance of the beliefs. All that remains is the irrationality of an atheistic faith severed from reason and science, a faith held despite the demands of reason and the implications inherent in science and its methods.

Consider what the universe looks like to atheists. In their quest for knowledge, their exaggerated, scrupulous skepticism leads them to destroy any way of knowing. Their need for demonstrable, physical proof defeats their search for real truth at its very inception. Their insistence on demonstrable, physical proof is not really skeptical or cautious, but a commitment to physical, tangible evidence alone. It is a narrow view of knowing, not a wider one. And, as we will see in the next chapter, even science and reason cannot meet the criteria of their narrow, restrictive, and erroneous field of view.

But, for now, reflect on a universe of only matter and energy. Think about the devastation this causes for reason and science. Don't dwell on the despair or purposeless horror of such a world. The atheistic, material universe is a universe dark and diabolical. But it's nothing more than the product of an empty and distorted mind, a mind that denies so much of what we know and experience without just cause or rational grounding.

Remember, the universe we live in is the one we're trying to understand, comprehend, and discover. If the answers of atheism and materialism don't represent the universe we inhabit and know, then they must be false and wrong. Their hypotheses about the kind of universe that exists are not true. And if you can't fully see their errors yet, the next chapters will make them clearer, as we review the basic evidence of science and the witness of reason for the existence of God and the universe He created.

Take some time really to inspect what I've explained above. Really work through this. Look at how much we use reason every day, how much we rely on its certainty and application in science, engineering, and technology. Think deeply about not just the loss of reason, but of the human mind and consciousness, of virtue, beauty, and love. And know how important it is for us to recognize these deficiencies. For when we see deficiencies in our fellow human beings in areas such as these, we know them as true and important deficiencies. They betray the materialists' hardness of heart, their slowness of mind, their willful avoidance, their lack of sensitivity, their inability to form human connections. And our perception of deficiency is true and accurate, as is our perception of the more positive depth and range of all these crucial human faculties.

So again, think. Think long and hard. Think carefully and correctly and you'll see the errors I've laid out. And be critical. Through your critical and skeptical thinking, the truth of what I have said will become all the clearer. So don't hesitate to take exception to this case, but really deal with it. For the case for materialism is virtually self-refuting, if you just examine its claims clearly and coldly, if you look rationally and thoroughly.

6

Matters of Science

As we continue our pursuit of the truth about God and His existence, we come now to science. This is the bastion of atheism, its impregnable authority, the source of its strength. Here is where religion, particularly Christianity, is broken and left bereft of truth and power, except to its zealous and irrational adherents, with their blind faith and primitive worldview. Such are the claims of atheism and its use of science.

Atheists believe science has disproved God, and they defend this claim primarily with science. But as we've seen, a sound use of the scientific method is embedded in reason, and reason is required in every step in this method's proper application, be it in the pure or applied sciences. Scientists and atheists also use reason as they defend science and as they do science. Yet if reason is nothing more than biochemical activity, then we can't have real science, because it is so infected with biochemical illusions generated merely by neural activity.

Whoa! Too much? Well, just ruminate on some of this for a moment. It will become clearer as we go.

Atheism and Science

Now, it isn't as if atheists don't believe in science or use it to justify their view of the universe. They simply don't understand science properly. As a result of this, they misrepresent science and its findings.

For Catholics and atheists alike, science approaches the physical world from the perspective of gathering evidence about the things we are curious about and are observing. By making systematic observations of the things we want to know about, the object of our investigation, we can generate hypotheses, which we can then test to see if our educated guesses are correct. Finally, we can judge the degree to which our hypotheses are true and adjust and refine them accordingly.

This all seems like reasonable, patient, rigorous investigation: it arises from curiosity tempered by prudent and cautious skepticism, all driven by the desire to know the truth about how the world works. Indeed, science should take its time and remain cautious until it reaches a high level of certainty about the object of its inquiry, the behavior of the portion of the physical world under investigation.

Not only does science rely on reason in its basic definition and as it is carried out; it also relies heavily on mathematics. For much of science is guided by mathematics, allowing us to extrapolate experimental evidence to determine its logical conclusion and application. And as we know, mathematics is grounded in reason and built on the certainty of logic in its theoretical, pure forms and in its practical applications and everyday uses.

Additionally, any scientific investigation requires some important philosophical assumptions. We must assume that the physical universe behaves in a fairly orderly manner to allow us to investigate it. We also must assume that our senses, the means through which we can investigate the universe, are fairly accurate, so we can make accurate observations. We also must believe in the truth of logic and reason, which we must be able to apply in an accurate, sophisticated manner. For our ability to reason is the only way we can make any sense of our observations at all. That is what reason does: it makes sense of things.

Since science is wed inextricably to philosophical assumptions, such as a lawful and ordered universe and the reliability of our senses, why does this create a problem for atheists? Because reason, logic, and truth are not material facts but immaterial concepts.

As we will see in later chapters, proofs for the existence of God depend on such concepts. Religion not only includes facts about history and the physical universe but also relies on reasoning from such realities all the way up to a totally immaterial God.

The Catholic faith makes claims about history and the cosmos, about how the world works and where it is going, about the presence and nature of man and about God Himself and His presence in history in the person of Jesus, the Christ. So the Catholic faith must use science and deal with the knowledge science generates.

Now if, as atheists think, all concepts are only biochemical mirages, then science is as off base as religion. How can we reason properly and perceive accurately when the best observation we can make is that everything is essentially a biochemical illusion? In such a case, we can have no real knowledge at all. Paraphrasing J. B. S. Haldane, if all we are is biochemistry, we have no way of knowing that all we are is biochemistry.

You can see the need for something other than the physical to explain and describe our human experience and consciousness, as well as our experience and use of reason, sensory perception, and science. Even explaining reason itself beyond our personal, individual reasoning needs another something beyond the singular reality of matter or energy, beyond the grinding, lifeless, mindless reality of biochemical materialism, to be accurate and accurately used and applied.

Atheists who use science as their primary form of explanation and defense comprehend neither the science they use nor the information it provides. Oddly, the same is true for the many scientists who are atheists. Weird, huh? But surprisingly true. How can that be?

Understanding the philosophy of science and the philosophy of mind isn't necessary or essential to conduct science. Most scientists use the scientific method without seriously examining its underlying philosophies and reasoning. Science is so common and widespread that it has become merely a methodological technology we can employ easily and rigorously, without fully comprehending its philosophical and rational basis or even its theological roots and implications.

Also, over the last four hundred years, science has been so often portrayed as the enemy or antithesis of faith that the inherent harmony of science and reason and faith has been lost. To most people nowadays, promoting this organic, inherent harmony seems foolish, if not ridiculous and ignorant.

But the Catholic understanding of knowledge admits no conflict between science, reason, and faith. Such conflict is neither rationally supportable, nor is it in keeping with Catholic teaching. Science, reason, and faith overlap and are integrated, enlightening one another and yielding a fuller, more sophisticated understanding that touches all our ways of knowing and harmonizing them. And it harmonizes all parts of our being: our minds, our hearts, our experience, not just our ways of knowing.

The Law of Cause and Effect

One way this harmony of science and reason and faith is evident is through crucial principles of logic and reason. In the principles of reason used by science, we can see the harmony of true science, valid reasoning, and our faith, even in the face of science's apparent challenges to religion. Not only do these ways of knowing harmonize with and inform one another, but they do so by design, as will be apparent as we look at the dynamic of causes and effects.

As we grapple with the problem of the origin and the order of our universe and our world in the next two chapters, we will see evidence not only of God's existence but also of His plan and purpose. These two scientific challenges to our faith will prove not to be challenges at all. The harmony between our ways of knowing will be evident. The agreement between science and reason will be clear, and it will support and affirm the knowledge that comes from faith and revelation. Finally, the intention and plan behind this harmony will be manifest.

Let's begin by examining a critical principle of reason and of science: the law of cause and effect. This law simply establishes a link between prior causes and their immediate and long-term effects. When we see some effect, we know it must have had a preceding cause. If we see an accident along the road as we travel, we know with absolute certainty that something must have caused that accident, though it may not be readily apparent what that cause was, because, after all, it was an accident. But it is highly likely there was some malfunction in judgment or mechanics that led to the accident.

If we pass a building as we travel, we know it must have been constructed by people—by builders, craftsmen, and laborers. Buildings don't just appear without having been designed and built. We know absolutely that that building is the result of many prior causes: the owner's initial decision and designs, the municipality's approval, the bank's financial underwriting, the builders' organization and coordination, the craftsmen's skills, the laborers' physical efforts.

Seems obvious—too obvious to need further examples. Effects that we see come from causes seen and unseen. Again, it's just that simple; it's just that profound. And most importantly, it's just that true.

The cause-effect relationship is true in the absolute sense of the word, true in the practical and scientific sense, true in the logical and rational sense, true in the religious and theological sense.

Cause-effect relationships lead to absolute truth, to undeniable truth, to objectively true truth.

In summary, not only can we see the role of reason's law of cause and effect; we can also see how reason has an integral role in science. In fact, you can't have science without it. Also, we can see that if there is nothing but matter and energy in the universe, we can't have reason. Without reason, we can't have science. So, despite atheism's claim on science, atheists tend to use it as a technology, a mere method, without understanding its reliance on philosophy and reason.

Because of these errors and omissions, these distortions and misapprehensions, atheists get science wrong. They get the universe wrong, too. They fail to understand their belief system properly, and so they miss its fundamental properties and miss the basic contradictions of a wholly physical, materialistic belief system. They fail to use science and reason properly, and, in the process, they fail to give reason its rightful place, power, and authority.

Within this more accurate understanding of science and reason, let's examine some of the more common and crucial claims that science and atheism make against the existence of God. Let's turn to the origin of the universe in the light of our robust, rigorous view of reason and science. And let's see if atheism is still a viable or rational or scientific alternative.

As always, take your time and reflect on the truths in this chapter. Read it again if necessary. Dwell on the law of cause and effect and why it works logically and practically. Think about what it means to have an objective principle of reason beyond the limitations and illusions of mere biochemical brain function.

I'm sure the more you comprehend this, the more you'll understand our pervasive reliance on and use of the intangible aspects of the universe, especially human consciousness and rational thought, which is possible only in a universe that is more than the tangible realities we see with our senses, more than just matter and energy.

7

Matters of Origin

When it comes to questions about whether God exists, we must look for answers in the origin of all things, the origin of the universe and everything we know that already exists.

We do this because things exist in space and time. And so we must trace this obvious, observable string of cause-effect relationships back to its source, back in time.

Reason compels us to look for the beginning of all things, because we know that everything in the cosmos must have begun at some point in time. From the law of cause and effect, we know that something cannot come from nothing. So, it is plausible and necessary to search out the initial cause of all that exists.

Our curiosity arises from our reason. We look for a reasonable answer, a reasonable cause for our existence and the existence of the cosmos. Reason compels us to seek some answers to the question of existence in the physical world and in reason itself.

Let's first look to the physical cosmos for evidence of God's existence. It is reasonable to expect to find some evidence here, some artifacts of His handiwork that point to His existence.

Let's begin with the beginning of the cosmos, for the logical law of cause and effect all but compels us to begin here in our search for answers about whether God exists. This is one reason why the Bible begins with an explanation of the origin of all things. When considering God, human reason turns almost automatically to questions of existence and origin. Such is our innate sense of rationality, our innate sense of cause and effect.

Additionally, the Bible begins with Creation because it is telling a story—the story of existence and, most importantly, the story of human existence and our relationship with God. For history is simply a form of narrative cause and effect.

The Origin of the Universe

The cause-effect relationship is crucial in exploring questions about our lives and how we came to be, how the universe and all its many facets and features came to exist. And it is crucial in getting answers about them too.

Science and faith are two good places to begin our exploration of the origin of the universe. Let's see what truth exists and how much of it we can know, and let's look at what the origin of the universe says about God. Then, in the next chapter, we'll see what the order of the universe tells us.

First of all, it's common knowledge, based on extensive scientific investigation and rigorous mathematical extrapolations, that the universe had an absolute beginning. Scientists and Catholics alike call this beginning the "big bang." This initial cataclysmic event was the very birth of everything in the universe: its space, its matter and energy, even time itself began at the initial instant, at the first moment of the universe's existence, at the very birth of our cosmos. It began with this dense singularity and with this unimaginable explosive force. This cataclysmic explosion, this "big bang," caused everything that exists to exist.

At this "singularity," the beginning of the universe took place. At this "big bang," this explosive event, the universe began to exist. Virtually all scientists agree with this. So does Catholic teaching.

The apparent conflict arises when we ask where the singularity and the explosion came from. According to the law of cause and effect, the matter and energy that banged in the big bang—the singularity, however small and dense, and the initial force, however powerful and long—had to have come from somewhere, from something, from someone. The initial matter, no matter how dense or how small, the initial force, no matter how powerful or long-lasting, all had to come from a prior cause from outside the physical universe. At the very least, it must have been caused somewhere else other than within the space and time or from the matter and energy of our universe.

These are our essential choices of cause: something, someone, somewhere else. Catholics claim it was someone; most secular scientists claim it was somewhere. For the moment, let's see what reason demands as we formulate our answers and test out the veracity and viability of our faith and its relationship with science.

This dense singularity and its explosive force are causes of all we see and know. Science tells us this with a high level of certainty. But the singularity and force are both effects too. And these effects came from something else, something prior, something more powerful. That is equally certain.

For that is the nature of the universe and of the science that investigates the universe and its nature. It investigates the causal nature of the universe. For the law of cause and effect is the core of the scientific method And the law of cause and effect is a crucial part of reason as well. And so is the very idea of "law," of logical laws, scientific laws, practical laws, and moral laws.

And reason demands that, sooner or later in our investigation, we must confront something uncaused that causes everything to exist. Sooner or later, we must meet an uncaused cause or an uncaused cause, an uncaused something or an uncaused someone.

Otherwise, we would be stuck with an "infinite regression," a string of prior causes without end. And this does not make sense logically. For the law of cause and effect requires that the string of causes and effects cannot go on infinitely or indefinitely. It must end at some point with an uncaused cause or an uncaused cause. And the physical universe demands the same ultimate causation.

So at the dense singularity as the explosive force initially erupted, we have a beginning to everything. But where did the singularity and force come from, after all? And what about the order of these initial things? For the initial singularity and its explosive force had to have some kind of order or properties, some structure, some compositional organization. And, that suggests an orderer, just as a beginning suggests an uncaused cause. They must have come from something else, a designing orderer, an uncaused cause.

In the Beginning . . . Infinity?

That something else, that someone else, must have the ability to create the initial singularity and to create its explosive power. We can see this as we investigate our universe with reason, science, and mathematics.

And everything must begin with something that was not caused —something that caused the singularity and the force but was not caused by anything else; something that just *is* without prior cause; something that is not an effect, but rather an uncaused cause that starts the string of causes and effects that our senses and our science observe.

And it is just here that reason and science agree, despite what atheists and skeptics, scientists and philosophers may argue. Because the law of cause and effect is as much a scientific law as it is a logical law. And when we investigate the physical universe, we find we need an uncaused cause that causes all the other causes and effects to occur. That is the implicit reality of the big bang made explicit.

To think that there is an infinite chain of causes and effects stretching back in time is nonsense—utterly and absolutely. For in space and time, infinity is merely a concept, not an actual reality. There is always a finite amount of matter and energy, a finite number of things, a finite degree of force, no matter how large or numerous.

While really big numbers of things or stretches of space may be huge, vast, almost unfathomable, there is a categorical difference between really, really big numbers and infinity. This difference is so immense that it defies description and measurement, for infinity is a limitless number compared with just the really big numbers of the universe. So don't be fooled by the scientific rhetoric of the "virtually infinite" universe, because infinity is way beyond any really big numbers.

And this is the odd twist of recent discoveries supporting the big bang theory. For the big bang validates the logic of cause and effect in its ultimate origin and leaves modern scientific man on the threshold of discovering God, by implication, as the universe's uncaused cause.

This is one reason why some scientists have argued for an infinite universe or a universe that regenerates itself. You see, by offering this hypothesis, they eliminate the uncaused cause, for an infinite universe does not have a beginning or an end. It just *is*. Or so those scientists think.

Because a universe infinite in both directions (past and future) is without beginning or end, the question about its origin is moot. But this is just a way of temporarily dodging the inevitability of the law of cause and effect scientifically and logically. If a universe is infinite in only one direction (extending without limit into the future), then that universe began at a moment in time: the first moment in time. Such forward-focused infinity is possible, but its initial moment had to come from something or someone outside of everything.

And despite the lack of real evidence of a regenerating universe, a universe that expands and then collapses an infinite number of times, this infinite oscillation of expansions and contractions just begs the question of origin anyway. This is what you have to come up with when you try to avoid the law of cause and effect. You avoid it with infinity.

A Bouncing Universe?

And this avoidance leads to the "bouncing" universe, the idea that the universe has expanded and contracted an infinite number of times and will continue to do so an infinite number of times, despite the absence of real evidence, despite the contradiction in reason, despite our inability to test it in a lab. You see how some scientists abandon their science when it leads to inevitabilities about God, as the law of cause and effect must inevitably do.

How did this theoretically oscillating universe come to be? The atheists' and the secular scientists' answer is that it just *is*. It always was and always will be. Not very scientific. Nor is it very logical. In fact, it sounds more like philosophy and theology than science. But it avoids the logical and scientific necessity of the origin of our cosmos and avoids the implicit question about the existence of God.

The Multiverse?

And this leads to another hypothesis designed to avoid the God question at the origin of the universe, the beginning of all that exists. Some such scientists also promote the idea of the multiverse as an alternative to the expanding-contracting universe of the infinite oscillations. It is another attempt to circumvent the question of origin, of beginnings.

The multiverse theory offers us the idea that there are multiple universes in other dimensions or in parallel states undetectable to our investigations, because they are composed differently from our universe. This is an interesting idea, in that science proposes a concept of multiple universes that are essentially undetectable to scientific investigations and are the product of some questionable theoretical mathematics. Essentially this is a form of scientific imagination, not hard, practical science.

If the physical universe we now inhabit and observe is just one of an infinite number of other universes, how can we investigate them? Is this merely a way of stating that we have a single, infinite universe that perpetually morphs into new versions of itself every fifty billion years or so? How can we know this?

And how do we explain some of the laws of physics that guide so much of our science, even simple laws such as the second law of thermodynamics, which says that all things will lose heat over time? Such fundamental laws don't apply to other universes? Really?

So what we know, we don't know. The laws of our sciences aren't laws. They are just local ordinances in our particular universe. But don't these scientists use these local ordinances to establish some of their rationale and evidence for these other universes? So these local ordinances of physics provide the rationale of the supposed truth of other parallel universes where the laws don't apply. I mean, you can't say these laws aren't laws and simultaneously say they are. That just doesn't make sense.

And it doesn't make sense because it is wrong, illogical, irrational. And it is unscientific. Are these laws of physics to be understood only as local laws without any jurisdiction beyond our present universe? And how do we know that, except by raw and unsupportable assumptions, by acts of deliberate irrationality in spite of what science and logic tell us? Can you see how science is hijacked again to serve a philosophical predisposition, a particular opinion about God and religion and reason? Can you see how such science is not only irrational and anti-logical, but in fact anti-scientific?

We see the same principle operating here as we noticed in the discussion earlier about biochemistry and reason, where biochemical materialism destroys reason. On a grander, cosmological level, the same problem occurs for atheists who must insist on a "multiverse" or an "infinitely oscillating universe" rather than the big bang beginning. For a "big bang" necessitates an uncaused cause, just as reason necessitates an intangible certainty beyond mere biochemical materialism.

The multiverse hypothesis avoids the logical inevitability of the law of cause and effect, but at the expense of science and reason. Making the universe infinite is a way of substituting the material, tangible, infinite, and eternal multiverse for an infinite, eternal, intangible being beyond the universe.

And, because there must be an uncaused cause, this being must be outside the physical universe. God must, by definition, be intangible and not subject to the limitations of space, time, and material, which are by nature finite and physical. God must be eternal and intangible and all powerful, among other things.

The Uncaused Cause and Order

But let's take a step back before we take it a step further, when we examine the order of the universe. Our reason tells us clearly and explicitly that sooner or later we must have an uncaused cause for all that exists.

This is not news for modern times. This idea is grounded in reason itself. The idea that something must have caused the beginning of the universe has a long history, though the supporting scientific evidence is relatively new.

We see how reason can tell us what can or must be. And science, guided by reason, discovers evidence to support it. It discovers evidence in the physical world that is orderly and predictable. For our universe is stable enough to investigate. And its laws and order make these discoveries replicable, predictable, universal.

And unless we believe that the universe perpetually oscillates or that we live in one of an infinite number of universes, we must confront a universe that had a definite beginning. And if everything began at the explosive singularity of the big bang, from what or from whom did that singularity come?

It must have come from something uncreated, something intangible, something outside the physical realm, something powerful beyond comprehension. It had to have come from something capable of creating from nothing all that is, all that exists. This something is what all theistic religions and some deists call "God."

For God spoke all things into existence. He commanded everything to be, to exist, to begin. This has always been a logical necessity. As science has advanced, it has essentially validated this logical truth. Guided by reason, science has given us a better understanding of how and when the world began. It has also given us a sharper understanding of how this universe works, of its intricacies and its simplicities, of its vast expanse and its infinitesimal depths, of its inherent order and its marvelous beauty. And it is to this order that we now turn.

But let us remember that reason and science are not competitive, but mutually supportive. For reason properly used is the mind of science. And science properly used is reason applied and validated in the physical world. There is no essential competition, no inherent conflict here, though it may seem so at times.

For science helps us to know and manipulate the tangible world, the physical universe. It can demonstrate the need and necessity for an uncaused being powerful enough to create all that there is from absolute nothingness. It can demonstrate the limits in time and space of the tangible physical universe too. It can even provide mathematical and physical proof of how existence began and progressed.

Our universe is lawful and predictable and knowable through reason and through reasoned observation and experimentation. This is the charge, achievement, and legacy of science—a reasoned and methodical investigation of the physical realm. And as the discussion above shows, science also points to the necessary existence of God, though it does not prove it. For science deals with the physical, tangible plane. And God is neither physical nor tangible.

And so we find evidence of God's existence and His nature in the universe we inhabit and investigate. Through the law of cause and effect, reason reveals to us the likelihood of such a being as God; through the big bang theory, science points to the necessity of God. We find evidence for God in the fact of existence itself—in the universe's very existence, even in our own existence. We find existential evidence that something, someone, made all this, made us and all that surrounds us.

And though many of us may never have spoken this desire for truth out loud, it has reverberated in our hearts. When we have gazed at the stars in the night or watched the rising and the setting of the sun, we have marveled and wondered. And all our wondering has led many philosophers, and even the philosopher within each of us, to reason that all this must have begun somewhere, at some point.

And this question of a beginning points unmistakably to God through reason and through science.

Before we go on, let's take an even closer look at the universe and the evidence of science. Let's look at the structure and order of the universe to see what they reveal about atheism and Catholicism, whether they will validate the atheistic picture of the cosmos.

Remember, think about the topics we've discussed. Take the time to investigate them. Be sure to apply reason to this case and to every preceding discussion.

Ask for God's help in this. He encourages you to ask questions, just as He exhorted His first disciples. Questioning is part of seeking, an essential part of honest and thorough investigation. Don't neglect it.

Be sure to seek to know God personally, not just conceptually. For God is a person, and He invites us to reach out to Him in a relational, personal manner. He sees us not simply as followers or believers, but as His sons and His daughters. He longs for us to know Him. He longs for us to see the bounty and beauty all around us in His creation. He longs for us to know the depth and the richness of His love for us. And He seeks a relationship with us, in which we can fully know and experience His unfathomable love for us, and in which we may come to love Him ever more deeply, intimately, purely.

8

Matters of Order

Whenever we investigate and analyze the tangible world, we have some basic expectations. One of those expectations is order.

Think about it for a moment. We expect things to happen in an ordered and orderly way. That is why, when we try to fix something and we can't, we get frustrated. We get frustrated because we expect there to be an order to the thing we want to fix and we are unable to restore that order. Or our knowledge of the order of the broken thing is inadequate, and we can't find someone who can fix the broken order. In fact, most of our frustration comes from the expectation of order and our inability to restore it or find someone who can.

You see, we expect the things of the physical universe to be ordered, to follow the scientific rules of the universe that we know through the sciences and engineering. Our knowledge and expectation of order is what tells us something is wrong or broken. When we attempt to fix the broken thing, we apply our knowledge of the order of the universe to fix the problem. If we're unsuccessful, we often conclude we don't know enough to fix it, and so we try to learn more. Or we try to understand what the source of the problem is.

Our search for the answer assumes an order, a lawful predictability, that we must discover, understand, and apply in order to fix the broken thing. This expectation applies to man-made things and also to natural things.

This is how we have advanced technology and science over the centuries. We assume there is an order to the things we build. And, more importantly, we assume there is an order to the universe and all its many materials and processes. Our knowledge of the universe's order, its structures and processes, allows us to build things, to make things, to create things. For if we did not have any knowledge of the universe's behavior and material, we would not be able to do much or to build much.

We expect the realm of the physical universe to be lawful, to be ordered. We do not expect things to be disordered or to behave in an arbitrary way. If things behaved arbitrarily, we wouldn't be able to know anything, because our science and our reason depend on the universe's lawful structure and logical function. The entire universe would be inscrutable, unpredictable, unknowable.

And all this absence of order would defy our reason and our science because both depend on order, a lawful structure and function. The absence of order would defy our ability to discover, to know, to apply any knowledge of the order as well.

Thankfully, we inhabit an ordered universe, a universe whose order we can know, a universe whose order is revealed through our investigations and our applications.

Intentional or Accidental Order?

This is precisely where atheists and agnostics slip into error. For order is a particularly strong clue. Order offers strong evidence about the existence of things, where these things come from, whether they are purposeful, whether they were made by someone or something.

For we observe an orderer, a maker of the order; we see a cause of the order. And we can know this sense of order and its link to causes and effects instinctively and logically. When it comes to man-made things, atheists would agree that order indicates a design, a deliberate effort toward a specific end, function, and vision. But when it comes to naturally occurring order, most atheists and agnostics assume that all the order of the universe, its natural properties and processes, arose by accident. Atheists look at all the order of the universe, from the minute to the cosmic, and they assume that it must have come from random chance, from blind accident, from sheer serendipity.

It doesn't seem very consistent or rational to observe such order, such complexity, such harmony, and to conclude that such order arises accidentally. But that is what atheists would have us believe.

Gambling with the Atheists

For most of us, such a huge number of ordered accidents seems to strain credulity beyond reason to the point of fantasy or stupidity. It doesn't make sense to believe that such cosmic and minute order comes from nothing but mindless chance, from such improbable luck. That is why most of us are surprised when we find unlikely or improbable order happening by accident in the mundane circumstances of our daily lives. And we are even amazed when this accidental order is neither very complex nor very large.

Let's look at an example. Let's say you're playing blackjack, a simple card game, and the dealer keeps making a perfect twenty-one every hand. While you may not be particularly suspicious at the beginning, three or four or five hands in, you will begin to wonder if the purportedly random dealing of cards is, in fact, random.

In short, you will begin to sense that maybe this accidental, random card dealing is really ordered. And you'll think this because your intuitions based on the observed data and your logic tell you this kind of order is outside of natural probability, outside of what should be randomly produced order.

When you face such an unlikely order, you naturally and rightly look for a cause behind this order. For as we all know, when it comes to playing cards, if the results are so stilted as to suggest someone is "stacking the deck," then you are really looking for a cause of the order. And the first person you will look at is the dealer.

Or imagine walking through a forest and coming upon the ruins of a small village. You would rightly assume these ruins could not have sprung into existence all by themselves. You would rightly conclude that someone or some group must have built it, because order such as what is evident in the ruins does not come about by accident. The ruins had to be built from natural materials by intelligent beings using some form of tools. No natural causes could ever assemble such ruins all by themselves.

The idea that order, in all but the simplest and narrowest sense, is accidental is nonsense. Order of any scale or degree strongly, even irresistibly, suggests an outside cause, a maker, a designer, for even the simplest order defies the laws of mathematical probability. It defies the laws of reason and common sense to see all but the simplest order and to conclude that it is accidental.

Yet that is what atheists believe. Because atheists believe that the universe is all that exists, they must also believe that the order we observe arises accidentally. They must explain everything in the universe in terms of the physical and material things only. Their view of an entirely random, accidental universe seems ridiculous, irrational, almost delusional, in light of what reason and logic, intuition and common sense, tell us about order and its causation.

But that is what atheists' view of cosmological evolution is. This is what a wholly material universe actually means. For atheists, all order is the product of random chance; all order is accidental—period.

Faith in Blind, Random Accident

Now, this blind faith in cosmic accidents, despite the cautions of reason and common sense, reveals the underside of atheism's explanation of existence. It reveals an almost unquestioning confidence in accidental order, despite the natural cautions of reason, common sense, and mathematical probability, which inherently push us to seek a source behind any observed order.

This blind faith in random chance makes you want to play poker with these atheists. You could stack the deck on them all day long, beat them in every hand, and they would still blindly assume it was all accidental luck. With their blind trust in accidental order, you could retire early simply by playing poker with these guys.

But we all know atheists wouldn't stand for such abuse. They weren't born yesterday, though their beliefs about chance might make you think otherwise. They simply cannot live in a manner consistent with their blind trust in chance. Yet on a far more important level, on a grand, cosmological scale, that is precisely what they try to do. They set aside their common sense and reason and insist that everything—and I mean everything—in the universe is the product of random chance over time.

This is why, when the question of observed order is considered seriously, the atheists' case fails to pass muster. It fails to meet the demands of mathematical probability. It fails to meet the demands of accumulated scientific investigation. It fails to meet the demands of the law of cause and effect. It fails to meet even the basic laws of reason.

Order and Mathematical Probability

If we intend to ascribe to chance the order we observe in the universe on the minute, microscopic level and on the vast, cosmic level, we have every right and obligation to subject that conclusion to scrutiny. But how? How do you examine accidental processes when you can't see them? How can you observe accidents? You'd have to be everywhere and observe everything. Not very practical or possible, especially over time.

But we can subject such assertions of accidental order to a mathematical analysis, given the impossibility of direct observations across the length of the universe over the course of all time. This type of analysis does not involve direct observation of chance occurrence, but it does provide a mathematical, statistical model to analyze the possibility of chance occurrences over time. This analysis accounts for and predicts the likelihood of accidents.

So what does mathematics, particularly statistics, say about the order we observe in the universe? There are such studies that give us a sense of the likelihood of our universe's order arising from sheer chance. And these numbers are ridiculous in the extreme. The probability of the universe's arising from blind chance is so unlikely as to be virtually impossible.

But don't take my word for it. After all, probability is a numbers or odds thing. And the numbers almost speak for themselves. But just in case the numbers aren't enough, we can also draw out their conclusions with words and descriptions.

Roger Penrose, a British mathematician and colleague of physicist Stephen Hawking, calculated the probability that our universe arose by chance. He examined the universe's order and complexity, its harmony and dynamism, its size and structure, and he concluded that the odds against the universe's spontaneous existence were $10^{10\wedge 123}$ to 1. That's 10 to the 10th power to the 123rd power to 1. Pretty steep odds, given the fact that the number generally accepted as zero probability is only 10 to the 50th power. So according to statistical norms, the probability that the universe arose by chance is so close to zero as to be virtually impossible. The universe is too ordered and too complex to have come about through any such accidental processes.

And this is only one piece of evidence. But it is a piece of evidence that affirms what we can see with our eyes—the universe is too vast, too complex, too dynamic to have come about through some form of dumb luck. It just couldn't happen that way.

The Tuning of the Universe

Not only is the accidentally evolving universe a virtual impossibility according to statistics, but there are other scientific measurements that support this conclusion as well.

In physics and cosmology, the study of the cosmos, there are certain physical constants in the universe that structure it in various ways. Gravity is one such force. There is also a relationship between many of these constants that create the order and processes essential for the universe's behavior and structure.

Some scientists who studied these constants and their dynamic relationship with each other theorized that the array of physical constants and their interrelationships seems too great to have arisen accidentally. And as they studied these constants, they found that these constants seemed "tuned" to permit and to promote the development of not only our balanced universe, but also carbon-based organic life.

In short, these constants, in and of themselves, and in their relationship with each other, seemed too finely tuned to be accidental in origin. And their fine-tuning seemed to promote not only the finely balanced universe we observe, but the very possibility of organic life. They called this principle of fine-tuning for life the "anthropic principle."

When this principle was first presented at an international cosmology conference in 1973, the number of identified constants supporting this idea was fairly limited. Nowadays, the list of tuned constants has grown to over one hundred. (Remember, these are scientific constants, not some evidence generated by people of faith.)

The anthropic principle claims that the mathematical properties of these identified constants indicate their purposeful nature, given the number of constants involved and their fine-tuning relative to each other and to biological life. For example, if one exponent was changed by one number in one formula for one physical constant, the entire universe would be made of helium. This fine-tuning seems to indicate the likelihood of intentional and intelligent design. So the sheer number of the constants suggests the absence of chance as the originator of the universe's order.

And the nature and fine-tuning of the constants and the overall number of them indicate a fine-tuning for biological life, particularly human life. That is why they called this theory the "anthropic principle."

One such example might be an anomaly; two might be a curiosity; three, a puzzle. But over one hundred suggests some serious scientific evidence. And all this evidence suggests a universe ordered, tuned to bring about the development of biological life. Our reason tells us there should be evidence of God in His creation. We can see some of this evidence in the universe's fine-tuning and in its order, no matter how much atheists try to write the evidence off as coincidence.

The evidence against atheism continues to mount: the big bang as the origin of the universe and the fine-tuned constants as its order. Even the existence of biological life increasingly reveals purpose and intention unexplainable through blind evolution.

Biological Adaptation

The dominant paradigm of evolution explains the existence of everything in the universe in terms of accidental activity. Organic life, in its many forms, arises solely from accidental mutation and adaptability. But let's take a very brief look at some of the problems inherent in this claim of random evolution. The basic atheistic view is that genetic mutations occur accidentally. These accidents, if they provide some adaptive advantage to the organism, will tend to dominate and eventually, over time, will become part of the new form of the organism's basic equipment.

Though this may indeed be the process for some variations, other changes attributed to this simple, accidental process are not so easily explained. For example, the dual principles of irreducible complexity and minimal function have challenged the traditional atheist view of the gradual evolution of biological life.

The principles of irreducible complexity and minimal function may be seen most clearly when we look at compound organs, such as the eye. For an eye to exist, it must be adaptive, according to the atheistic evolutionary paradigm. It must provide some kind of adaptive advantage to exist and to be present throughout a species. It must allow a creature to see, and sight must be an adaptive advantage.

But an eye, even a primitive one, is composed of many smaller structures, which are dependent on the brain and its capacity to interpret sensory data. In order to offer an adaptive advantage, the eye must provide information that eventuates in better decision-making or, at least, better instinctual responses that enhance survival.

Well, think about that for a moment. Think about all the many tiny structures in even a simple and primitive eye. Think about the neural connections between these structures and the brain. Think about the capacity of the brain to process such information. Think about the connection of this sensory data to decision-making and instinctual centers in the brain of the species.

Think about all these many components that must be present at the same time for an adaptive advantage to exist. If things that evolve are composite things, as most are, this composite complexity can't be broken down over time in order to explain the compound organ's ability to function minimally. If the organ doesn't have a minimal function at the very outset, it has no adaptive advantage. Unless everything is present at once, it doesn't work. It doesn't give the species an adaptive advantage.

So the idea of gradual, accidental adaptation is not a viable option, because it cannot explain the need for simultaneous mutations integrated across many biological structures, including cortical and neural pathways. The sheer number of things that must be present at once indicates intentional order more than it indicates accidental adaptation. Even if we assume that complex adaptations could occur by chance, this process would require far more time than has elapsed since the big bang. In short, it is the "tuning" principle on the small and microscopic level. This kind of thing might happen in extremely rare occurrences, but as with the "tuning" constants, the sheer number indicates intentional order.

In addition to the logic and data of irreducible complexity and minimal function, as well as "cosmological fine-tuning," the collective probability of these principles defies statistical criteria for chance activity. This type of statistical analysis indicates something beyond chance occurrence. It indicates something more purposeful and intentional.

And all the many sophisticated adaptive species we now see would have taken much more time to evolve to this level since the big bang. So, even if these adaptations might have occurred, it doesn't seem that there was enough time for all this adaptive activity to occur, even if it operated very efficiently.

The Uncaused Cause

So the universe exists. This we all know. We know it by our senses. We also know it by our reason. Why, we even know it because we are simply asking the question about the universe's existence. The reality of our consciousness and our mental activity tells us that we exist and that our world, our universe, exists.

Not only do our world and our universe exist, but they came into existence at a definite instant in time. Science indicates that our universe began with a dense singularity and a cataclysmic explosive event. And this happened from no prior cause within the physical universe.

Indeed, the universe began from an uncaused cause outside the universe, an incorporeal being of immense power capable of creating things from absolutely nothing. A creator who can simply will things into existence. A being who can simply command things into existence. We call this creator God.

And this creator is a necessary being, for without such an uncaused cause, we must face a universe that leaves us no way to investigate it. It leaves us a universe without science or reason, without accurate perceptions and reliable reasoning.

Even if the universe's origin is found in infinity, as the multiverse and "bouncing" universe theorists claim, we still face a universe whose law of cause and effect requires a truly uncaused cause. For the universe tells us that the law of cause and effect does apply when it comes to the origin of everything, even if the universe had a beginning or has merely oscillated infinitely. If the universe's history is infinite, then we still face a universe that appears to be reasonable and lawful. Whether there is a beginning or not, we still must have a cause for all these effects, regardless of their extent.

So if we have a universe that has no origin, a universe that is eternal and infinite, it is a universe that defies reason and science. It is a universe whose expanse in time and space shrouds itself under dimensional infinity by denying the essence of the law of cause and effect by appealing to a multiverse, many universes where the laws of logic and physics do not apply. It denies the inherent demand of the law of cause and effect. It also denies the necessity and reality of order. For the law of cause and effect requires a necessary beginning, a beginning from an uncaused cause. When an ultimate origin is denied, all of the order we observe becomes, in essence, an illusion, a merely local event.

When it comes to a multiverse or an oscillating universe, in the end, the law of cause and effect mocks us by leaving us an infinite regression without origin or end. And an infinite regression not only denies a beginning but also defies logic and reason. For it tells us that our reason is simply applicable in a local sense, not in an ultimate sense.

For our observations of causes and effects are valid only in a near sense in our local universe, not in any ultimate or inclusive sense. Our observations and the logical laws that govern them are valid only here and now and nowhere else.

If the law of cause and effect is true, then sooner or later we must have an uncaused cause that begins the chain of causes and effects we know, observe, and rely upon. Still, atheists claim our universe is infinite, without origin, without ultimate order.

And order is a manifestation of reason, a mental order. In fact, the presence of reason is the presence of order. But an infinite universe denies reasoned order by casting all things in an infinite ground in direct contradiction to the laws of reason. And if reason is so undermined and denied, so, too, is science, for, again, there is no science without reason.

In the end, an infinite universe is a universe of apparent order and logic whose logic and order arise from nothing, a universe grounded in the destructive condition of relentless infinite regressions, a universe whose observed order indicates nothing more than accident, a universe that reduces all reason, all science, all perceptions to mere biochemical illusions generated by other accidentally ordered means. Our reason becomes irrational, a mere mirage coming from biochemistry without any validity or certainty.

And, this is why atheism, when examined carefully in light of reason and science, fails to satisfy the demands of both reason and science. For the existence of all that exists tells us there must be something outside of the physical realm that has caused everything to come into existence. We know this logically and scientifically.

The Meaning and Truth of Inherent Order

Here we turn a corner of great significance. As we look at the order of the universe, we must face a rising tide of certainty, a deepening deluge of dogma about the existence of God. And as God becomes an inevitable reality supported by science and reason, atheism and agnosticism lose their intellectual viability as legitimate explanations of existence, the universe, our world, human nature, and science and reason themselves.

Atheism must give way before the weight and breadth and depth of evidence of a reality beyond the mere material plane, beyond simple matter and energy, space and time, accident and chance. Agnosticism must surrender to the body of real evidence that defies its claims about the absence of evidence for God's existence, its insistence on God's obscurity, and its belief that we can't know anything much about God.

Why is this the end of atheism and agnosticism? Well, to ask questions about order is a natural and reasonable impulse in all of us, as we've seen above. It is at least one of the reasons you are still reading this book.

When we ask such reasonable, natural questions, we know that our curiosity is reasonable. Our impulse to seek the truth is reasonable; it's a function of order, an implicit order: the order of reason, the order of logic, the order of common sense. In other words, asking questions about order presupposes and recognizes the existence of order. Our questions about order are themselves a form of order.

For order indicates truth; it indicates the truth of reason; it indicates an important clue about the nature of the universe and of God's existence.

Reason and science tells us that order exists. Many of the observations they make about the universe, its order, its tuning, and its biological development indicate the high likelihood of God's existence. These observations are upheld by trained scientists, mathematicians, and logicians, some of whom are investigating on the very frontiers of their fields.

Though many such scientists do not talk about God openly, the few who do see in the physical cosmos and in biological life the fingerprints of God: His design, His creativity, His beauty, His character, and His plans.

Given the evidence for the existence of God, let's now look into the nature of God and His relationship with us. What kind of a God is God? Why did He make us? And why did He make us the way we are?

But remember to think about this information, keeping in mind that science hasn't proven that God doesn't exist. Quite the opposite. Much of modern science indicates the likelihood of God's existence, just as our reasoned proofs do.

Check it out. Look into the science and ponder the rational proofs. If you need to, consult more sophisticated and elaborate references. Be sure to do your homework on this. For the existence of God is the biggest, most comprehensive, most crucial of all questions. And it is the foundation for all other questions about God, who He is, what He wants.

So take your time. But don't waste your time by neglecting this question. Pray, even if you don't believe yet. Ask God for help and insight and desire and discipline. He encourages such prayers.

God wants you to know Him, not just to know about Him. If He created us, He is our Father, our loving and perfect Father, our Daddy, so much more than an all-powerful being who rules over us. He desires that all of us love Him with all our mind and all our heart, with all our will and all our strength.

He asks you to seek Him, not just to believe in Him blindly. And He promises that those who sincerely seek and keep seeking Him will, in fact, find and keep finding Him, for He is God.

9

Matters of Reason

When we investigate the physical world, we use the experimental method, a logical, objective approach to finding out what is really going on in our physical world. And this is appropriate and essential for coming to true knowledge about the world of our senses.

We use the scientific method to safeguard ourselves from the distortions of our senses and the potential bias of our beliefs. That is why we replicate experiments. To determine if the knowledge we found by using the scientific method is true for any and all circumstances, we test the experiments and examine their conclusions.

Reason and science are inseparable when it comes to investigating the material, physical world. As I mentioned before, you cannot do science without reason, for science arises from reason and is replete with reason in its conception and in its practical uses. Reason is an implicit and inherent aspect of all science. And as people of the twenty-first century, we all should know this.

Falsely Limiting Reason

But when it comes to reason, things in the modern world and in the modern mind are different. For it is almost a cultural given that reason on its own can prove virtually nothing. Culturally, we have seriously undermined the power and usefulness of reason, unless it is tied to science and the investigation of the physical world.

That is why many of us have come to believe there are no real truths other than scientific truths, truths about the physical world only. When we believe this, reason's power and the truths we can know are lost. Science and the physical truths it generates become the only truths, and reason is seen as more about manipulation and rhetoric. That is why we have come to believe that truths beyond the physical plane are all personal truths, not actual and factual ones. That is why philosophy is merely philosophy and not a source of truth.

But reason can also give us truths just as reliable as the most certain of scientific truths. It can do it all by itself without an appeal to science. Like mathematical proofs, reason can prove things with only an appeal to the laws of reason. And it is right here that our cultural bias against reason and its power is manifest. But let's take a minute to make reason's power more evident.

The use of reason as an independent means to finding the truth can be seen most clearly in simple geometric proofs, though it is inherently evident in mathematics itself. For instance, through reason we can know that the sum of the angles in any triangle must be 180 degrees or that the sum of the squares of the base and the height of a right triangle is equal to the square of the hypotenuse. And these can be proven without an appeal to science, as we all know from our high school math courses.

Also, independent reason tells us truths even about the physical realm that we do not have to subject to direct physical observation. For instance, we can know things about the origin of the universe, the initial "big bang," without having directly observed the event. By using reason, we can extrapolate from what we know about physics and chemistry to some evidence and artifacts of this initial event.

And as a result of these extrapolations, we can determine what occurred at the initial singularity. In fact, the very idea of extrapolation is based on reason. And the process of extrapolating is a direct use of reason applied to a body of knowledge. You see how reason is implicit and crucial to science, to knowing, to truth.

Also, experimental science cannot tell us directly about the need for an ultimate uncaused cause of all that we observe in the physical realm. Science can tell us only about the effects and the immediate and distant causes of these observed effects. It can't tell us about the absolute necessity of an uncaused cause at the very beginning of the universe. Only reason tells us that.

Our simple yet powerful reason tells us there must be an ultimate initial cause to everything in the physical universe. Otherwise, we are faced with an infinite regression of causes and effects without end or beginning. And that just begs the question and defies the laws of both reason and science.

These simple but profound problems reveal the limits of science and the real power of reason, which gives us access to a wide range of knowledge and truth about the ultimate things of life and living, about God as the necessary being. So let's just use our simple, powerful, yet profound reason and demonstrate some absolute conclusions we can know about the universe and about God.

We explored this earlier in our discussions of the law of cause and effect, biological materialism, and the origin and the order of the universe. Now let's take a brief look at how powerful reason is on its own and what some of these truths that reason reveals to us are.

Change

Let's begin with change. When it comes to change, most of us understand how that happens. We have the potential for something, and when we act or move, we turn our potential into something actual. We have the capacity to do or move or act. And when we use that potential, we convert our potentiality into actuality.

When we observe these changes, we can see that they are made up of other changes, as well. For example, when we scratch our heads, we move our arm and our fingers. But these motions are performed by muscles and nerves and individual cells, all of which are involved in the change or motion or action. And all of these smaller components have a potentiality changed to actuality too.

Even we who initiate these many changes from potentiality to actuality are also a mass of potentiality. But behind this string of changes, according to the law of cause and effect, there must be an unchanging ground for all change: an unchanging being. Not only that, but this unchanging being must also be all actuality and no potentiality, a perfectly actual being—a completely actualized, unchanged being.

This logical necessity for a perfectly and completely actualized being is the same as the logical necessity for an uncaused cause. Otherwise, we have no way of explaining this change from potentiality to actuality.

Both the perfectly and completely actualized being and the uncaused cause are logical necessities, things that are necessary truths. They have to be true. For there must be an uncaused cause to the universe, because the law of cause and effect demands it. And similarly, there must be a completely actualized being, an unchanged changer behind each and every act, each and every move from the potential to the actual. And this unchanged ground must be there at each and every moment. And we call this necessary ground "God."

Reason, as it is manifested in the law of cause and effect, requires these two significant and irrefutable conclusions. One is the need for an uncaused cause as we look back in time. The other is the need for an unmoved mover as we look down in time.

These are necessary conclusions. If we disregard or ignore them, we break the laws of reason and move into irrationality. And we can't pick and choose which laws of logic and reason we want to accept. Because reason is lawful, we must accept its conclusions, just as we do with irrefutable scientific findings.

Reason Is Universally True

If reason is denied in and of itself, then we must also deny its legitimacy and practical usefulness in other places. For instance, we can't use reason in science when it is convenient and helpful, yet ignore it or diminish its utility and certainty when we find it inconvenient or difficult to comprehend. It must be valid in examining the physical things of this world as well as the intangible things that seem more philosophical, more religious. Reason is legitimate and valid everywhere or nowhere, particularly when the same law of logic is operative. It is just that simple. It is just that reasonable.

As with proofs in mathematics and logic, proofs such as these prove the absolute necessity of their conclusions. And this proves the validity and importance of reason. Reason is essential to scientific methodology and to making scientific observations and conclusions. It is also crucial to mathematics and to reasoned proofs. It is no less important or crucial when examining the ultimate things of life.

Oftentimes, reason's critical importance to science is overlooked, just as it is omitted or devalued as an autonomous way of knowing. This is why philosophy is often viewed so skeptically, because reason is its primary methodology. And in our culture, we have come to believe that reason cannot help us discover the truth about anything except some fairly basic scientific laws.

But as this chapter explains, reason tells us a great deal more about science, its discoveries and laws, its technological and engineering advances, and its mundane and rudimentary applications.

More than we might have thought. More than we may imagine. It even tells us what is unscientific, false, illogical, irrational, and imaginary.

Truth and the Necessary Being

It tells us all this and more. It tells us truth exists. It tells us philosophy is legitimate. It tells us God exists and can be known. It tells us there is scientific evidence and logical proofs for God's existence. It tells us our reason is real and an important path to truth.

And it tells us our limitations. While we may know many truths, we cannot know all truth. For our reason situates us in our proper and ordinate place in the universe. For we are neither the uncaused causes nor the perfectly actualized beings. We are the crown of creation. But we are not the creator. We are the creatures, the children of the necessary being—the uncaused cause, the unchanged changer, the creator.

In our universe, we see evidence of this necessary being. In our logic and reason, we see that this necessary being must exist prior to the existence of everything in the physical universe. We know this necessary being created everything that constitutes the physical universe. We also know that this being created an ordered universe that can be investigated through the proper use of reason and observation. We know the universe is tuned for biological life, even for human life. And we know the universe created and ordered by this necessary being is reasonable and logical.

Yet this necessary being seems hidden, obscure, mysterious. Even though we may know that this necessary being, this God, actually exists, we're not really sure who or what this necessary being is. But should that surprise us? Let's use our reason and look at this necessary being and the idea of mystery in our universe and in our human experience. And let's look at our capacity for knowledge and truth.

First of all, mysteries come in degrees. I mean, the fact that we cannot know everything about something does not mean that we cannot know anything about it. For instance, take most of the machines we use. We know only how to operate them, not how they work or how to fix them. Our knowledge of most machines is enough for our needs. And though we may not know the intricacies of these machines, we know the basics necessary to use them and maintain them properly; so, on a certain level, the machines are a mystery.

It is important to understand the idea of the degrees of mystery when we are talking about things that are somewhat obscure or mysterious or complex. When we talk about knowledge, we must recognize the difference between exhaustive knowledge and functional knowledge. And we must recognize that this difference in degree between comprehensive knowledge and functional knowledge is inherent in our human condition.

We are the crown of creation, beings of immense talents and capacities. We are the thinking beings, the self-aware beings. But we also know we are limited in our capacities, limited in our ability to know because some things may be too sophisticated, too comprehensive, too complex for even the brightest of us to understand and to express. So some of the differences between exhaustive knowledge and functional knowledge come from our essential limitedness.

Some of these differences come from our differences in intelligence. Some of our limits come from our beliefs and from the presuppositions upon which our beliefs are based. And some of them come from our subjectivity and our perceptual bias, as well as our interests and talents for different things.

Some of the differences between exhaustive knowledge and functional knowledge come from what we seek knowledge about. When God becomes the subject of our quest for knowledge, we can know by definition that our knowledge will be limited to some degree, because to know about God fully would make us gods ourselves. And we are clearly not gods.

So our knowledge of God will be limited, though the degree of these limits is not clear so far in our discussion. But in the coming chapters, we will explore the knowledge and mystery of the necessary being, of God. And we will push the limits of our current knowledge of God and our capacity to know. We will also spend time examining whether God communicates with us.

Our reason tells us that there is a God and that we have limited capacities. Yet even though there are limits to our general capacity to know and our capacity to know about God, let's push those limits. Resolve to push yourself to know more, to learn how to reason more effectively and incisively, to discover the real frontiers of knowing and knowing about God. Be willing to strive relentlessly in pursuit of the limits of knowing and knowledge. For the rewards are great.

And though you may seek understanding, knowledge, and truth, you also seek something more than information, knowledge, truth, or even wisdom. When you more fully comprehend all this, you can then turn your mind and heart to the idea of revelation, the fact that this necessary being actually communicates with all of us generally and with each and every one of us personally—maybe even at this moment. Pretty wild, huh?

But as we move on and explore the nature of this necessary being, you will find that, though such revelation may appear odd, it is really consistent with the very nature of this necessary being, this God, the God of the apostles.

So, as always, seek God sincerely and with an open mind and heart. For God desires you to know with certainty and to experience the joy and confidence of truth. And you should seek not just with your mind or your heart, but with every facet of your being and with every act, every behavior you can muster.

Whether you pray to God or read about God, whether you strive to love others and give yourself to serve them, whether you are actively making the world a better place for those you encounter or you are sitting back and gratefully appreciating the beauty and wonder of our world—remember, these are all ways you seek God. Just remember that more deliberately and you will realize it more definitively.

10

Matters of the All

Now that the existence of God is clear and certain, the next crucial corner we must turn involves who or what God is. What kind of a God is He? Exploring this critical question will consume the next few chapters. And as we search for answers and the truth about this question, we will use reason and human experience as our primary means of discovering the truth about who God is.

We will look at all the basic possibilities from which we must decide. Remember: we can choose the right answer only from a list of real possibilities. Some may propose choices not on this list, but those are sheer fantasy. There is not a list of infinite possibilities from which to choose, nor even a very extensive list. When it comes to basic questions, there's a limited number of real and distinct answers. Any new religion or belief about God is just a variation on these basic choices. If our list is thorough and incorporates all the basic possibilities, then it must be exhaustive, however short. And if it is exhaustive, then we can know with absolute certainty that the right answer is on that list. That means that the truth about God must be one of those choices, among which we must decide.

The World according to God

A Separate Being?

First, we must decide if God is apart from the physical universe, a separate force, a separate being. Or is our word "God" really just a way of expressing the idea that everything is really just a part of the whole cosmic consciousness, that we are all part of God, who is everything? This is the first crucial choice we must make.

Again, is God a separate being different from the universe, outside though immanent in the universe? Or is God everything in the universe? Each of us must decide from this short list. Either God is separate from the universe, or God is the universe.

This idea that God is the universe is called "pantheism." The prefix "pan" means "all" or "everything." If we connect this prefix to the root word "theism," which means "belief in God," then we see "pantheism" essentially means a belief that everything is God. Pantheism is the theology of Buddhism, New Age spiritualism, and other such holistic religions and movements.

The *Oxford Dictionary* defines "pantheism" as "the belief or philosophical theory that God and the universe are identical . . . the identification of God with the forces of nature and natural substance." According to the *Modern Catholic Dictionary*, "pantheism" is "any of a variety of views that claim that all things are divine, or that God and the universe are really identical, or that there is really no distinction between God and what believers in creation call the world." So I'm God. You're God. My dog is God. Your car is God. The forces and substance of nature are all God. Everything is God. Everything. Get it?

I mean, can I really be God if you have to tell me? Wouldn't I already know? Actually, as a pantheist, I wouldn't, because my consciousness and the content of my thoughts don't matter: I'm a mere infinitesimal part of this pantheistic God, this cosmic consciousness.

Or, to take it a step further, if everything is God, no part of this holistic God would know that it is God. That means God doesn't know He exists. Whoa! Wait a second. If God doesn't know that

He exists, how can pantheists know that God is everything? Do you see what I mean?

Don't you find this weird and nonsensical? Pantheism shouldn't be taken all that seriously, for it is built on a major contradiction and on a fundamentally nonsensical notion. And what is pantheists' evidence for their belief? Do they have any? Could they have any?

Well, actually, they have no evidence. Their belief consists in simply extrapolating from their personal consciousness and guessing there must be something beyond what is. Often some of the more spiritually inclined atheists and agnostics find pantheism appealing, because it allows them to find a measure of reality in human consciousness and experience, and it provides a degree of hope that atheistic materialism can never provide.

Also, the crucial contradiction that arises from the pantheistic idea of God as the divine consciousness of everything in the universe is not a benign contradiction. It is a contradiction of consequence, a crucial and fatal contradiction, just like the contradictions of atheistic materialism. Let's take a look at this fatal contradiction in more detail.

A Critical Contradiction

If the universe had a beginning, then the pantheistic God must have had a beginning too. As you know by now, this leaves us with the same problem that the atheists have with the law of cause and effect and the uncaused cause. Who or what caused the universe to exist, so that everything could then become God? The contradiction is that God depends on the universe for existence or, at least, for complete development, for fulfillment, for full realization.

Or, even funnier and more ludicrous, there is no way rationally to prove to any degree the existence of this pantheistic God, because our reasoning is really just a very minor thought in the deep recesses of this holistic and cosmic consciousness, which is somehow not conscious of its own consciousness. Pantheism thus resembles atheistic materialism in claiming that all consciousness is simply a composite but contingent phenomenon dependent solely on biochemical activity. We, the pantheistic God's local consciousness, are incapable of knowing or participating in this holistic consciousness in any discernible way.

Do you see the divide between our consciousness and thought and this idea of pantheism, which is by definition outside our capacity to know through reason, experience, science, and so on? Do you see what human thought means for this holistic consciousness? Do you see how pantheism disregards and destroys reason?

Problems of Pantheism

This is why pantheism has such a strong appeal to New Age movements and spirituality: it offers ways of knowing and being outside of human experience, with a particular emphasis on denying reason. It exhorts us to look beyond reason, beyond science, beyond our rational faculties, beyond our everyday consciousness, for truth and relational intimacy.

Pantheism offers spirituality without reason, concrete content, or definite doctrine. It gives only a descriptive invitation to an experience in which we shed our specific, personal consciousness and enter the great "all." It invites us to enter a consciousness that empties us of our thoughts and our consciousness. And it invites us to join the all, the one, the whole of the universe.

The implication is that we must abandon our consciousness, our reason, our sensitivities, our emotions. Joining the all or becoming one with the greater whole requires obliterating our very selves, denying who we are, as we succumb to the "all." Pantheism involves our willful abandonment of ourselves by plunging into the obliteration of the all.

In the end, pantheism simply makes each and every one of us a part of God. As with atheistic materialism, our consciousness and our unique personalities are passing mirages, illusions we live by, but with no reality.

In both cosmologies, this means that each of us is obliterated at death. When atheists die, they no longer exist. When pantheists die, they no longer exist as themselves. They become part of the great all, a mere part of God without their personal, individual identity, without their unique individuality, without any and all consciousness of who they are or were.

As you see, at death, it is still obliteration couched in terms of ascendancy and final fulfillment, but the fulfillment comes at the expense of who you are. And could real fulfillment be attained by the obliteration of who you are? Isn't fulfillment the completion and perfection of who you are? I mean, the word "fulfillment" means "completion and full realization," not "destruction and obliteration" (at least in the English language).

Once again, we encounter a serious lapse in logic, which betrays an utterly flawed understanding of human consciousness and human nature and what our human experience is all about.

Modern Error

No one could find pantheism appealing or true without setting aside reason, don't you think? No one would believe this, unless he was running from something far worse: a secular universe and its atheistic, materialistic presuppositions.

But oddly enough, this is what many moderns either implicitly or explicitly believe. They believe truth is beyond reason and not in any degree subject to reason's rules. Because it is apparently beyond reason and in no way subject to the rules of logic, pantheism comes down to a deliberately blind faith, an entirely psychological faith, with an inherently irrational personal spirituality. It is a faith beyond truth and morality, a faith beyond good and evil, a faith whose real truth, purpose, and being are beyond the mind and its faculties.

Pantheists believe that truth, goodness, purpose, and being are outside our capacity to know and to understand—at least to any degree beyond the existence of the "all." Pantheism is a theory about "God" that asserts that we are all part of "God" and will become "God," even though we won't know it, because when we know it, we won't be ourselves. When we reach an enlightened state and transcend this earthly world and our very being and personality, we will no longer be who we are.

Pantheistic Implications

Let's take a closer look at some of the implications of a pantheist view of God. First of all, it is not reason that gives pantheists enlightenment and truth. The truth comes from emptying ourselves. Knowledge as information or wisdom or truth is not the goal, nor is it even possible.

Pantheists seek truth in a method of deliberate self-destruction. They become enlightened by denying and eliminating their personality and consciousness. Their goal is to become empty.

Now, the denial of personality does not happen at the beginning of a pantheist's journey. Pantheism generally asserts a few moral claims, most of which are intended to deal with our selfishness and our senses. Over time, as pantheists proceed on their journey, they leave behind all the struggles of selfhood to seek further enlightenment. Often, they do so through transcendental meditation and the repetition of mantras to seek higher levels of removal from their worldly state. This spiritual and psychological approach and its desired state tells us a great deal about the type of "God" pantheists believe in.

Pantheists are not called to contemplation or deeper thought. They're encouraged to leave behind their thoughts and seek an experience that almost defies description. They are to go beyond good and evil to a higher plane of existence. Notice how pantheism therefore defies morality in addition to reason and thought.

By going beyond good and evil, how do we know that such a state is actually better? If this state of existence is "higher," "better," wouldn't it have to end with the ultimate good? It sure should, if the law of cause and effect and the laws of reason hold. The word "better" implies some ultimate perfection. Better and better requires the best, the ultimate in goodness, the highest good. Logic requires it. But not for pantheists.

Plus, isn't the idea of "better" an inherently moral statement? Yet if our ascent through this pantheistic path to the heights of being and consciousness takes us beyond goodness and evil, how can we know that that state of ascended consciousness is better? Doesn't it mean there is a perfection of which "better" is a reflection, at least to a certain degree?

And if it is the ultimate good to get beyond good and evil, doesn't good win? Isn't the balance between good and evil a mistake or a lie or a semantic misnomer? So, the ultimate good is to get past goodness. Do you see the problem here? How could the ultimate good be beyond perfect goodness?

Just consider this for a moment. Either the pantheists seek a higher plane that defies description and can be experienced only beyond human consciousness. Or the pantheists contradict themselves by maintaining there is a better state of being beyond goodness that is actually better than real goodness.

This is why pantheism must deny reason even if its adherents don't think so. Reason must be set aside or denied outright because it contradicts itself or because it has no place in the theology and philosophy of pantheism.

The contradictions just keep coming. The reasons for the pantheistic view of "God" lie outside of reason. But this contradicts reason. It relies on some form of emptying and ending consciousness, without any real shred of rational, logical, historical, scientific evidence. Many pantheists would claim that the absence of this evidence proves their point.

Can you see the smoke and mirrors here? We're instructed to leave behind all our thinking, but without sound reasons. Having reasons would imply the existence of a logical order, and pantheists want none of that: it causes their whole view of things to implode.

Like atheists with their multiverse and bouncing universe, pantheists appeal to evidence that cannot be observed. Just as the multiverse is beyond investigation, so, too, does the "all" of pantheism exist outside reason, observation, analysis, and even description.

Pantheism is a raw, experiential view of "God" without any real content or information about the divine consciousness of which, supposedly, we are all a part. It's just a blind hope for a blind faith. And that is fatal for pantheism as a viable view of the universe and human consciousness, as a theory of knowing, as a moral and ethical system, and as a philosophy of purpose for living in time or eternity.

Modern Seduction

Many atheists and agnostics are allured by pantheism's denial of reason and its offer of fulfillment through self-obliteration. Pantheism provides an experience of transcendence and spirituality that fits with the secular ideas of a godless universe, where reason affords us no path to knowledge or truth, except in a rhetorical or scientific sense. In other words, pantheism builds on the atheistic assumptions that permeate our culture. That is its great deception. Oddly, it offers some vague hope, too, although this hope defies reason, science, natural morality, and even the desire for transcendence. It meets Western secularists at their point of weakness and need.

Pantheism attracts those who cannot face the cold, lifeless, empty, and silent universe of mere materialism, this pitiless and dehumanizing view of life and the cosmos. It offers some nebulous, ephemeral hope, without making any demands or requiring much thought or truth. Ultimately, the hope of pantheism is no real hope at all. Remember, if everything ultimately becomes one, then death obliterates every human being, every single soul. Our individual identities are lost as we meld into the universal consciousness, as we slip beyond reason and morality, as we leave behind everyone we love.

The Antidote

Because there is such an emphasis on the spiritual experience in pantheism, a brief comparison can reveal the real destitution of pantheism's worldview. In Judeo-Christian spirituality, the goals are far different. They seek a deeper vision and understanding of God. Most importantly, they seek a direct, personal experience of God. And He seeks us in return.

Sure, we wish to improve ourselves as outlined in the Scripture and doctrinal formulations, but not at the expense of our worldly life, our personality, our service to others, or our love for all. Quite the opposite. We are called to pray, to serve, to love, and to become a clearer and fuller reflection of God. To enable us to pursue this perfection, God has given us life, talents, and time, as well as reason to help us discern and approach the truth.

Also, the Judeo-Christian God is separate from His creation, and the universe is contingent on Him; for pantheists, the inverse is true. For pantheists, "God" is contingent on the universe. Those with a Judeo-Christian worldview seek wisdom, truth, and a relationship with God, but for pantheists, such things prevent the ascent to the "all." Those with a Judeo-Christian worldview strive, however inconsistently, to please God and to become better disciples. Pantheists believe this striving prevents us from emptying ourselves and leaving behind our human consciousness.

Think clearly and critically about these distinctions, and consider what pantheism really means. If you do, you will see both its seductiveness and its silliness.

The modern secular world predisposes us to find some comfort in pantheism, as long as we don't directly confront its logical consequences. Pantheism claims no truth other than the truth that lies outside of human consciousness and reason, which fits well with modern secular ideas. Adrift in our culture, we are susceptible to such appeals. When we are blind to the nonsense of our modern ways of thinking, we leave ourselves open to such equally extreme and nonsensical ideas as pantheism.

The nearly imperceptible influence of modern culture leaves many of us drifting in and out of secular atheism or a confused agnosticism. Even if we don't embrace pantheism completely, we fall prey to its hidden, implicit presence in our world. This happens because we don't trust our reason, our moral sensitivities, our common sense, our experience of human consciousness. And that is because we do not fully understand science as a rational process, as a rationally reliant method, as a use of reason applied to the physical realm.

So take your time with this. It is crucial to dig deep here, just as it was with atheism. Modern assumptions and presuppositions have stacked the deck against you. You must recover the power and utility of reason and the truth of your moral sensitivities to grasp the truth about pantheism.

And as you do, you will see the logical and scientific necessity of a God who's more than just the creator of all things. You will see the absolute necessity of a God who is separate from His creation.

Just as with atheism, you will see that the edifice and substance of pantheism cannot withstand even the most rudimentary inspection and critique. For pantheism is built on sand: the sand of irrationality, the sand of materialism, the sand of intentional blindness, the sand of the modern beliefs that so many of us have ingested without any direct inspection or review.

So again, take your time. Do your homework. You will see that the logic and reason are inescapable, not because I am a Catholic or a good debater, but because these belief systems are fundamentally false, flawed, and foolish.

After all, I'm not looking to be disrespectful to other beliefs. You and I are simply searching for truth. That means we must analyze and critique all competitive truth claims. Only through this process can we come to the truth. For truth means the right answers about life and living. That means the truth is out there waiting to be discovered, and not everyone can be right.

So, read, think, and pray. Be patient but determined. For the truth beckons but waits. As Jesus said, seek, keep seeking, and you will find, keep finding. It is God's desire that you know the truth. But you have to look for it. You will indeed find it, when you seek it with all your mind and heart and being.

11

Matters of Divinity

By now, we know that there is a God. We can know this with rational certainty and scientific evidence. And we know that God cannot be the holistic sum of all physical existence or just some form of emptying spiritual experience. Neither atheism nor agnosticism nor pantheism meets the tests of logic, reason, common sense, or even science.

So we have dealt with the existence of God and our capacity to know that God exists. And we know that God is a separate entity outside the universe. The next big question is about the nature of God. What is He really like? Is God a force or a person?

Inevitably, because our reason and our curiosity compel us, we must face these questions about the deity we call God. If we are honest and even remotely sincere, we must face the question of what it means to be divine, to be God. Again, what kind of a God is God?

As we saw in earlier chapters, if the various beliefs about God are substantially different from one another, then one of them must be right. Determining which is right is a matter of examining the claims of each choice and gathering supporting evidence in science and logic, in human experience and human history. That's exactly what we've been doing in this book.

Once we've settled the question of whether God is a force or a person, we must consider His interest and involvement in our world, as well as His purpose and plan for us. Is God near and active, interested and involved in human affairs? Or is God distant, disinterested, uninvolved? Is God some intangible essence and, to a large degree, beyond our knowledge, or is He knowable and communicative to any degree? Does God have a reason and a purpose for the universe and for human affairs? Is there some implicit or explicit connection between this plan and human life?

The Nature of God

Let's turn first to the nature of divinity itself. What does it mean to be divine, to be God? I expect that anyone who is curious or serious about God would answer this question by considering first whether God is a force or a mind, a power or a person. Is He self-aware, conscious, and rational? Is He personal, and can we know Him as such?

Many more questions follow. Can we know about God only as we might know about someone by reading his resume or story? If God is a being, are we limited to the facts *about* Him? Are the scientific evidence and rational proofs and the witness of history the best we can hope for when it comes to knowing God? Or can we know all the scientific evidence for His existence and His nature and still experience Him more personally, more spiritually, more intimately? Can we encounter Him face-to-face?

Force or Mind?

Well, let's look at the force or mind question first, because once we've answered this question, other questions about knowing God personally and determining His activity and proximity will make sense. For if God is only a force, only a power, then other questions about spirituality and intimacy with Him are nonsensical. Powers and forces are not the least bit personal. They are impersonal by definition.

So if God is a force, He would lack consciousness, self-awareness, thought. As such, this "God-force" would be incapable of reason and making decisions. Such a God would be incapable of morality and affection too. These are all essential aspects of consciousness and mind, which forces don't have.

In short, if this divinity we call God is a force and not a mind, He would somehow have to be less than human, less than the beings He wrought. God would be a lower life-form than we are. A Godlike force would exercise no judgment, make no decisions. It could only act. It would simply be a blind, relentless, mindless power acting as it is compelled, without any consciousness, thought, or decisions.

Seeing God as nothing more than a force differs little from materialism and evolution. It leaves us without a means of explaining what everything actually is. If God is a force without consciousness and free will, there is no way to explain how the universe began.

For such a beginning must be related to a decision. To call everything into existence is a willful act, a deliberate decision. If God were simply and utterly a force, a power, then something or someone must have acted on this God-force to make it create the entire universe.

We saw this same problem in our discussion about the origin of the universe and the absolute necessity of an uncaused cause. If God is a mere force, then something had to cause this force to act. Here, too, we can see the logic of what it means to be the uncaused cause. Now we can look even more deeply into the nature of this first cause. If all effects come from causes, then God, the uncaused cause, can't be a force. Our uncaused cause must be a mind—a mind capable of making decisions, of choosing, and of willing things into existence in and of themselves, without recourse to other causes or situational influences.

That means if God is a force, He can't be God. Being God requires a mind capable of making decisions with real, practical implications, even in the physical plane. A God who can't decide certainly isn't God. A God-force subject to other causes or effects in the physical or even the logical realm can't be God as we normally think of Him. This force may be powerful. It may exceed our comprehension. But it's not God.

For these reasons and others found in morality, aesthetics, science, technology, and our common human experience, God must be self-aware. He must have a mind; He must decide. Otherwise, He isn't God. It's just that simple; it's just that certain; it's just that startling.

Still, many moderns find the idea of a God-force a compelling answer to life's big questions. Why? Well, they find it compelling because it fits with their view of the universe as a machine, a grand, interrelated scheme that mechanistically chugs along, compelled by an unseen, unknown, uninterested force beyond our vision and our comprehension.

This idea, by which many of us have been influenced, is really just a variation of the atheists' materialism and the agnostics' ignorance. Attributing a force-like nature to God keeps atheistic and secular beliefs intact, while eliminating any need to grapple with a God who is near, involved, communicative, and relationally bound to human beings.

The secular, modern view of the universe as the product of blind chance and mechanistic dynamics makes no demands, creates no obligations, and provides no purpose. If God is a force, without consciousness or reason, then intentionality is absent from the universe, and we don't have to wrestle with the possibility of a purpose to our lives. We don't have to grapple with what a transcendent purpose might mean for us, whether in the everyday or in the ultimate sense.

In addition, the idea of God as a force absolves us of any moral obligations, except in the broadest sense of social practicalities and individual preferences. Our lives are our own, because moral order is not inherent in life to any degree, nor is there any real certainty regarding the content of all but the most basic moral imperatives.

Reason and Order

If God is a force, reason can tell us nothing about truth. As in a materialistic world, reason becomes a mere pattern of thought, a neural configuration shared by most people. Nothing more.

As with materialism, those who see God as a force cannot explain reason in any other terms except as normative neural brain patterns. Thus, those who insist on God as a force fail to explain reason. By necessity, they fail to explain science too. There can be no science unless reason is absolute and unless it yields objective and factual truths.

If reason is just biochemical, if its laws and principles are nothing more than social norms arising from neural activity, it can't get us to truth—not even close, because it just isn't reason.

According to this materialistic mechanical view, the content and application of reason are just customary patterns of thought arising solely from habitual neural patterns. That's it. Period. They are nothing more than habits of our minds.

Reason in this type of universe has no direct link to the God-force, nor is it an aspect of this force's nature. Reason is not a means through which we can know God and discover His order and plan. Reason is nothing but a human activity with some limited utility in science, but no real explanatory or obligating power.

Reason thus becomes more a means of rhetoric and persuasion than of knowing God, truth, morality, or beauty. Reason is for lawyers and politicians to use in order to manipulate opinion and is otherwise impotent and without meaning or value.

Can you see how this resembles our earlier discussions of the modern mind and its atheistic and agnostic beliefs? The idea of a force-like God allows for some form of ambiguous supernaturalism or extra-naturalism, while dismissing reason and truth. It shrouds the divine in obscurity and distance, for forces don't communicate. A force-like God must be distant and noncommunicative, because it has no consciousness, no thoughts, no ideas, no emotions. Nor does this God-force make any decisions, ever. It's just a force. That's all.

Yet, in earlier chapters, we noticed the artifacts of reason and order in the universe, both of which indicate intelligence, even in practical, worldly ways. For example, if we observe the presence of order and reason in the artifacts of a lost civilization, we would know intelligent life must have been in that location. So, too, with God.

When we see the level of precise order and predictability inherent in both the vast reaches of the universe and its minute recesses, we know that some form of intelligence is at work. Our universe, in total and in part, is replete with order everywhere we look. Sometimes, this order is as simple and mundane as the fine balance we see between the force of gravity and the mass and motion of things in the universe. Sometimes, it is so sophisticated, refined, and complex that it all but defies our limited intelligence and technology. Take, for example, the behavior of quantum phenomena or the simultaneous, interrelated forces at work keeping the earth rotating on its axis each day and revolving around the sun each year.

We also find conclusive artifacts in reason itself: in our rational faculties and the many crucial ways we use reason to further our understanding and to communicate with one another.

Just look at human reason and rationality itself. Logic, common sense, mathematics, and science are all based on rational principles. The same is true of morality and beauty. Also, because we all have a rudimentary capacity for reasoning, we can know things with certainty and confidence and have the means to communicate them. Our language is based on certain logical structures and relationships and on the surety of the rational minds we all have and expect others to use.

Simply by using reason to communicate with each other and to communicate the truth, we implicitly affirm the existence of reason and its principles. When we appeal to logic, reason, or common sense, we explicitly use these principles to demonstrate the strength of our opinion or case. Even in debate, when we oppose the ideas of others, we make our case with reason in a rational manner, according to the laws and principles of logic. This is true even when we are skeptical or cautious, as we try to discover the boundaries of rational certainty, ambiguity, and error.

If reason is used incorrectly or poorly, we can correct it by making the rationality of our case clearer and more sound. When people do things outside of rationality or apply reason incorrectly, we call their behavior irrational or arbitrary, because they are either violating the laws of reason or ignoring them altogether.

We even use reason when we determine that something is unknowable, unimportant, and too insignificant to warrant attention or debate. Regardless of what conclusions we draw about things, our decisions are first and foremost grounded in sound reasoning. Or, at least, they should be.

God and Mind

The very existence of reason offers significant evidence about the nature of God. God must be rational, because reason exists and leads us to real truth. To create a rational universe with discernible principles of reason, God would have to be perfectly rational and perfectly ordered. He would embody these and all other perfections that we know despite our inability to embody them ourselves.

God would also have to be the maker of all tangible and intangible things. He must be the creator of reason and its laws, just as much as He is the creator of the entire physical universe. For if reason is ordered and capable of grasping the truth about things in mathematics and science, in logic and living, then such rational certainties and faculties must come from some being, not some force.

The law of cause and effect stipulates that a greater effect can't come from a lesser cause. The effect must be equal to or less than the cause, and the cause must be of the same type and scale as the observed effect. Otherwise, we're faced with a universe that is unpredictable, where we can have effects without causes—a fundamentally irrational idea, a form of wishful thinking. The law of cause and effect thus provides further evidence that God is a rational being, not a blind power, for the law of cause and effect is a crucial rational principle evident in the tangible world of science and in the intangible world of thought, reason and mathematics. And that is evidence for God.

Similarly, if truth is found in accordance with the "rightest" reasoning, then truth is also a significant artifact. The presence of real truth grounded in and established by reason also points to God's nature. God is rational. God is ordered. God established an ordered and rational certainty in the universe and in us.

Because reason is a faculty of the mind, God must have a mind, a rational consciousness. God must think. Even in our secular world, consciousness, thought, and reason indicate intelligent life. Still more significantly, if this intelligence created human consciousness itself, then it must be the best, the first mind. And this mind we call "God."

His mind is not like the calculating "brain" of a computer. God is the epitome of mind, the integration of reason and emotions, morality and beauty, truth and love. God perfectly harmonizes every facet of consciousness in a manner that creates an inherent unity of mind and heart, which we so rarely and fleetingly experience. And He is all this perfection comprehensively by dimension and in perfect harmony.

It is just here that we see the clash between Catholicism and secularism. In the modern, secular view, the physical universe is infinite, and the mind arose much later through evolution. In the Catholic view, the Divine Mind is infinite and precedes the physical universe. And the human mind of mankind came about not by accident but by the intention of the Eternal Mind.

Finding and Choosing the Truth

So we must choose, and the correct choice is clear and straightforward: God is not a mere force. If He were, as some people think, then our intelligence would be greater than its cause. Our rationality would be a fortuitous accident, the product of some special, though limited, mind.

Rather quickly, we can identify two reasons why this can't be the case. First, the fortuitous accident would have to be intangible, because the mind is intangible. But what would that intangible accident look like, be like, act like? Where would it come from? Again, we have to explain the source of this accidental cause. Secondly, we would have to have some evidence that this mind that is more than human, but less than divine, was acted upon by some intangible causal agency to create a perfectly rational structure. Somehow, this capacity for reason and logical thinking was transmitted to human beings, without this less-than-divine being's capacity to understand it. Can you see how this slips into irrationality? Can you see how reason reveals that such a belief can't possibly make sense?

Do you see the problem that inevitably arises when a greater effect comes from a lesser cause, particularly when the effect is immensely more advanced than its cause? Do you see the absolute necessity of a perfectly rational deity in order to explain the existence of reason and its rules? Do you see the need to explain our capacity for rational thought and our ability to communicate with each other using reason and its rules? Our reason, like our existence, points directly, though subtly, to God's existence and His nature. It speaks about God and it speaks about the rational aspect of who God is.

Think about what a God-force would be like. No decisions. No purpose. No consciousness. No plan. Only a relentless power going nowhere and for no reason. Can you sense how our universe would be inevitably mechanistic? You can almost hear the grinding gears and the hum of surging energy. Do you really suppose our consciousness, our thought, and all the sensitivities and sensibilities that make up who we are as human beings came from such an empty, mindless entity, from some intangible power, from some pre-cosmic energy?

This view is irrational and unimaginable, except for those desperate atheists and agnostics scrambling to hold on to some faint hope in the face of the grinding, heartless, and hopeless specter of materialism and the distant, heartless, mindless God-force.

God Is a Being

But a God who is a mind, a being, a person, creates an entirely different vision of reality. God decided to make the cosmos and created us to reflect His nature. We can think just as God thinks, though not nearly as well or as vastly or as deeply. We love just as God loves, though not nearly as well or as fully or as perfectly.

We sense God's perfections, yet we know we are not perfect. We can see our flaws and shortcomings against the backdrop of

God's perfection. And in this way, we know God is more than a force. We know He must be a mind, a being, a person. And this is an absolute truth.

So think long and hard about this. This is a crucial tenet of the faith you are seeking and discovering. Be cautious and deliberate if you need to be. For the idea of God's personal nature, as well as the logical process by which we have uncovered it, is critical when meeting the challenges of modern culture and its implicit beliefs, which we have dealt with from the beginning of this book.

The beliefs of modern culture have shaped you more than you may think. These ideas, which are so much a part of the Western culture in which you were raised and in which you live, have influenced you more indirectly, more implicitly than you may know.

This is why many of you may have winced while reading the introduction, specifically when I said I became a Catholic because the Catholic Faith is the absolute, objective truth. You winced (and may still be wincing) because you've been programmed to think in certain ways that are wrong, illogical, false. Or you've been trained not to think at all, because our culture says science is the only way to know anything for certain, while reason can't prove anything important.

As you've read this chapter and seen how quickly and effortlessly such false ideas about the nature of God have been revealed as the errors they truly are, you may feel that the case for a personal, rational God can't be true. It's too easy and clear. I must be glossing over things, or I must be mistaken. Surely, I'm oversimplifying or missing some crucial observations.

Well, the ease and simplicity aren't mine. I'm not that smart or that talented with words, though you might think I am, if you're not in the habit of getting to the essence of things and thinking clearly and logically about these questions. I don't have to make the matters of this book simple; they're already essentially clear, as are most things. But because we've been trained to think there are precious few right answers—and none whatsoever when it comes to religion and God—we're just not used to thinking well, incisively, or at length about God. And that's why you're reading this book.

So think carefully about this idea and the other ideas you have encountered. Be sincere and honest in your thought and analysis. If you need to think more critically, do so. For God promises that all who seek will find.

Ask this personal God to help you discern the truth about who He is and what He intends. After all, in these early stages of your search, it's important to get to know this God-Being, this God-Person. And this search through prayer and meditation can also be another way to understand God and His nature in a real and intimately personal way that affirms the evidence of science, reason, and history. How this unfolds will be unique to you.

12

Matters of Proximity and Activity

Once we know that God is a being, not a force, all kinds of critical questions and possibilities come to mind. In contrast, if God is merely a force, an energy, a power behind the cosmos, then there's no real concern for who God is or what He's doing. God is just a vague, inscrutable force, an enervating energy. That's all.

We can't get to know God if He's just a force, nor can He respond to us or tell us anything. The only insight we can gain is to know that this God-force exists.

All theology is thus reduced to one relentless, ridiculously narrow fact. It's just like the materialism of the atheists and agnostics. And it resembles the same flaws of pantheism, in that all of reality is really made by this God-force, though there is no consciousness to the God-force or to us when we die. In the end, the God-force view resembles atheism and materialism in that our consciousness ends at death, while the God-force endures without consciousness.

Do you see how this one-dimensional view cuts off further inquiry and curiosity about God and the ultimate purpose of human life, how it reduces every theological and philosophical question to irrelevance? Do you see how this is an anti-theology like materialism? Do you see how all of human inquiry about God and meaning and purpose collapses before this type of God? God is a force, and that's that. Nothing further need be said. The rest is up to us. The rest is merely a product of our construction and ideas, without a trace of anything real, objective, or factual.

All of these problems—the absence of purpose and order, ethics and aesthetics, meaning and reason—don't just disappear once we understand that God is a being, not a force.

Some moderns think God is a higher being who is disinterested and uninvolved, unconcerned and distant, passive and removed from all human beings. We call this view "deism" and its adherents "deists."

Deism

Deism looks at God as obscure and mostly unknowable. The deistic God is a being or consciousness of some sort, though His mind is not like ours; consequently, He is inaccessible to us. Also, the deistic deity is chronically disinterested in the events of our universe and our lives.

Most deists believe that this distant deity probably created the universe but maintains a strict hands-off policy. Deism denies any supernatural communication, intervention in space and time, management of events, and purpose for our lives. That means we can have no revelation, no miracles, no providential occurrences. Basically, belief in this obscure and uninvolved deity makes deism a form of "natural" religion. By using the word "natural," I don't mean that deism is pure or basic or simple or unfettered by human interpretation and ideas, but that it denies the supernatural altogether.

For example, the *New Shorter Oxford English Dictionary* defines "deism" as a "natural religion," a "belief in one God who created but does not intervene in the universe." The *Modern Catholic Dictionary* states that deism accepts a "personal God and [adheres] to what is called natural religion, but with no recognition of a supernatural order." The dictionary further states, "Accordingly revelation, miracles, grace and mysteries are excluded from acceptance."

So when deists use the terms "natural religion" and "naturalism," they mean pretty much the same thing as atheists and agnostics, except they do admit some form of deity that created the universe, although this deity remains generally outside our capacity to know or comprehend. We can see its handiwork, but the universe is left on its own to operate independent of any divine intervention or sustaining presence or activity. And so are we.

Believing in this obscure deity does lead to some interesting implications, if you think about it for a minute. For example, believing in an obscure deity, whether a force or a being, requires sound reasons. This means deists must be certain that they can't be certain about the nature of God, while at the same time being certain that God exists. Let me say that again. Deists believe there is a God, but they can't know Him except to say that He's either a force or a being. They know this with a certainty that seemingly defies their fundamental absence of certainty about the nature of this God-being or God-force. Whew!

It seems as if you have to go a long way to say almost nothing when it comes to deism, particularly the form of deism that believes in a deity with a mind. That's to say nothing of their high level of certainty about the uncertainty about God and His nature. Pretty odd and shamelessly contradictory, don't you think?

Advantages of a Distant Deity

So why do deists believe what they do? Well, it's much easier to ignore and even avoid a deity who is distant and obscure than one who is near and involved. After all, a distant, uninvolved deity makes no demands and has no expectations. Its distance leaves us to act as we may choose without any real guidance, expectations, or evaluation of our behavior, attitudes, or beliefs. But a God who is involved, who loves us, who expects us to reciprocate and obey, is a God who can and wants to be known.

Despite its convolutions and contradictions, this kind of thinking attracts and infects a lot of modern people. But why? Perhaps because believing in a distant, unknowable deity is more comfortable for them. It also offers a great deal of personal discretion. In the absence of an active, involved deity, people can do as they please.

But how could deists swallow such a weak, superficial, contradictory belief with no evidence? Well, such shortcomings and contradictions don't often deter moderns, as we've seen in our earlier discussions about truth, reason, atheism, agnosticism, and pantheism. For all their professed uncertainty, and despite the dearth of reasonable evidence for their beliefs, modern people hardly lack confidence in what they claim to be true.

The Truth of Doubt?

One thing of which moderns are almost universally certain is the truth of doubt. They're so certain that not much can be known about God, about life's meaning and purpose, about morality, that this has become their dogma, the dogma of the certainty of uncertainty.

That's why we spent so much time restoring confidence in reason, and it's why we'll be spending a similar amount of time reviewing the core ideas behind many of the world's religions and philosophies. We have to do this because we've all been infected, to varying degrees, by the malady known as "modernity."

The presuppositions, assumptions, and basic beliefs that make up "modernity" often prevent many modern people from advancing beyond deistic views as they pursue the question of God. They're barely able to muster even the belief that there could be a God. Going any further seems ridiculous to most moderns, who groundlessly fear that a quest for deeper truth would entail severing their rational capacities, embracing irrational ideas, and just believing. So they stop here at deism.

We're not supposed to leave behind our reason and common sense. A blind leap is not what our faith asks of us. Ours is an informed faith, a rational faith, a commonsensical faith, a faith built on God and on familiar aspects of the human experience, from love and reason to beauty and truth. Our faith asks us to press on toward the frontiers of what we can actually know. Here, on the frontiers, there is a need for some faith, even in the smallest amount. Faith is necessary because we don't and, in fact, can't know everything. It shouldn't surprise us that exhaustive knowledge is beyond any of us.

After accepting some limits to our knowledge and our capacity to know, the next natural question is just how much we can know. How much faith do we really need in the face of what reason, science, history, spirituality, and our personal experience can show us?

Knowledge, Truth, and Faith

For when it comes to knowledge, truth, and faith, the real question is: Do we know enough to have reasonable, realistic beliefs? Do all our means of knowledge supply enough evidence to let us consider the possibility of a God who communicates and reveals Himself to us? Do we know enough to take that step with a reasonable degree of rational certainty?

When we step outside the deistic belief in an obscure and uninvolved deity, we ask some profound questions that the modern world finds provocative. Many moderns don't really believe that these questions have correct answers—at least, no answers beyond some broad generalities and simple superficialities.

Again, that's the influence of modernity and its deistic, agnostic, and atheistic presuppositions and assumptions. I mean, there are many religions from which to choose. Aren't they all true? Don't they overlap, if not in doctrine, then in the spiritual and emotional experiences they elicit?

Well, we'll handle that assumption in due course in later chapters. But for now, we must really grapple with the question of God's nature, because we have seen that the God-force really isn't an option: it's irrational and lacks scientific evidence.

So let's take a brief tour of the possibilities for God's nature. We have discussed how the law of cause and effect shows that God must be a conscious being. Simply put, you can't get thinking and consciousness, personality and purpose, decisions and morality, from an empty, silent, mindless force. So we know God is a conscious being.

Questions about God's nature contain two crucial aspects. First, when we ask about God's nature, we have already rightly assumed there are or should be aspects about God that we can know and to some degree evaluate. This directly contradicts the deistic assumption about what can be known and what God's nature could be.

As we have seen, we can know that God is a conscious being, a mind, a person. And this seems pretty straightforward. And, indeed it is. God must be a conscious being. And, as a conscious being, God can be known to some degree. Our consciousness, our intellects, our wills, and our emotions are artifacts of His nature. We bear His image.

Similarly, we should be able to know something about God's nature beyond that God is a conscious being. Though we are limited human beings who can't know everything, we are rational and conscious beings who can think and know. This directly contradicts the deistic assumption about what can know about God's nature and what He is like.

So, then, if God is a conscious being, what is His nature? As you might suspect, there are all kinds of answers to that question. Some say there are many such gods. Others say there is one God.

Some believe God is a king: a powerful, demanding supreme being. Others say God oversees and scrutinizes us, as might a boss or a supervisor. Two religions say God is a loving Father. One of them even says God came to dwell among us.

Each of these answers offers a different way of seeing God and the world. That's why we have to make a choice: a balanced, informed choice, based on reason and science, history and morality, truth and beauty, common sense and consciousness. The world's religions say different things about God—sometimes very different things. Thus, they can't all be correct.

So, it is a good thing these religions are all pretty clear about the nature of the God they believe in and follow. But which religion is right? Is it the polytheism of the ancient myths or the Hindu tradition? Or is it one of the great monotheistic religions: Islam, Judaism, or Christianity?

Those are the basic choices, with some slight variations that account for sectarian theology or governance. Though small, this list constitutes the full range of possible answers from which we must choose, unless we resort to atheism, agnosticism, pantheism, or deism.

Only one of the traditions on our list professes the full truth about God. The rest contain some elements, degrees, approximations, or distortions of truth. Regardless of their proximity to the truth, these other traditions can't be fully true. This is despite the modern penchant for encouraging ambiguity and compromise and for discouraging critical analysis. In spite of the modern desire to undermine reason and to distort science, so that nothing but the most basic physical laws appears certain, the truth about God is still accessible to the sincere, honest, rational, judicious seeker.

Though it may be comforting to know that many religions contain a degree of truth, what really matters in an ultimate and practical sense is which religion is true. Elements of truth make nice starting points for dialogue, but when it comes to belief and commitment, on which you must stake your temporal and eternal life, knowing and professing the one true faith matters profoundly. And it is surprisingly easy to know.

What's more, to the disbelief of the modern world, discovering the one true religion does not require blind faith at all. It requires open eyes. Our search requires reason and science, history and common sense; it demands an honest heart, a clear head, and a rich understanding of human nature. And yes, it requires some faith, but no more than a pinch in most cases.

I mean, if blind faith were so necessary, most of this book would be emotional appeals and exhortations to believe. This book would be about pathos and rhetoric, not reason and deliberation. But as you see, this book invites clear thinking and calm deliberation, tentative trust and measured faith, as you work out the answer to these profound questions.

The modern world sees religions as very similar, almost interchangeable. Any differences are minor, without any real importance or substantial variation in practical, personal, social, and political implications. This erroneous claim tells us more about the modern world then it does about the similarities among religions. Most moderns have not looked at any of these faiths with any degree of critical analysis beyond the idea that God is invoked by all of them. Their comparative analysis, when it is done at all, is woefully superficial. It lacks depth, discernment, and sophistication, even at the most rudimentary level.

God's Nature

A key to deciding between these many religions is evaluating how each one describes the nature of God, His involvement in human affairs, and His purpose for our world. We can determine the truth of these beliefs by comparing them to rational, scientific, and historical truths. We can also examine them in light of the many facets of human experience we already know to be true: the truths of beauty, goodness, love, justice, sacrifice, and even our intuition.

The accuracy of these core theological beliefs tells us a great deal about God and the truth about religion. These things tell us whose beliefs are true and whose are wrong. Additionally, they tell us what the errors are, where they occur, and how far they are from the truth.

Let me say that again. By examining God's nature, His interest in our lives, and His intentions for the world in light of our many means of gaining knowledge, we can know what's true about God and what's not. We can identify theological errors and their magnitude. I don't mean this lightheartedly, but sincerely and certainly. So let's begin.

First of all, it's a good thing these various religious traditions say different things about God. There is no way to combine or confuse their claims; thus, our choices are clear and distinct. In most crucial areas, each of them says different thing about who God is and what He does. And things that are crucially significant. That makes our job much easier.

Let's begin with what we can know about this intangible God through what exists tangibly and through human nature and consciousness. Let's begin by learning about the God who is a person and a mind, who can be known scientifically and rationally, spiritually, and personally.

In light of the modern tendency to look for physical evidence first, let's go back to the question of origin. If the universe began as the big bang indicates, we know our universe had a beginning. The scientific principle of cause and effect requires some prior cause to this beginning of space and time, to this beginning of the universe. Also, the law of cause and effect states that at some point we must meet an uncaused cause. Otherwise, the chain of cause and effect would extend backward and forward in time into infinity and into absurdity. This is part of the rational proof for the existence of God, as we discussed earlier.

So what does this say about not only God's existence but also His nature? A great deal. First of all, it tells us that, as the uncaused cause, God is infinite, because He exists outside of and before time and space, outside of and before all human consciousness and conscience. God *is*. It is just that simple and just that profound.

God is the only noncontingent being, for God is the cause of everything that is known and that has yet to be known. If God were not the first cause, then whatever other infinite, first cause there is would be God. God is the ultimate, first, and final reality behind all that exists.

God's Eternality and Infinity

Similarly, God's infinity takes on many other facets and dimensions beyond the obvious one related to time and power, as in the first cause of the universe. For instance, God's infinity is the first cause and the perfect fulfillment of the many perfections we observe in our universe and in human consciousness and personality. Again, any perfection we observe finds its cause and its completion and perfection in God. As I stated earlier, you can't get a perfect effect from an imperfect cause; no perfection can exist without a fully perfect source.

Though this may sound a bit heady and esoteric, it actually isn't. Every day, through small acts of kindness and love, sacrifice and generosity, other people offer us glimpses and glimmers of perfection: a perfect act of kindness, a perfectly wise insight. In fact, the very idea of wisdom gives us a glimpse of perfection and points toward the unity of all perfections.

When we observe, perform, or receive a simple act of love, we can see the perfection behind the act. This perfection tells us that we have witnessed a truly loving act, and it points to a God who must be the perfect embodiment of love. God would have to be perfect love and perfectly loving, for the source of any and all perfection must have a cause that is the perfect embodiment of any or all perfection.

As another example, we can see this same perfection and cause in sacrifice. We even have awards for such acts of love and courage. The Congressional Medal of Honor is given to individuals whose behavior was far beyond the expected level of heroism and sacrifice. It mirrors the perfections of sacrificial courage so perfectly that it warrants the highest order of commendation possible. In fact, this commendation recognizes an implicit ideal manifest in the explicit criteria that define the commendation itself. So even here, we can see the inherent morality and the perfections that define it. And these perfections must have a cause and a perfect embodiment.

Again, the perfections that we see imperfectly must have a perfect source. That source is God. So God is infinite not only in time and power but also in purity, holiness, justice, and love. Every perfection we can observe or imagine is fulfilled perfectly and completely in God.

We should note here that we often use figurative language, drawn from our human experience, to describe the nature of God and His many perfections. God's infinite and complete knowledge is often expressed in human metaphors, in anthropomorphic ways that say as much about our limited capacity to grasp infinity and perfection in its utter completeness as it does about the perfections themselves.

Hence, we sometimes speak of God "seeing" or "hearing" or "feeling" as we do, even though He is infinite and therefore beyond our capacity to describe and understand fully. These metaphorical ways of thinking about God's nature don't diminish His perfections; on the contrary, they point out the horizons of human thought, the limits of our language—not the limits of God.

Again, we can't know everything, but this doesn't mean we can't know something. Nor does it mean we can't know enough. Our artifacts of small perfections point to the source of all perfections: the infinity, unity, and perfection of God.

Unity and Simplicity

Two other necessary aspects of God's nature are His unity and His simplicity. By "unity," I mean singularity. God's perfections require that He be singular. A variety of gods would mean different gods, which would contradict the essential and logically necessary perfections of God. Different gods would manifest different aspects of perfection and would necessarily have deficiencies, however slight. Variability requires differences in perfection, which lead to a logical and practical contradiction. Therefore, a variety of gods is impossible, unless these many gods are not actually God.

Perhaps an example will help. Let's imagine a room full of good people—full of saints. In these people, we would perceive some amazing traits and some very clear reflections of true perfection. But we would not see the absolute embodiment of all perfections, because this embodiment would be a singular, absolute perfection, the perfection of all perfections. And so there would be no way to differentiate different gods in the face of the harmony of true perfection. This is why infinity and perfection necessitate one God. Here, we start to see one reason why polytheism cannot be the right answer.

Despite the logical evidence we've just presented, modernity struggles with the notion of singular perfection. Instead, moderns trumpet the existence of many perfections. But that's just nonsense. There are not different perfections. There are different aspects of perfection, which manifest themselves differently at different times and in different circumstances. But the unity of perfection is not just a logical necessity, but a practical inevitability.

First of all, though there are different dimensions of perfection, perfection can't be achieved in part, but only totally and completely. Partial perfection necessarily points to a deeper, fuller perfection beyond itself, which, in turn, points to God as its cause and source.

If perfection weren't complete and comprehensive, it wouldn't be perfectly perfect. This means perfection, in the truest sense of the word, is achievable only in completeness. Holistic perfection is the only perfection. Dimensional perfection is not perfection, though it is laudable when we humans achieve it, even for a moment.

So "perfection" means complete perfection, which requires oneness, not diversity; singularity, not multiplicity. This is the province of God, the one and only perfect being.

Finally, we see that God must be not only singular but also simple. He is simple because He is fully and completely actualized. In Him, all perfections are fully realized.

This goes back to the idea of potentiality and actuality we explored in our discussion on matters of reason (see chapter 9). God has no potential, because He is fully realized in Himself. His essence and existence are one and the same. God *is*.

Anything less than God's full actualization and perfection would contradict the law of cause and effect and reveal that the God we're thinking of isn't really God. Contrary to popular belief, this wouldn't mean there is no God, but that what we think is God isn't God. There would still have to be a real, fully actualized God behind the being we think of as God.

These three crucial aspects of God's nature—His infinity, His unity, His simplicity—prove that there is no logical or scientific basis for any form of polytheism. These are unavoidable aspects of God's nature, unless we abandon reason. Doing so makes our Faith inherently irrational and illogical and our beliefs completely wrong.

This shouldn't be troublesome. It may be a bit unsettling, because we need to think about all this a bit more to evaluate it properly and then to decide.

You should be unsettled, because whether you know it or not, whether you like it or not, you have been reared and educated in the modern world, with all its assumptions and presuppositions. Though you may have only an imperceptible awareness of its presence, modernity is there beneath the surface, influencing your thinking and undermining your reason.

All this will become clearer as we explore more fully the nature of the one God. Now we begin to leave behind these important, but rudimentary distinctions about the nature of God and get down to the details of who He really is. This is where we begin to encounter a God who seeks intimacy with us. This is where we come to know a God who loves us and exhorts us to call Him "Father" and "Daddy." This is where we meet a God who lived among us, as one of us, and who sacrificed Himself, so we might live with Him for eternity.

It is to this active and proximate God, who shared our very existence, that we now turn — to a God who seeks us; a God who communicates with us; a God who was so active and so proximate that He came and lived among us.

13

Matters of Revelation

When I tell you that divine revelation is real, you may think I'm out of my mind, off my crumpet, out to lunch. To the modern mind, the idea of divine revelation seems far-fetched, beyond reasonable belief. The very idea of a God who communicates with us seems more than a little fantastic and primitive; it certainly can't be a serious and sound basis for religious belief, nor can it have a place in our modern world. Isn't our desire for revelation just a manifestation of our search for meaning, nothing more than an artifact of our basic psychological need for purpose and our fear of the unknown or of death? Or couldn't this idea of divine revelation simply be an artifact of more primitive and ignorant times?

On some level, the idea of divine revelation seems superstitious and silly. Why—and how—would God talk with human beings? What relevance and purpose could these ancient and primitive messages have in our modern, scientific world, anyway?

By now, you should suspect that these assertions about the foolishness of revelation are wrong—and not just because they contradict Catholic teaching or the teaching of the world's revealed religions. These claims are wrong in the actual and factual sense: they are so considerably off the mark as to be wrong by definition.

Even those assumptions that are closer to the truth contain mistakes and misunderstandings about the nature of revelation.

Let's take some time first to explore revelation as an idea. Then we'll consider the two forms of divine revelation with which you may be familiar. As always, we will discuss revelation in the light of reason and science, history and human experience, so you can see the reasoned basis for belief and then make an informed decision about God and, down the road, about Jesus Christ and the Catholic Church.

Natural Revelation

Now, what could "natural revelation" mean? Isn't revelation something extraordinary, some sort of miraculous epiphany? Well, it can be. But that's not God's only method of revelation.

If we think even superficially about the very idea of natural revelation, we can see that it must be something common and obvious—something, well, natural. So, how could natural revelation be so natural, so obvious as to be a common human experience?

Just as we can understand intangible things by applying our sense of reason, so, too, can we use reason and careful observation to discover truths about our physical world through reason and careful observation. We do this every day.

As we saw in earlier chapters, our ability to reason and the principles of reason, in and of themselves, are crucial to proving the existence of God, to understanding His nature and His relationship with creation, and to discovering His plans for each of us. And they are also crucial to knowing and understanding and experiencing the very nature of God's being and character. This is the common, everyday way in which we encounter God's divine revelation.

Reason allows us not merely to know about things, but to judge them as well. We can know what is soundly reasoned or shoddily reasoned. We can know that an argument is rigorous and rightly argued. And, we can know an argument is flawed and fallacious because we know the principles of reason and we know we can rightly apply these principles to any issue or case at hand. Also, we can learn that some of our opinions are weak and others are strong based on the rules of reason and their proper application and use.

So, when we use reason rightly, we discover the truth. And this right use of reason is a crucial means for knowing about God and knowing His plan and understanding how we are to apply it and live by it. Our proper use of reason is a form of natural revelation, for we can discern the revelations of God by using our God-given faculty of reason. By using our reason properly, we can discover the truth.

This is why even non-Catholic faiths contain some degree of truth in their religious doctrines, in their system of thought, in their ethics and spirituality. It is also why the fullness of truth resides in the Catholic faith, for reason demands coherence and integration. It demands depth and breadth, the ability to explain the broad expanse of life and the details and depth of living. It demands a reasoned explanation for the full range of human experience: the mental, the emotional, the physical, the spiritual, the relational, the ethical, the aesthetic, the practical, the ecclesiastical, the political, the social.

And because we can use reason to know the truth about life and about living, as well as aspects of God's character and plan, we know we are discovering at least some part of God's revelation in a natural way through our reason and common sense. We can know this even physically as we observe the behavior of the physical world and process these observations with our reason too.

That is essentially what the scientific method is. It is the proper application of reason to our observations and manipulations of the physical world. This is what we discussed earlier in the chapters on origin, order, and reason.

When we discover any wisdom or truth by using our reason and reasoned observation and manipulation of the physical world (science), we can know this is as one form of natural revelation. This is why, until the early nineteenth century, science was usually referred to as "natural theology." The term "science" represents a secularized word for what was once "natural theology," a word inherently describing the integration of reason and tangible observation under the broad umbrella of theology, as reason would require.

So, whether we explore the physical realm only or look at the intangible world of the human mind, emotions, and character, we can know this is just another form of natural revelation, a form of natural theology. When we use our reason as it is or to understand what our senses tell us, we can know with absolute certainty that this is a form of natural revelation. And such natural revelation is a revelation that is plain to the eye and to the mind. Natural revelation is there for all of us to see and know.

It is deliberately democratic, a revelation that is simple and clear for any and all who seek and think. Yet this simplicity is not without sophistication and complex integration, for its profundity derives from its simplicity and its common accessibility. This common, natural revelation leaves all of us with a basic level of revelation, with a democratic access to God.

We are all without excuse because we can all know there must be a God, based on the fact of reason and the uses of reason. The same is true about science. It leaves us without any legitimate excuse for denying God's existence. Based on all that we are and all that exists, based on all that we observe in our world, in others, and in ourselves, we can and do know that God exists, that God is a mind, a person. This natural revelation is there waiting for us, inviting us, almost imploring us to look for God, the God who can be found.

Despite this abundance of accessible revelation, the Catholic Church does make room for ignorance—despite this general level of revelation. For none of us can be held responsible for what we don't know. This is a simple and glaringly obvious truth.

So in the Catholic Church, ignorance is a good excuse—at least to some degree. Despite the profusion of natural revelation accessible to our senses and our reason, we can know with similar certainty that God will not hold us responsible for things we do not know unless we deliberately avoid learning and knowing, though God encourages us to look, to seek, to desire to know Him. Such is the hope of love and of our heavenly Father.

So, despite the issue of "invincible ignorance," we *are* responsible for the natural revelation we know and for the things we can know but choose to ignore. We must remember that God knows what we do know. And He will judge us accordingly.

Now that you know that natural revelation is accessible to you and that you are responsible for it, you can't claim ignorance. You can't deny knowing this or anything else we have discussed in this book, at least to some degree. Be mindful of this responsibility.

Yet don't be troubled: as you'll see later, you have the teachings of the Church available for guidance. Don't forget, too, that you can rely on reason. Properly applied, reason will always guide you out of ignorance and toward the truth. All this should seem quite reasonable and just, a fair way of dealing with natural revelation and our responsibility in light of such a democratic and common form of revelation, for the Catholic faith is one of fair and reasoned principles.

It is also why the Church has always been a teaching Church. For the Church articulates and elaborates not only supernatural revelation, but natural revelation as well and often does both simultaneously. We can see this even in the sacraments and in the Mass.

And it is why we have been deliberately using reason and justifying its use and its power since the beginning of the book. It is a crucial clue, a definitive dimension of God's nature and a special endowment granted to all people as His image bearers. Human intelligence is a crucial but common key to knowing that God exists and to knowing God's nature and plan. And reason itself is both evidence for God's existence and evidence of God's nature, as we have seen.

Reason is also how we come to know God personally and how we come to understand what we experience personally, spiritually. Reason is also how we understand more direct revelation. It is how we even understand the specific content, the special messages of more supernatural revelations.

Our use of reason, when it is applied properly, will get us to the truth about all the important things in life. It will get us to the basic truths about God. But knowing that God exists and that He is a person doesn't give us enough information to know Him fully, let alone to love Him. That's why God must reveal Himself to us. By communicating with human beings directly, God takes the initiative to show us who He is and what His hopes and expectations are for us. It is to these immensely important divine messages that we now turn.

Supernatural Revelation

"Supernatural revelation" is simply the name we give to God's communication with human beings. It comes in two forms: (1) the personal or private and (2) the general or public. For now, we will focus on personal revelation, which we experience in prayer, meditation, the sacraments, and our daily lives. This personal experience of God is something we should seek and expect: God invites us to know and love Him, and He assures us of His divine love.

This love transcends mere reverence and obedience, although they are components of our relationship with God. We are called to personal intimacy with God; we are called to see Him as our loving Father. In this relationship, God reveals Himself to each of us personally.

This love of God for each of us is a relational bond of the highest and most inclusive order. And, given God's perfection, we can know we will be loved perfectly. This is also why we pray the Our Father. For our bond with God is a family bond in the perfect sense of that word. It is not a legal or contractual one; it is not a strictly moral one or a solely emotional or spiritual one. It is a bond of love, of intimacy, a comprehensive bond unifying and integrating all our dimensions as only love and intimacy can. And such intimacy with God is a form of divine revelation. It must entail God's disclosure, God's revelation of Himself.

While we will discuss this form of personal revelation in later chapters as we explore the essence of God's relationship with us, it does bear some mention here as a form of revelation. For God reveals Himself to us as we seek Him. He lets us come to know Him and about Him. And that can seem quite natural, but it can also seem quite special and revelatory.

In this book, we have, so far, come to know God in a general, natural way as we have gradually made the case for theism—the belief that God is a mind and a person. But now we will begin to separate from the other theistic religions according to their conception of God's nature, based on the content of the revelation they each claim is supernatural, and what this supernatural revelation says about the nature of God and His plan. It is to this that we now turn our attention as we consider how God has revealed Himself and what He wants us to know.

But when it comes to our relationship with God and all other public forms of supernatural revelation, we must remember that we can't reason our way to Him, as we do with natural revelation. Here, we encounter God's active public communication and self-disclosure to anyone who seeks His voice. Here we encounter

God speaking or communicating directly to His prophets—and, through His prophets, to anyone who will listen, who will seek, who will strive to find Him. For we all know that hearing and understanding come from listening and paying attention. This is why Jesus often says, "to all who have ears, let them hear" (see, e.g., Matt. 11:15; 13:9).

Whether these communications are heard by many or by few, by crowds or by prophets and priests, the idea that God actually communicates, that God actually speaks, seems a stretch to most people, particularly in modern times. But is it? In my early skeptical days, I would have said yes. It would have been a stretch for me. As I thought more about God and reason and truth, supernatural revelation seemed a much shorter stretch than I initially imagined. The more I learned and thought, the more plausible I found divine revelation. Gradually, reason convinced me that divine revelation was necessary. Some ideas simply take time to germinate and grow. I came to believe that God could or should communicate with us. It almost seemed a necessity.

I expect you will take a similar road from cautious skepticism to tentative belief as you grapple with the idea of supernatural revelation and the idea of the supernatural, period. But as you wrestle with these ideas, recall how much of our everyday human experience points to an intangible dimension. And the reality and truth of this intangible dimension are part of our everyday lives, and our minds and beings already give evidence of the existence not only of God but of human nature too. And reason is just such an intangible aspect. So are love, morality, justice, and all the other virtues we all admire in others and strive to attain ourselves, at least when we remember to do so.

And it is here, in the realm of the intangible, on the threshold of the supernatural, that most modern people get a bit squeamish, a bit skeptical, a bit cautious. It is here that we enter into the miraculous, the supernatural. It is here that we begin to think deeply about what miracles truly are, about what the supernatural truly is.

Supernatural revelation and miracles present a significant boundary for most of us, particularly those of us who've ingested lethal doses of materialism and modernity. Most modern people think the supernatural is just a fantasy, a viral delusion inflicted on us by our parents, our past, or our weakness in the face of a wholly mechanistic material universe. Or they may believe in a hard boundary between the natural and the supernatural, which confines faith and belief to the subjective, personal realm and science and evidence to the objective, natural realm.

Most moderns believe the natural domain is grounded in science and in reason, whereas the supernatural is based on belief and spirituality. But no such separation exists. Reason, love, and morality create unifying bridges between the tangible and the intangible, between the natural and the supernatural. So too with science and spirituality, but in different degrees and with different emphases. Science relies heavily on reason, an intangible faculty of an intangible mind; likewise, personal spirituality must meet the basic demands of reason. Both aspects are intangible experiences experienced by each and every intangible personality and being.

The apparent boundary between the natural and supernatural is much more fluid than we may think. Our reality, therefore, is much more integrated than most moderns believe.

If we pause to ponder this, we will discover that we are all an integrated amalgam of tangible and intangible, material and immaterial, natural and supernatural. Any boundary we may sense between these dimensions is essentially conceptual. And, this integration, this synergy of dimensions, might even surprise you.

With this in mind, let's take a deeper look at the idea of supernatural revelation and the miraculous, as we consider the role of revelation generally and the content of these messages specifically. In the process, we'll naturally deal with the very idea of religious truth and the assertion that all other world religions are mere shadows of the blazing truth we call Catholicism—the idea that Catholicism is the one true faith, that the Catholic Church is the one true Church ordained by God.

Let us learn why the Catholic faith is the one true Christian faith. Let us learn why the various Protestant denominations, sects, and movements are really distortions and deviations from the original, historical, and doctrinally correct Christian church, as later chapters will make clear and certain. We'll encounter the reality that the Catholic faith possesses the fullness of truth, and that the Catholic Church is the only church directly and personally established by the God who became man and dwelt among us.

This is *the* preposterous claim to which our investigation of natural and supernatural revelation must lead: God came to us in a tangible way, spoke to us in a natural way, died for us in a real way, and rose from the dead in a historic and factual way. All these supernatural activities unfolded in the natural world, the world of tangible realities, the world of space and time.

The greatest miracle is that God Himself lived among us and spoke to us as a human being. This man, Jesus, gave His life for us so we could become the sons and daughters of God. The Catholic Church was begun by Him and comes to us now, even in our modern times, just as it did in its earliest days, despite the heresies and distortions of other faith traditions, despite our modern proclivity for inclusion and diversity at the expense of reason and truth.

Our consideration of Christ and His Church will lead us to the very threshold of informed belief and committed discipleship, for we are responsible for what we know and for what we do with this knowledge. As the truth about God, Jesus, and the Catholic Church becomes ever more certain, we become ever more obligated to make a decisive commitment.

Let's move forward with rising curiosity and courage. Let's open ourselves spiritually, emotionally, and intellectually to the presence and activity of the supernatural. Let's meet the man who lived among us as God incarnate, who performed the greatest miracles, who is the sum and substance of the Catholic religion: Jesus, the Son of God.

14

Matters of the Miraculous

For many of us who have received the gift of faith, miracles provide another level of evidence for God's existence and His nature. They tell us He is active and near, and they reveal to us His plans and His priorities. But for those who are uncertain or uninformed about their faith, miracles often challenge long-held ideas about our world, our universe, and the presence and nature of God. In the realm of the miraculous, ideas run right up against the reality of the physical world and the practicalities of daily living. This is where our very concept of reality is challenged, where our implicit beliefs in materialism are revealed. And this is one area that often reveals a belief in the wholly mechanical nature of the universe and its latent materialistic basis. It reveals the unspoken belief that the universe is only and completely physical, matter and energy. That's it. And that is all there is.

On the surface, miracles seem to contradict the lawful limits of the universe: the predictability of science, the certainty of order, and the reliability of our senses. By implication, miracles also challenge the comfort that comes with belief in a wholly materialistic universe, for this entails the illusion of certainty we think science provides. For many moderns, and even for some of the faithful, it's one thing to say that God exists and that we can know Him; it's another to claim that He intervenes in our universe and our lives. It's an even more extraordinary thing to say God intervenes on our behalf or in response to our pleas and prayers.

But let's set aside prayer and providence for the moment and just examine God's initiatives and interventions in the reality of reality, God's miraculous activity. Let's step back for a moment and return to basic questions. Could God really intervene in our lives? What might His intervention look like, and what would it tell us about Him?

Let's think about the very idea of supernatural revelation and the miraculous. For it is crucial to understand supernatural revelation and miracles in order to grasp more fully who God is and what God does.

The Basics of the Miraculous

Let's go back to some earlier ideas and facts before we move into the realm of the miraculous. For, as with so many things in our modern world and so many principles of reason and common sense, it is in the core and foundational issues and facts that we so often find the answers to perplexing questions. It is here that we find not impenetrable mystery and obscurity but rather sophisticated simplicity and inherent and integrated complexity.

So let's begin our recap. First, if God has a mind and is a person, He must have a purpose and a plan. God acts upon His plan to ensure its fulfillment, especially because human beings have free will, which is also part of His plan. We humans can make choices; we have the freedom to cause things to happen and to prevent things from happening. Our choices may, and often do, run counter to God's plan on the grand scale of the world at large and in the details and small scope of individual practical lives and living.

So let's begin at the beginning of all things. Our universe was created according to a preconceived plan. When God created all that exists, this was not some whimsical thought, some passing impulse, some irrational, pointless decision. It began with a vision and an end in mind. Reason tells us this. For such a grand and creative act would have to have a reason, a purpose, an end. When we see something we can't explain, our first question is usually how this thing came about—how it got here. Our second question is why it is the way it is—what its purpose is.

You see, we all expect things to serve some end, to have some point, to move toward some goal. Reason and reality demand such a purpose and plan; otherwise, we wouldn't bother to ask why things are as they are, nor would we be surprised by things that lack a point of origin or an intended goal.

As a mind and a person, God creates things to serve some purpose, even if its purpose is not readily apparent. Given what we already know about the nature of God, His perfection and His mind, we know He creates intentionally, purposefully. The wealth of evidence we find in both the physical and the mental world demonstrates order and purpose As mentioned earlier, the tuning of the universe, its lawful behavior, and its existence all point to design and structure, so much so that if it weren't for this inherent order we see all around us, we would not be able to know much of anything about our universe. The same is true of reason itself and our application of reason to our investigation of the physical world. All physical and reasoned evidence points to an inherent order. And inherent order reflects both a plan and a purpose.

It's not far-fetched at all to expect some plan, some goal, some purpose for our world and for our lives. If we can recognize the truth of such a commonsensical and critical idea, we shouldn't be surprised that God might intervene in the affairs of mankind from time to time, even outside the laws of the physical world He created, for the existence of everything was intentional and designed with an end in mind. An interested, involved, and intimate God could and would intervene in whatever way He chooses in order to realize His plan.

God intervenes in the physical realm and in the realms of the mind and heart. So, if God exists and created the universe with a plan in mind, He did not create all that exists and then leave mankind alone to figure it all out. This is why He reveals Himself miraculously in His spoken word, in His miraculous action, in His providential provision, and in His proximate and intimate relationship with us.

Similarly, if God created everything, including us, and then just watched disinterestedly, as deists and modern Westerners believe, then He just would not be the God of the Bible, the Judeo-Christian God. He would not be the God who loves us, who exhorts us to know Him and to follow Him. Because He loves us, He intervenes, He communicates, and He ultimately came here, spoke to us, and acted on our behalf.

Perhaps an example might help. Think of a good parent. A good parent loves his child, provides for his child, protects his child, teaches his child, corrects his child. If we who are imperfect, flawed, and fallen know this, how much more would God, who is perfectly good, perfectly just, perfectly merciful, and perfectly loving, intimately and actively intervene in our lives!

We know this almost intuitively, viscerally. God is perfect, good, and loving. In the end, God does intervene in our world because He is not just some powerful deity. He is the embodiment of complete moral perfection. And our intuitive and rational moral sensibilities are approximations of His many perfections, reflections of His very nature.

Not only does God have the power and authority to intervene in our world and our lives, but He intentionally acts to advance His plan and demonstrate His love. And as we see in Scripture and in history, God has intervened and continues to intervene in this world, in space and time, in the physical world and in the intangible world, the world of the mind, the intangible world of men and women.

A God Who Intervenes

All these interventions constitute God's personal initiative, His active intervention, His supernatural revelation. For God has a long history of changing physical circumstances both subtly and dramatically. He also reveals Himself to people in an intangible way, within their minds. Such occurrences have been recorded in the Bible and in Church tradition and history. You may have heard of the Old Testament stories of Abraham, Isaac, Moses, Samuel, David, Elijah, Elisha, Isaiah, Jeremiah, and Ezekiel. Peter and Paul, James and John are examples of people mentioned in the New Testament who received God's revelation. There are many others named in Scripture and throughout history. We may know these people as prophets, mystics, saints, or Doctors of the Church. They all claim to have heard the voice of God, whether interiorly or audibly.

These people recorded the messages God gave them: messages of destiny and deliverance, rebuke and repentance, love and encouragement; messages that foretold coming events, that proclaimed the coming of the Messiah, and that spoke of His return.

Just as there is a long history of God's subtle, providential interventions, so, too, is there a rich collection of intangible, supernatural revelations. We read these dramatic, miraculous stories in the Bible, especially in the Gospels.

Dramatic Miracles

Let's start with some obvious miracles. The first miracle of all is the existence of everything. Yet it's also the most frequently overlooked, and, oddly, it's the miracle unbelievers tend to use to disprove miracles.

Most unbelievers, even some who are curious about Christianity, assume that the universe came about by accident, or that it is eternal, with no beginning. But as we discussed in the earlier chapters about origin and order, our universe must originate from an uncaused cause. The first effect of this cause—the creation of the world—is a most magnificent miracle. Equally miraculous is the finely tuned order of our universe. And over time, as Scripture and science tell us, the universe became full of living creatures. In all this, we see a God who continues to produce miracles as He reveals His plan little by little, at each new stage of the world's development.

At the climax of God's miraculous creation is human life. Our conscious existence, too, is a great miracle. God created us to be self-aware; He made us to think, reason, choose, and love. Ultimately, He designed us to be able to know Him in a direct and personal way. And as we know all too well, the first human beings eventually chose badly and began to love poorly and jealously. Our thinking became irrational and flawed. This was the fall of mankind from our original perfection to the imperfection and iniquity with which we're so familiar now, by our misuse of the gift of our free will.

Even so, the origin of the universe, in all its order and with all its living beings, including us, is inherently miraculous. Everything we see, everything we are, everything we take for granted is unbelievably miraculous, regardless of the eons it took to achieve its current level of diversity and complexity. Existence itself is a clear, unmistakable, magnificent miracle that exceeds our imagination and comprehension. At the same time, it seems so natural and predictable that we often miss its miraculous manifestations and the glimpses of God present at every moment of our lives.

As we look back in time toward the ultimate origins of life and existence, we can see the constant dynamism of divine intervention and providential circumstance and timing. We see creation and elaboration, initiation and expanding sophistication, a beginning and later developments. We don't see a single or short series of creative acts and then nothing; instead, we see ever-unfolding development.

Even the fossil record demonstrates this dynamic process of providence and creative initiation. We can see scientific evidence of the initiation of life, the first forms of which grew, developed, and experienced significant providential changes, such as mutations and adaptations. These new initiations arose naturally from earlier ones in circumstances strongly suggestive of divine intervention, divine providence. New abilities and structures—sometimes entirely new species—came about through God's intervention.

Our modern world typically attributes this process of biological development to chance, luck, or coincidence. That shouldn't be surprising: according to the modern, atheistic view, everything that exists is the result of chance. A universe without God is blind and mechanical, made of nothing but matter and energy. That's all anyone can appeal to.

In other words, if the universe is only matter and energy, then everything must be explained by matter and energy, the two forms in which the physical universe is manifest. If the universe is only one thing, everything must be explained with that one thing. Anytime an organism experiences an advantageous mutation that perfectly suits its circumstances and surroundings, we must attribute this serendipity to blind chance. The same goes for mutations and other adaptations that give rise to entirely new forms of life.

Such is the nature of an empty, silent, mechanistic universe. Without a second thought, without considering the possibility of divine providence, those who believe in such a world write off the sheer number of these advantageous mutations. They ignore, too, the ridiculously low probability that such perfectly adaptive mutations could arise by chance, as you'll recall from our discussion of Penrose's number.

But as the Catholic Church, science, reason, and practical experience show, such "chance" occurrences arise from God's sustaining power, with which He maintains the very existence of the universe and its lawful, predictable, moment-by-moment existence. He holds everything in existence, even if we can't see His providential actions. His active interventions, which we call miracles, account for seemingly random, chance events, in keeping with the overall logic of reason and mathematics.

God's miraculous, providential development of life is in harmony with what science tells us about biology. Even secular scientists have noticed sudden leaps in complexity and differentiation in the fossil record, such as the Cambrian explosion. These changes reveal a form of punctuated progress: a pattern of sudden growth in an existing species or the emergence of an entirely new form of life, which then gradually differentiated and developed.

These punctuations in the equilibrium and development of the universe are dynamic, purposeful acts of God to advance His plan and to demonstrate His love and His perfect nature. These punctuating events, these new initiatives, these fortuitous circumstances show us His active presence in our world. However seemingly coincidental, these events are providential, revealing our world's divine origin and order.

Free Will and the Mundanely Miraculous

Our world offers some pretty strong evidence of the miraculous and of God's activity and proximity. When we take these things for granted, we often become blind to our maker and His activities. The things that constitute our everyday reality—consciousness, reason, matter, time, space, and life itself—came not from blind accident or from the eternal ebb and flow of mindless matter in motion. They came from an uncaused, rational, perfect being. We are awash in clues and consequences of His existence and His nature.

This is why we are without excuse. For existence, consciousness, reason, space, time, matter, and energy all began at one point in time. They all have an order, a lawful structure, no matter how complex or simple. And they all constitute the reality we walk around in each and every day.

How could we deny miracles and revelation when God's handiwork is all around us? We are His miraculous creatures, made in His image; we are the crown of His creative activity and plan, the very object of His love and care. In the miracle of our consciousness and reason, our moral sensitivities and sensibilities, God chose to reveal His nature.

As if all that weren't enough, God also used dramatic miracles to reveal Himself to mankind and to bring about His plan for us. And He did this all while preserving the freedom of choice that is essential to relationship, to love, and to goodness. This is precisely why some of us see miracles and others don't. If God always acted so dramatically, so inescapably, we would have no choice but to do as He commands, though we might not truly love Him. We would be compelled against our will by the sheer scope and size of evidence.

That's not what God wants for us. He wants us to know Him, not merely to know about Him. He wants us to know Him personally, emotionally, spiritually, intellectually, as a free decision of our will. He wants us to know and love Him as sons and daughters should.

While knowledge may be grudgingly admitted and accepted, love must be freely chosen. Love must be a conscious and deliberate decision grounded in affection, intention, and intimacy. Our love cannot be compelled by anyone, human or divine. It must be given. It must be given freely and fully, willingly and joyfully, exuberantly and trustingly. Love can never be commanded, demanded, or compelled.

In keeping with the idea of love and its inherent need for intimate self-disclosure, if God didn't give us any revelation, we wouldn't know Him personally, intimately, lovingly. We would simply be solving a puzzle: the puzzle of existence. We would be tackling an intellectual challenge, not boldly striving to find our beloved. That's why the Scriptures and the Church continually remind us of the goal of our quest: to find the God who made us out of love and who sought us before we ever thought to look for Him.

God doesn't simply want us to find Him in the philosophical, rational, scientific, physical, historical, moral, or ethical sense, though all these ways reveal some of God's many facets. He wants us to find Him, in the harmony and fullness of all these many dimensions; He wants us to find Him and know Him personally, so that we can truly and fully love Him.

For God reveals His truth and His nature to those who will simply seek. His desire is that we should know and love Him generally and personally, specifically and deeply. And unless God reveals Himself, we can't possibly fully love Him, for love is intimate disclosure. The very nature of love requires disclosure and intimacy, as is evident in our most intimate personal relationships.

This is why God acts dramatically, but in a manner that doesn't overwhelm our free will. It's just that simple. And as you will find as you contemplate the reality of our human free will, it's just that essential, just that deep, just that wondrous.

To see this, we need look no further than history. Some of God's greatest actions in space and time, in history and in practical events, are recorded in the Scriptures. For instance, one of the most significant miracles in the Old Testament was the deliverance of the Israelites from their captivity and slavery in Egypt. Under the inspired leadership of Moses and with His miraculous acts, God delivered an entire people from their abject, inhuman station in a foreign country that had relied on their forced labor for generations. The Israelites left their captivity in Egypt without an armed revolt, without a negotiated release, without persuading the mind and softening the heart of Pharaoh. They left because circumstances outside the control of human beings, outside the control of slaves and kings, softened Pharoah's heart and secured their release.

According to God's plan, as communicated to Moses in an epiphanic encounter in the desert at the burning bush, the entire nation was to abandon the slavery they had endured for centuries, pack up their belongings, and set out on a journey to a place they had never seen, a place they had never lived in, a place they were promised by God in His earlier covenant with Abraham, the nation's forefather. God promised to set this people free, despite the practical circumstances and wisdom that would preclude such a liberation.

Through Moses' trusting obedience in the work of divine providence, God enacted His plan to lead His people out of Egypt and to break their yoke of servitude. Forty years later, after a period of disobedience, trial, and eventual maturation, the people of Israel were ready to enter the land God had promised to Abraham.

Beyond this signal event is a thread of dramatic miracles, recounted in both the Old and New Testaments. This is significant, because it demonstrates historical continuity, as well as the continuity of divine intervention. God uses the same kinds of miracles to reveal His nature over time. For example, God miraculously fed the Israelites in the wilderness with manna, just as Jesus fed the five thousand who gathered to listen to Him preach in a deserted place. God manipulated physical matter when He parted the Red Sea to allow the Israelites to escape Pharaoh; likewise, Jesus calmed a storm, walked on water, and directed His disciple Peter to join Him on the waves. In both testaments, we see God reveal Himself to individuals, offering instruction, prophecy, discipline, and inspiration to men and women like us.

All these examples of divine intervention are the acts of a kind, loving Father who longs for an intimate, loving relationship with His children and whose divine spark is evident at every moment, no matter how dimly and distortedly. All these miracles point to a God who is there, a God who is near, a God who is neither silent nor passive nor distant. They point to an active and intimate God, who desires that we freely reciprocate His eternal love.

His desire for intimacy with us is so great that He acts in time and in space and speaks in ways discernible to us imperfect beings. He makes His love physically and historically evident, even beyond these miracles of obvious intervention, providential guidance, revelation, and inspiration. For not only did God continually reach out to us in all these revelatory and miraculous ways, but He actually came to live among us.

This fact is so startling, so ridiculous, so deeply miraculous, that it seems hard to entertain as a thought or a real possibility, let alone as historical fact. But this truth is exactly what the Catholic Church has maintained since its inception two thousand years ago. It's what the Gospels proclaim and the New Testament expounds. It's what the faith has relentlessly and rigorously explained, defended, and taught right down to our modern times, with all our secular, and scientific bias, with all our skeptical and irrational prejudice.

It is to this fact that we now turn our attention. Anyone who seeks God must examine and deal with this outrageous claim, this ridiculous belief, this preposterous idea that God would live among us as one of us. For it's the only belief of its kind. Some religions appeal to so-called prophets of God, to obscure deities, or to intangible dynamics. But only the Catholic Church has preached and lived and died for the truth of the God who came and dwelt among us, who made Himself visible, who taught us directly and in person. From its inception, the Church has taught that God

Himself suffered and died for our sins; that He rose from the dead so that we might know, love, and live with Him eternally; that His Spirit dwells within each person who seeks and loves Him; and this same Spirit guides the Church, God's chosen instrument for bringing salvation and revelation to all men and women.

God became flesh, just as He promised His prophets throughout history. God came to us naturally, yet miraculously as a human being, fully man, yet fully God. He was the child of promise, whose birth was foretold by the prophets. He was the coming king and the suffering servant, the longed-for liberator and redeemer. He was the priest, the king, the prophet, the very Son of the Living God. He was the Messiah, the Christ of God. And His name is Jesus.

15

Jesus in History

Why are we talking about Jesus now? Isn't this a little premature? Shouldn't we consider the other non-Christian faiths before looking at Jesus?

Well, perhaps we are getting ahead of ourselves a bit. But I don't think so. And as we go along, you'll see that my decision isn't a simple matter of style or rhetoric. Nor is it a sly move designed to convince an unsuspecting future convert.

My decision comes from none of these reasons; rather, it's simply a matter of good thinking. To delay by scrutinizing the other revealed religions misses the point of our quest. For the goal of this book is to find the truth about God, not merely to amass knowledge about world religions and their different views of God. We are here to find the truth, plain and simple.

For many modern people, approaching the question of religion in an exhaustive manner doesn't lead to clear, logical answers and facts. Instead, we risk getting confused by similarities between religions, which can lead us to minimize their many crucial differences. The truth becomes hidden in this mirage of complexity.

Approaching the world's religions from the standpoint of commonalities rather than from the standpoint of distinct differences tends to push us implicitly toward a mindset that prevents or obscures the discovery of truth, rather than bringing us closer to it.

This method of inquiry can foster the conclusion that there is no truth about God, that all the world's religions have similar levels of truth, or that God's nature is a compilation of all these different theologies. We may mistakenly decide that no matter how strongly religions disagree with each other, their differences don't matter. By taking only similarities into consideration, many moderns may think the truth about God can be found in any religion whatsoever. Thus, we have a form of truth by consensus, a form of truth that overlooks religious differences and distinctions, the existence of right answers, and the very nature of truth.

It's true that many of the world's religions do possess truth, but only in certain amounts. Some possess a very small amount. Others have more. But to one degree or another, all these religions are merely shadows of the one true faith. For the fullness of truth is found only in the Roman Catholic Church. This is a fact, as the remainder of this book will clearly demonstrate.

But don't take my word for it. Don't be taken in by my strong belief, my confidence, or my ability to make the case for the Catholic faith. Truth doesn't reside in zeal, confidence, or rhetoric. It resides in sound and logical reasoning, in the historical and practical and actual facts of things. This is the case even if some of the truth we find comes to us miraculously or through revelation. If God communicates with us and desires an intimate relationship with us—as He must, because He is both perfect and loving—then we can expect revelation to be an important part of our faith and a significant source of truth. The revelation we receive will tell us things we can investigate, criticize, and evaluate, not simply things we must accept without analysis and critique.

In contrast, if God doesn't communicate directly and personally with each of us, then all we really have is a distant deity who commands our obedience. We're left with a God shrouded in obscurity, distant from our lives and our concerns, indifferent to what we do and whom we worship. And that's just a form of deism, which we've shown to be false.

When searching for truth, what matters most is the differences between the various theistic faiths, not their similarities. In order to find the truth, we must have clear, distinct alternatives to evaluate. We need to know what the different truth claims are in order to evaluate them for their accuracy, for their sound reasoning, for their purported truth. Finally, we must determine which alternative is the truth. And we must pick a single answer.

I am serious when I claim to present *the* truth about life and living. Truth is a certain, singular thing, not one arbitrary answer among many. It isn't constructed from a collective decision or agreement, nor does it arise from some form of democratic consensus.

That's why I intend to deal with Jesus now. I do so because no other faith claims what Christianity claims.[3] No other revealed religion is like Christianity. Its dogmas are so distinct as to make any compromise impossible, or at least insignificant.

It's simple, really: Christians claim that Jesus was God incarnate. They claim Jesus was God, the God who became flesh and dwelt among us. This single claim is so important and so revolutionary that, if true, it makes all other faiths and philosophies irrelevant, mere shadows of the real truth. A God who cares for us so much that He would become flesh and dwell among us is a God unlike

[3] Here, I use the word "Christianity" to refer to both the Catholic faith and the various Protestant denominations who hold the same basic view of who Jesus Christ is, what He did, and what mission He fulfilled according to the New Testament. Later, I will explain why the Roman Catholic Church is unique among the Christian churches.

any other, a God of reckless love, a preposterous God. He is a perfectly good and just God, whose power was manifest on a cosmic level in the Creation of the universe and on a personal level in the Incarnation of Christ.

Christianity did not invent this claim; rather, Christians profess nothing less than the words of Christ Himself. Jesus claimed to be God. His teachings and miracles, His signs and wonders, His resurrection and ascension all proved the truth of His divinity. So did the emergence and endurance of His Church; so did the lives of His disciples and His followers down through the centuries.

No other religion makes such a claim. Polytheists might admit that Jesus was a god, but only one among many. Islam and Judaism claim Jesus was a great prophet and teacher, but neither claims He was God. Deists might agree that Jesus was an admirable person, but His Incarnation is incompatible with their view of God as distant, passive, and inscrutable. Like deism, agnosticism professes a form of theological ambiguity arising from the absence of evidence. So agnostics would reject Jesus, because He claimed definitively to be God, and His existence proved that God is knowable and near, not obscure and hypothetical.

Jesus' claim of divinity would obviously be beyond atheism, which repudiates the very idea of God, let alone the idea of a man who claimed to be God. To atheists, Christianity's belief in an incarnate God merits nothing but a tirade of sarcasm and scorn, because it's too ridiculous to take seriously.

So let's cut right to the chase and see whether Christianity's claims about Jesus are true.

Jesus of Nazareth was born under the rule of the Roman emperor Augustus. His public ministry took place in the Roman province of Judaea, during the reign of Emperor Tiberius. Jesus was a Jewish man who said He was the Son of God. He claimed He was God incarnate. He claimed He was the long-awaited Messiah foretold by the Hebrew prophets. He claimed He was the Savior sent by God for the redemption of mankind.

He performed miracles. He healed the sick, the lame, the blind, the maimed, the leprous, the deformed, the possessed. He taught openly for all people in a manner that was incisive and inclusive, that drew on what people already knew. Yet His preaching articulated the truth in an unprecedented and unrepeatable way. He taught with power and authority, as only God can.

He also gave His life to redeem mankind, so we might be free from the bondage of sin and able to spend eternity with Him as His beloved disciples.

Okay! Okay! I just wanted to give you a quick overview of some of the preposterous claims Jesus and His Church have made about who He was, what He did, and what He still does, two millennia after His resurrection following His death on the cross for supposed blasphemy and sedition.

Remember the earlier chapters, when we spoke about the nature of God and God's proximity, intimacy, and activity? Well, rather than dwell on the various religions and their views of God's nature, I thought it would be clearer, more effective, and more efficient to go right to the heart of the matter and look at Jesus. For He is the deal breaker.

If these claims are true, then Jesus is the crucial turning point of all things temporal and eternal. He is the hinge of history and the hope of humanity. He turns our idea of divinity on its head. All the deities of the world's religions pale in comparison with the God who became one of us, who dwelt among us, who died for us.

Jesus is just that crucial, just that significant, just that pivotal. If He is who He says He is, nothing, absolutely nothing, about life and living stays the same. For Jesus claimed He was God. And so does His Church, down to this day. That means that God actually became man and lived among us. He spoke to us in words and ideas we could understand. He lived among us as one of us. He ate, laughed, cried, worked, walked, and washed just as we do. But He was and is God.

You won't find a nearer or more active or more intimate God than Jesus. Nor will you find a more wondrous and joyous faith than the Christian faith, which, if true, is a faith of loving intimacy with God, not of esoteric ideas or ephemeral practicality. Because God came to us in the here and now of space and time, in flesh and blood, we know He loves us as no other god could. God loves us even more than our closest friends and family do. He loves us perfectly and completely without any lapses or misunderstandings, without any reduction in intensity or selflessness. For He loves us perfectly.

In Jesus, we have a God who is concerned about us in a manner that can only be described as personal, proximate, intimate, active, loving. Even nonbelievers know that the other monotheistic faiths have nothing like Him.

History shows that Jesus Christ is Christianity's one absolute distinguishing mark. Down through time, in all places, cultures, and circumstances, Jesus' followers have echoed His claim that He is the God-man, who lived among us in the flesh and shared our humanity; who taught us; who humbled Himself to the point of suffering and dying on our behalf; who rose from the dead; and who is with us even unto the end of time. Christians claim Jesus did all this in a specific geographic location and at a particular point in history. And we claim this Jesus, the Son of God, did all this out of love of each and every one of us.

This is what separates Christianity from Judaism, Islam, and any of the other revealed religions. Islam and Judaism see Jesus of Nazareth as simply an inspired teacher or prophet or a holy man committed to God and saintly living. But Jesus did not leave us that option. He claimed to be God, and that purported blasphemy led to His crucifixion. Any religion that does not accept Jesus' claim to be God incarnate must see Him as nothing more than an imposter, a liar, a blasphemer. This includes Islam and Judaism.

That makes things easy and clear for anyone sincerely searching for the truth about God. For Jesus, His nature, and His mission make a clear and deliberate decision possible. Jesus makes the claim of Christianity unmistakable and uncompromising to everyone. He poses the question of the ages, which can be answered in only one of two ways: either Jesus is God or He isn't.

And as you now know, we can uncover the truth when the choices we confront are clear, comprehensive, and mutually exclusive. Such is the nature of truth. For the truth is the truth. Anything less, whatever it may be, just isn't the truth. And the truth is knowable when all the options are in front of us and the evidence is clear—logical evidence, historical evidence, scientific evidence, moral evidence, revelatory evidence.

Jesus is just such a choice. You are either for Him or against Him. Either He is God or He isn't. Either the Church is right or it isn't.

This clear and compelling choice is both a comfort and a challenge. It's comforting because we can indeed know the truth one way or another. But like so many things in this book, the choice about Jesus will challenge your reason and your resolve, your curiosity and your conscience, your complacency and your comfort, your honesty and your humility.

Truth inevitably leads to just these kinds of challenges. The comfort of truth is won only when the battle for understanding is fought fully and fairly, passionately and purposefully, relentlessly and realistically. Make no mistake; it is a battle: a battle for the very idea of truth and a battle for the very facts and ideas through which we find the truth.

So let's look at the life of this man Jesus and see if He is, in fact, God. Let's see if such a preposterous claim is more than some fantasy or myth. Let's see what evidence there is to this claim. Let's begin with history and the facts of His life, so we may be certain this man actually existed in space and time in the manner the Church has claimed from the beginning.

History

Probably the first place to look for the truth about Jesus is in the historical accounts of His life. These are found in the New Testament in the Bible. The more detailed accounts of His life are found in the Gospels, while the rest of the New Testament details the life of the early Church and its teachings about Jesus.

The four Gospels—according to Matthew, Mark, Luke, and John—recount the life of Jesus. They tell the story of Jesus' birth, life, death, and resurrection. Two of the four Gospels were written by the apostles Matthew and John, who accompanied Jesus during His ministry. According to tradition, the other two authors were disciples of Jesus and also relied on the testimony of the original apostles. The apostle Peter was the source for much of Mark's Gospel, and Luke's Gospel relies similarly on the apostle Paul.

These accounts traditionally were written within twenty to thirty years of Jesus' resurrection and ascension, between A.D. 60 and 70, though many modern scholars date them between 70 and 100. Given the modern mind and its strong tendency toward radical skepticism, the earlier, traditional dates seem more likely, given their dominance for seventeen hundred years. But both sets of dates indicate documentation in close proximity to the actual events, though oral preaching and the oral tradition behind it began within forty days of Jesus' ascension, as the Acts of the Apostles indicates.

The Gospels document the facts of Jesus' existence, His nature, His mission, His teaching, His ministry, and His purpose. Though the Gospels tell the same story, each tells it differently, because each was written by a different author and for a different audience. Their differences are not substantial: they differ in emphasis and in approach and even in some minor details, but the Gospels are remarkably similar. This is probably because their authors all relied on apostolic eyewitness testimony and because all the events the authors recorded occurred within their lifetimes or just before they were born.

From a historical standpoint, all the important details and substance of the Gospels are the same. Their minor differences bear the implicit stamp of real and practical history recorded by different people for different audiences. In fact, these discrepancies make the Gospels all the more believable and reliable. They show that the Gospels are genuine accounts, not a managed or manipulated message. Think about it for a moment: even if you and I witnessed the same event, we wouldn't describe it in the exact same way. We might emphasize different details, depending on our audience, our interests, and our background knowledge of the event, to give a few examples. But the basic facts of our stories would be the same.

The Gospels are reliable for the same reason. While their minor variants reflect the individuality of the authors and their audiences, their core historical facts are the same. The overwhelming similarities contained in all the Gospels and in the teaching of the early Church bear witness to the same essential truths and the reality of Jesus' presence in space and time. They testify to the miraculous events of Jesus' birth, ministry, message, and mission, as well as His crucifixion and resurrection.

This is why it's important to read the Gospels as they were written. For they are not just stories along the lines of myths or fables or even fiction. They are written in a manner and style indicative of a historical account, though not the dispassionate history with which we have come to be familiar in our modern era. For the history of the Gospels is history with a point and a purpose.

The Gospels do not merely record the facts, because the facts themselves have meaning and a message, just as most facts of our lives do. Even in modern times, the bare facts of things tell us little unless we know what they mean, what their purpose and their message are. So too with the Gospels. Their authors want to communicate more than the bare facts. They want to communicate the point of these facts, their meaning, their significance.

The apostles who witnessed Jesus' ministry knew His teaching was profound and His life miraculous. They couldn't omit these miracles and still claim to offer a historically accurate account of Jesus and His life.

I mean, that's the story of the Gospels: the story that Jesus' life is more than a story. It's news, real-world news. It's unbelievable, extraordinary, miraculous, wondrous news. It's good news beyond anything we can imagine or concoct, good news for this life and for eternity.

That's precisely what the word "gospel" means: "good news." How else could you possibly tell the story of God's becoming man without incorporating miraculous events? The very idea of God incarnate is inherently miraculous. This is why the Gospels are accounts not only of real, historical events, but also of the meaning of these events: the meaning that God has come to live among us in order to fulfill His mission of loving redemption. If true, that is indeed good news.

Removing the miraculous elements and events would make the Gospels neither accurate nor historical. I mean, if God intervenes miraculously in space and time, then it has to be recorded that way; otherwise it is not true to the facts of the occurrence.

Think for a minute about how you could write a historical account of a miracle. The only way is just to say what you saw. So if you saw Jesus pray over a small amount of food and then distribute the food to five thousand people, and then you saw a large amount of leftovers after the meal, that's how you'd have to record it. That's what you saw. That's what actually happened. To write the story any other way would be to leave out the obvious miracle and the truth of what happened.

This is challenging to accept today, because moderns don't think miracles are possible. They think miracles are matters of personal perspective, because they unconsciously or deliberately believe in a mechanical universe, a closed system of cause and effect with no room for miraculous interventions or events.

But as we know from earlier chapters, a system of cause and effect requires an uncaused cause. This uncaused cause is God. That means our universe of cause and effect does not leave out apparently miraculous events initiated by the uncaused cause. Additionally, it means any human being who performs miracles must be God or, at the very least, has received God's assistance in some way.

For moderns who require historical accounts other than the Gospels, there are at least five other manuscripts that tell us about Jesus, His presence in history, His ministry, His death and resurrection, and His Church's early beliefs and practices. That is, they recount the core facts and features of Jesus' life and ministry.

And given the obscurity of His life and location, it is all the more remarkable that such an obscure man in the Roman world of that century would be mentioned by Tacitus—the preeminent Roman historian of his day; Pliny the Younger, a Roman senator; Josephus, a Roman Jewish historian; Lucian, a Roman orator and writer; and the authors of the Babylonian Talmud, a Jewish religious text.

These are five historical sources from the first and second centuries after Christ. They mention Jesus and His followers at a time when there were few widespread publications or means of communication. It is therefore significant that Jesus would be mentioned at all, especially so soon after His public ministry. The obscurity of His life and homeland, too, make any mention of Christ all the more remarkable.

While none of these documents asserts the truth of Jesus' many miracles and His divine nature, they all do record some of the earliest Christian practices and the Church's essential beliefs. So even in the infancy of our faith, we can find an essential continuity and unity of belief in Jesus' identity and mission.

Now, if you are like most moderns, you don't have much difficulty accepting the fact that there was a religious and moral teacher named Jesus during the early years of the first century. That fact seems virtually certain. But believing this teacher was God incarnate, fully God and fully man, is another matter altogether. It is a matter of great significance to say Jesus was God, more than just a holy man, a wise sage, an anointed prophet. Divinity is a much bigger claim than holiness, wisdom, or sainthood. In fact, it borders on the ridiculous. So naturally, this claim requires significant proof.

We do have extensive evidence that Jesus was divine. But before we dive in, I must offer you one caution: the Christian faith is still a faith. While its evidence is extensive, it's not overwhelming. It does require that we make an act of faith and that we freely decide one way or another.

But it requires less faith than you might think. The Christian faith is not a faith of blind belief, nor is it the enemy of reason and science, practicality, and common sense. It is a faith similar in type and amount to the faith we rely on throughout our everyday lives. When it comes to Jesus' identity as the Son of God, we may need some faith. But in most cases, we don't need all that much.

A Forced but Free Choice

So we know we need some amount of faith to fill in the gaps between the facts we know and those that are likely yet obscure. Faith is the mortar binding the facts of science, history, reason, common sense, morality, human nature, and love to the more miraculous and revelatory aspects of Christian doctrine. Faith is the glue between what we can know for certain and what we can know with incomplete but considerable certainty.

That's not all that surprising if we think about it even briefly. I mean, everyone knows that no one knows everything. As a result, we must routinely act and decide according to incomplete knowledge and guided by what we do know. Faith is a necessary part of our everyday lives. This is no less true when it comes to the big questions in life—questions about God and about Jesus.

Free will is also at the heart of our human experience. But our will is free to choose only between real options, not imaginary choices. Nor can we avoid making choices by seeing all alternatives as equally viable and possible. We can choose only from mutually exclusive alternatives. And this list of clear, separate, real alternatives forces us all to make a decision, but a freely chosen one.

So let's begin.

Jesus' Witnesses

Before the Gospels were written, the original apostles and disciples were the first real witnesses of Jesus' divinity. They knew Jesus personally; they heard Him teach and saw Him perform miracles. These first witnesses, many of whom were with Jesus from the beginning of His public ministry, saw Him tried and crucified and buried. They watched His tragic death on the cross in a very public execution, conducted by the Roman governor and his soldiers at the request of the Jewish council.

After watching Jesus die, they buried Him in a donated tomb, which was guarded by Roman soldiers at the behest of the Jewish council, who feared that Jesus' disciples would steal His body and claim He had come back to life. These same disciples saw Jesus after His resurrection, three days after His death. At different times and places, many of these disciples talked to the resurrected Jesus. They touched Him and ate with Him. They walked with Him. They knew He was truly risen from the dead. He rose bodily and physically, not merely spiritually or intangibly. For they saw Him with their eyes; they touched Him with their hands; they watched Him eat real food.

When Jesus ascended into heaven to be with God the Father, these same disciples waited, as Jesus commanded them, to receive the promised Holy Spirit, under whose unction they were to go forth and preach the good news. After a period of prayer and fasting in Jerusalem, they received the Holy Spirit and went public with the first proclamation of the Gospel, which Peter preached in Jerusalem.

In this proclamation, Peter cited many Old Testament passages that foretold the life of Jesus. He gave an account of the recent events of Jesus' life, death, and resurrection, with which everyone in Jerusalem would have been very familiar. Peter singled out the resurrection as a crucial piece of evidence for Jesus' divinity and His salvific mission for all of humanity.

At this point, it would have been all too easy to refute Peter's description of the recent events surrounding the execution of this Jesus of Nazareth. It would have been easy to dismiss this "cult" figure, this "religious" fanatic, this "snake oil" salesman, this preposterous prophet with delusions of grandeur, this uneducated man with a "messianic complex."

But that's not what happened in the days following Peter's initial preaching. Instead, the numbers of disciples began to grow daily and disproportionately. The facts of Jesus' resurrection were near in time and accessible to anyone wishing to refute or reinterpret the apostolic accounts. It would not have been difficult to find out the truth about Jesus. Had the apostles lied or embellished the truth about Him, their stories could have been easily debunked.

But that isn't what happened. In Jerusalem, the most prominent city in Israel, the Roman provincial center, the apostles preached the good news of Jesus' death and resurrection, and people believed. The people of Jerusalem had witnessed firsthand Jesus' crucifixion; they knew the facts of His life because it was all so public. According to the Gospels, before His death, Jesus was considered a holy man and teacher, a prophet anointed by God and sent to Israel. And so He would have remained, were it not for His claims of divinity and the masses of people who hailed Him as the Messiah.

After His resurrection, and in light of His repeated claims to be the Son of God, Jesus' divinity was almost without question for many. Because of His teaching and miracles, Jesus was deemed to be a man favored and aided by God, although many religious leaders held grave doubts about whether He was a prophet, the Messiah, or just another fraudulent manipulator preying on the ignorant masses.

Following Jesus' resurrection, people converted in droves. For the men and women of Jerusalem, the resurrection confirmed the truth of Jesus' teachings and claims. It was the one indisputable fact that made sense of all the other facts: the fact of Jesus' crucifixion, the facts of His many miracles, the fact of the truth of His teaching about God, and the facts of His moral teaching.

The resurrection changed everything. For here was a God who cared. Here was a God who loved us enough to suffer for us. Here was a God who actively sought our welfare and intervened on our behalf. Here was a God who was near and personal. Here was a God who loved us even before we loved Him. Here was a God who gave His life for us, so we might know His love and live with Him for eternity.

While this all sounds nice and spiritual and a little too fantastic, many of the people who knew the facts of Jesus' ministry as their own personal experience in space and time, who witnessed that ministry and the crucifixion, came to believe in Him and His resurrection. Why? If they were here to speak with us directly, they would tell us that they saw Jesus' teaching, miracles, death, and resurrection as real historical facts. And that's why they converted to this new faith, which professed that Jesus was the Christ of God.

Their conversion didn't win them any friends among the Jews or the Gentiles. From the very beginning, Christians suffered at the hands of their countrymen and their religious leaders. Soon, they suffered at the hands of the Roman rulers, as the gospel spread beyond Jerusalem.

The persecution of converts provides another piece of historical evidence for the truth of this new faith in Christ and His resurrection. What person would suffer for something he knew to be a fabrication? Who in his right mind would accept martyrdom for believing in a myth, a fable, a fiction?

Realistically speaking, no one would choose to die for Christianity if he knew it to be a myth, a fraud. Suffering and dying as they did, these martyrs must have known that Jesus truly died and rose from the dead. The willingness of these first witnesses to die for their beliefs testifies irrefutably to the truth of Jesus' resurrection from the dead.

At the very least, we must accept that these early martyrs knew that the resurrection was actually and historically true. They believed that Jesus was God and that He died and rose from the dead. They believed because they saw Him die and then saw Him alive again. Jesus didn't appear to them as a ghost, as some moderns claim; rather, the disciples encountered the resurrected Christ in the flesh. As the Acts of the Apostles clearly states, the disciples saw Jesus living and breathing again only days after His death.

This is not a subtle point. Many of the early believers suffered and died for their faith in the truth of Jesus' resurrection. In their blood and pain and death, they left to us their testimony of who Jesus was and how He accomplished His salvific mission.

They left us their definitive witness to the actual and factual certainty of Jesus' death and resurrection. Because martyrdom was always a public event, the death of the martyrs was a public and definitive declaration that the gospel message was true.

Their attitude toward their suffering and death also provides remarkable witness to the truth and beauty of Jesus' moral teaching. As did Christ, the martyrs prayed that God would forgive their persecutors. They also encouraged one another to embrace their suffering as a joy and a privilege. They considered their trials an opportunity to share in the work of the kingdom of God and to deepen their relationship with the risen Christ, with whom they would spend eternity.

And this historic and historical witness to the truth of Jesus' divinity and His resurrection also testifies to the morals and ethics that Jesus taught, to the love that He elicited and embodied, to the certainty, wisdom, and truth of His moral and philosophical teaching as well.

For their suffering and martyrdom, the manner in which they endured this, and how they understood such persecutions testify to the truth of what Jesus taught openly and in public for all to hear, just as it testifies to the truth of His resurrection and the claims He made to divinity.

Thus, the sum of all this historical evidence points to Jesus as an actual person, who lived and taught in a specific place and time, and yet who was divine. So, too, did the lives and deaths of His followers and the many converts they made.

The teaching and preaching of His followers, the witnesses to these historical events, affirm the truth of the Gospel accounts and the oral traditions of the early Church. For the early followers taught the miracles and resurrection of Jesus as facts, first to the people of Jerusalem before they moved into other Roman provinces. And the people of Jerusalem converted to this new faith in Jesus the Messiah in large numbers.

This large-scale conversion indicates the truth of the Gospel accounts and the claim of the early Church of the historicity of Jesus' divinity and resurrection. And it indicates the absence of real contradictory evidence against these claims of divinity and resurrection. Not only is the evidence against these two claims not evident, but some of these same converts faced social and religious reprisals, persecution, and even death because they knew these two claims were historically and factually true.

While you may not consider the written and oral truth about Christ and the actions of first Christians in Jerusalem to be definitive proof of the truth about Jesus, these historical realities are not insignificant. For they situate the Faith in history, rather than confining it to the realm of religious myth.

In light of the historical evidence we've considered, let's look at what Jesus taught, to see if His preaching contains further evidence for His divinity and His resurrection. For the truth should also be present and accessible in His direct teaching, in everything He told us.

Let's continue with a soft but determined curiosity and interest. Let's bring our hearts and our minds to the subject of His preaching. For here, the truth you may find equally concerns your heart and your mind, your thoughts and your deeds, your being and your behavior.

Let's prayerfully seek the truth of Christ's teaching and its meaning for our lives on a grand and on a small scale. Let's take up this matter of mind and heart, of reason and intuition.

Set aside your doubt, and just be open to the resonant ring of truth that reverberates in your heart and your head, in your bones and in your spirit. And, when it does, you will find more truth than you may now imagine. And even if you already believe in Jesus, you may find Him to be more than you have imagined.

16

Jesus' Message

As we look at Jesus' teaching, we cannot look at Him as a merely human teacher. Because He claimed to be God, we must apply the standards of divine perfection. We should expect Him to be a truly remarkable teacher and an inspiring preacher. We should expect a truly holy, loving, and joyous man of deep sensitivity and sharp intellect, who communicates effectively and clearly.

In the substance of what Jesus said and in the significance of what He taught, we should see evidence of His claimed divinity in the very words He spoke and in the meaning of His teaching and preaching. We should hear the tone of divine authority and the ring of real, transcendent truth. For He claimed to be God, and He should be subject to the standards of perfection applicable only to God.

In short, we should see flawless content and incisive methods. Above all, we should see in Jesus the perfect embodiment of His teaching. When claims of divinity are at stake, we can permit neither mild hypocrisy, nor minor manifestations of human weakness, nor accidental omissions of even the smallest variety.

Any God who claimed to walk among us would have to look, act, think, and talk as God does. If Jesus is God, we will find perfection in everything He said and taught. For the standards God must meet are the standards of perfection. It's just that simple. And it's just that challenging, for these are high standards. But they are fair.

Now, the four Gospels are our definitive sources for Jesus' life and teaching, because these historical documents preserve the very words of Jesus for us to read, review, and reflect upon. More importantly, the Gospels preserve the meaning of Jesus' message. They preserve in detail the ideas that Jesus proclaimed, by which He wanted us to live. They preserve the essence and substance, the message and meaning, the words and wisdom that Jesus wanted us to know, to comprehend, and to embody.

Jesus came to speak to us and to teach us. If He is, in fact, God, this is no small or minor matter. He wanted us to know what He taught. He encouraged us, because He wanted us to act more perfectly. He corrected and rebuked us, because He wanted us to live by the standards of perfection and goodness and holiness. He wanted us to recognize the many ways we fall short of these standards.

He wanted us to know how perfect, forgiving, and loving God is. He revealed God's nature to us by living, suffering, dying, and rising for us, so that we might have an intimate relationship with Him through His Holy Spirit.

But let's not get too far ahead of things. Let's look at Jesus' teaching and preaching, His message and method, and see if they bear the imprint of divinity, perfection, and purity.

Jesus' Assumptions

Let's start with the things Jesus assumes—the things He expects us to know and accept. Unlike modern scholars, He doesn't begin with skepticism and science; unlike classical philosophers, He doesn't begin with doubt and dialogues. He begins pretty much where we do: with practical reason and common sense, grounded in our conscious experience of daily life, the certainty of our rationality, and the reliability of our intuition.

Jesus treats human consciousness, reason, and moral sensibilities as givens, as part and parcel of what we are. With confidence, certainty, and sincerity, He talks to us, knowing that we are capable of understanding Him.

These assumptions tell us some significant things. They tell us Jesus treats our consciousness as a real thing, even though it is intangible. He affirms the truth of our rational capacities and the reality of our moral impulses.

In fact, by using reason, Jesus tacitly endorses it, just as He implicitly endorses our sense of goodness and morality, beauty and truth, right relationships and real intimacy. Most of all, He assumes we know what truth and love are, even if we don't fully comprehend them.

You see, Jesus begins with many significant matters already settled. He begins implicitly, without the lengthy disputations and discourses of worldly thinkers, philosophers, theologians, or psychologists. Similarly, by appealing directly to our reason, intuition, emotions, and consciousness, Jesus denies the merely biochemical nature of human consciousness and thought. This is significant for modern men and women, whose radical and relentless doubt obscures even the certainty of their own existence.

As He travels through the Roman province of Judea, Jesus meets people from many cultures. While encountering them as they are, with all their differences, Jesus appeals to their commonality. He appeals to the innate sense of morality, goodness, and truth that they all hold in common. And having done so, He presents a more perfect way of morality, which He demonstrates by His suffering and death.

So keep these assumptions in mind. You will see that they make sense and may even be familiar. In earlier chapters, we established the intangible nature of human experience and the human mind. Having done so, we can begin to explore human nature and consciousness, particularly what we seem to know innately, intuitively, inherently. For it is logical, reasonable, and practical to begin here. It's just as reliable to begin with our shared sense of goodness and morality, beauty and order, truth and certainty, reason and practical logic.

So what did Jesus speak about? Well, He spoke about many things. He spoke about who God is and what He is like. He spoke about God's perfection and plan, His promises and revelations, His truth and love.

Truth and Love

Let's turn now to divine truth and love. These two dimensions of Jesus' teaching underpin all the others. Every part of His mission makes plain His concern for the love of truth and the truth of love. Such is the simplicity and profundity of His teaching.

We see this in His actions too. When Jesus performs a miracle, whether it is one of healing or of safety, whether it sustains life or restores life, God's love is on display. So, too, is the truth of God's love and of His nature.

Nowhere in the Gospels is divine love clearer than on the cross, in the culmination of Christ's mission, in His redemptive offering of His body and His life, so as to repair our right and righteous relationship with God. Perfect love is evident in Christ's sacrificial suffering and death. This is clear even to those with the hardest of hearts and minds. We all know intuitively that sacrificing oneself to save another is the most perfect and most complete act of love.

Just as Christ's death manifests His perfect love, so, too, does it manifest perfect truth. Jesus sacrificed His life to atone for the sins of all mankind. We sin when we fail to abide by the truth—the truth we know, the truth within our very bones. The intuitive truth of real moral goodness we all recognize so easily and readily in our daily lives.

For instance, when we experience the warmth of affection or the sting of sarcasm, we inherently know the moral truth of these occurrences. When people are polite and friendly to us, in even in the most minor interactions, we know that they are acting in accord with goodness and kindness. We know they are showing us love.

Similarly, when we witness people telling lies and performing small, selfish acts, we know their behaviors are not right. These actions violate the basic moral truths we all know; therefore, these behaviors are wrong, unloving, even when they're small and insignificant.

We view these everyday actions through our innate sense of right and wrong, of love and selfishness. These senses are what Jesus appeals to when He instructs us. But let's take a little closer look at what is really behind these ideas of right and wrong, what is loving or selfish.

You see, "right" and "loving" inherently refer to the same things. Those behaviors and attitudes that are right are also loving. Similarly, behavior and attitudes that are bad or wrong are unloving. Consequently, doing something wrong is not just a matter of breaking a rule; it's a violation of a relationship.

This is why sins are best understood as violations of our right and loving relationship with God and with our fellow human beings. Sins are more about breaking a relational connection than about breaking some code, law, or moral standard. Sins break our relational covenants, not just contractual laws or cultural codes. We can see this even in the Ten Commandments, which are all given in a relational context, in the context of our relationship with God and our relationship with our neighbors.

So Jesus affirms the truth of morality and the truth of love in His teaching. He does all of this in the most accessible manner, for He taught the learned and the ignorant, the wise and the foolish, the good and the bad, the loving, the unloving, and the unloved. This is the case even today. Open up the Gospels to any passage where Jesus is teaching and you will see. He goes right to the heart of things, right to our intuitive sense of things, without ever disregarding our more explicitly reasoned sense of right and wrong.

Let's take an example. In the Sermon on the Mount, Jesus teaches about love. He affirms the essence of love, particularly as we experience it in our existing relationships. But He goes on to challenge us to love those who do not love us. In fact, He challenges us to love our enemies.

Read the passage and see:

> You have heard that it was said, "You shall love your neighbor and hate your enemy." But I say to you, love your enemies, and pray for those who persecute you, that you may be children of your heavenly Father, for he makes his sun rise on the bad and the good, and causes rain to fall on the just and the unjust. For if you love those who love you, what recompense will you have? Do not the tax collectors do the same? And if you greet your brothers only, what is unusual about that? Do not the pagans do the same? So, be perfect, just as your heavenly Father is perfect. (Matt. 5:43–47)

Here, Jesus affirms our moral intuition that it is right to love our fellow human beings. But He also uses this foundational moral knowledge to show us a more perfect way of thinking, being, and behaving: loving our enemies and praying for our persecutors. Right away, we see both the truth of His teaching and the difficulty of it. We know, almost at once, we should do this. And we know this will be difficult, if not impossible, without some divine assistance. Yet Jesus means to challenge His listeners, and to focus their will, so they may truly love their enemies and pray for those who persecute them—not reluctantly or superficially, but willingly, with a truly loving heart.

Lest we miss the point of His teaching, Jesus uses the example of pagans and tax collectors to show His listeners how unremarkable it is for us to love only those who love us, without challenging ourselves to love even our enemies. Jesus extends our obligation to love even those who are not our brothers, with whom we may have no real personal connection or concern.

Jesus does more than offer extreme cases as examples; He applies His teaching to our everyday lives. He talks about the simple act of greeting, saying "hello" to people we meet throughout the course of the day. He also wants us to greet our personal enemies and those who are different from us; even to these we are to extend our love, and not just as an internal affection or an observed disposition. We are to love them actively and aggressively. Jesus drives this point home by using God the Father as the measure and model of the love we must have for our enemies.

Can you see the morality and method of Jesus' teaching? Can you see the wisdom and righteousness of this, even though it convicts and challenges us? Jesus does not let us off the hook. He tells us to be more like God. And by doing so, He leaves us no retreat, no shelter, no excuse. Simply and profoundly, we are to love others just as God loves them. Period.

Common Sense and Iniquitous Objections

Jesus makes such a clear and incisive case that even our questions will be laced with our own iniquity, as we seek to find limits and boundaries to this exhortation to love others as God loves. In another scene from Matthew's Gospel, Peter asks Jesus, "Lord, if my brother sins against me, how often must I forgive him? As many as seven times?" (18:21). Here, Peter asks a practical question not about the need to forgive, but about the extent to which we have to show forgiveness. It's a natural question. But it's tainted with iniquity: it looks for limits to love, limits to forgiveness, limits to our obligations to others and to God.

Jesus answers Peter's question in clear, certain terms. He does not explicitly rebuke him for asking, but His answer cannot help but do so implicitly: "Jesus answered, 'I say to you, not seven times but seventy-seven times'" (18:22). Peter received a most challenging answer to his question and to his character and will. For he knew, as did the people of his time, that Jesus did not literally mean we must forgive seventy-seven times. Instead, He used a number that traditionally symbolized infinity. Jesus meant Peter was to extend unlimited forgiveness.

In both of these passages, we can see how Jesus draws on our common experience and moral sensibilities without making any direct appeal to Scripture or to religious tradition. He expects His audience to know what He means. Though we live in a different time and culture, we can still see the truth of His teaching intuitively, and we can see His vision of love just as clearly. Jesus does not have to dwell on the meaning of words or ideas. He does not have to come up with a string of examples illustrating the nuances and implications of how we must apply His teaching. He simply and clearly appeals to our innate knowledge and wisdom, as well as to our innate sense of perfection, which He links directly to God and His infinite love.

Jesus does not let us off the hook even when we raise questions that reveal our latent selfishness and self-righteousness. He simply raises the standards of perfection and teaches again about perfection, God, moral truth, and beauty. Jesus does this with wonderful brevity, remarkable clarity, and beautiful charity. He is a teacher without equal, whose capacity for clear and comprehensive communication is peerless.

Jesus' economy with words is also noteworthy. He says just enough without extending His discourse. He manages to say just enough to cover everything, and His silence and brevity communicate the wisdom and breadth of the message He wishes to drive home. His silence answers questions by preventing them or compelling His hearers to reflect for themselves. His examples, when He uses them, make the lesson's essence plain and unmistakable, except where He intends otherwise.

Paradigms of Knowledge

To appreciate Jesus' teaching even more richly, we must understand the operative paradigms of His day, so that we may hear Him as His contemporaries did. Viewing the relationship between truth and love through the Hebrew paradigm of knowledge can be particularly fruitful, because it differs so greatly from the way in which we see knowledge.

Our idea of knowledge is closer to that of the Greeks and the Romans than that of the Hebrews. In the Greco-Roman world, knowledge was considered to be essentially informational. We see it as the opposite of ignorance. Either we know something, or we do not know something.

But to the Hebrews of Jesus' time, the opposite of knowledge was not ignorance, but estrangement, rebellion, interpersonal distance, and the loss of intimacy. Knowledge was essentially relational, not just informational. Thus, we see how love and truth are bound together so naturally as to be virtually inseparable. This is what Jesus teaches in the two scenes above. This way of thinking about love and truth prevents any fragmentation or separation between the two aspects of love and truth. And, as such, it sheds greater light on Jesus' refusal to separate love from truth and to place limits on forgiveness.

This underscores the distinction between a contract and a covenant and the relationship between love and morality, which we briefly mentioned earlier. All the more clearly, we see how truth is love and love is truth. Here we understand the Commandments not as rules and legal statutes, but as relational promises and covenants. Here we can see how committing adultery is not simply breaking a rule, but breaking a relationship, a covenant. Here we can see how worshipping other gods is a form of religious adultery, as the Old Testament prophets so clearly and frequently showed.

Take a moment to think about all this, about the idea of truth and love as bound inextricably together. Think about loving your enemies and even simply greeting them. Think about forgiving without limitations.

Think about how challenging this all is. Think about how right it is, how absolutely essential it is and how necessary.

And think about just how clear and concise Jesus' teachings are. How deliberate and direct, yet how kind and compassionate is the tenor of His teaching. How perfect is His vision; how simple yet profound is His message. How democratic is His perspective. He makes the ideal real. He makes perfection more accessible, truth more knowable, love more visible.

And keep in mind how all this is just a small piece of His teaching and message, a small segment of His greater mission.

You should hear the echoes of divinity. Even if you do not really hear the words of God in the two Gospel passages we examined, they should surely make you more curious. Surely, they should move you to entertain the thought that Jesus' claim of divinity might be true. Surely, this is a growing possibility, if you are not yet convinced.

Resolve to read some more of the Gospels in your free time. For they contain abundant and sufficient truth that is yours for the taking. But you have to be willing to look and consider. You have to be willing to be challenged. You have to be willing to take the time to think. You have to be willing to engage the very idea of what love really means and what truth really is. And it is all worth your time. For if anything in life matters, it does so only through God.

17

Jesus' Mission

Jesus, the Son of God, became a man and lived among us. He did this for a reason—actually, several reasons. His presence demonstrated to us that God is near and that He loves us, wants the best for us, has great hopes for us, desires intimacy with us.

Jesus came to enlighten us. He taught us and exhorted us, informed us and inspired us. He wanted us to know the truth about the big things in life. He wanted us to know many things about God, His plan and purpose, the order and destination of things, and the ultimate end of human existence.

He wanted us to know the little things too. He wanted us to know there is significance even in the small matters of our lives. He wanted us to know each and every person as a child of God. He wanted us to recognize God's love and wisdom in the everyday moments of our lives.

As the Gospels document, when Jesus met people in need, He responded not just with encouragement or wise words, but with miracles. He healed people and fed them. He calmed storms, cast out demons, raised the dead.

Yet perhaps the greatest of all Jesus' miracles was His forgiveness of sins. At first, we might think forgiveness is the easiest of miracles. Everything else we just listed requires divine power. None of us can calm storms, exorcise demons, or raise the dead on our own, because we are human. We exist within nature, not above or outside of it.

But think about it for a moment. How could anything else be greater than the miracle of forgiveness? Ultimately, only God can forgive sins, for they are an affront to His nature and our relationship with Him. They separate us from Him. Yet God desires a real and intimate relationship with each of us so much that He acts to fix this rupture.

All of the other miracles we described have to do with the physical, but sins pertain to the eternal: they transcend temporal life and space and time. That is why the most crucial part of Jesus' mission was to forgive our sins; to make us heirs of the kingdom of God; to empower us to live more righteously and intimately with God as His children; to preserve the world from sin and error; and to share the good news of redemption and salvation with all people.

Jesus accomplished our salvation in a most unusual way: by dying on a cross, like a criminal. He proved His divinity and fulfilled His mission by His resurrection from the dead.

Now, you may have heard this all before, but it bears repeating. For if Jesus was truly God and saved us from our sins, His death is no small matter. In fact, it is the hinge of history, the turning point of the human drama.

Today, most of us know the story of Jesus' death and resurrection, but our familiarity with the narrative may serve more to obscure than to reveal the meaning of these events. So let's revisit this story to understand better just why Jesus chose to save us through His suffering and death. Let's do this not just to examine every detail of the story, nor even just to understand the divinity of Christ. Let's strive to comprehend the reality of Jesus' actions and the legacy He left to His Church and to each of us.

The Dying God

Now, as we saw in the previous chapter, Jesus' mission was to teach us, to encourage us, to discipline us, and to assure us of God's love and truth. But He did something else that didn't seem to have an explicit purpose, though it was, in fact, of great importance. He died.

Jesus' claim to be the long-awaited Messiah and His claim to be God were both considered blasphemous by contemporary religious leaders. His apparent crimes precipitated a string of events that led to His betrayal, arrest, trial, and punishment. According to the majority of the Jewish leaders, Jesus spoke and behaved like a false prophet and a demon-possessed conjurer. He claimed to forgive sins, heal the sick, and perform miracles by His own authority, as if He were indeed God Himself and not just a teacher or prophet like His contemporary John the Baptist.

For all these reasons, Jesus was convicted and sentenced to death by the ruling religious council, the Sanhedrin. But the law prevented them from executing Him under their own authority; the Sanhedrin sought permission from the titular monarch of Judea, King Herod, to no avail. Failing to get Herod's permission, they sought the permission and assistance of the Roman governor, the real authority of the Roman province. Finally, after much prodding, the governor, Pontius Pilate, consented to flog Jesus as punishment for His religious crimes. After relentless lobbying and threats of rebellion from the Jewish religious council, Pilate consented to have Jesus crucified.

All this took place overnight, and the following day, Jesus was crucified, along with two other criminals. When He died, He was buried in a donated tomb, which was guarded by Roman troops for fear that His disciples would steal His body. For Jesus had claimed that He would be raised from the dead.

Despite these military precautions, Jesus did rise from the dead and was seen and touched in the flesh by many people in Jerusalem, for many days and at many times. Finally, Jesus ascended to heaven and sent His Holy Spirit to empower and inform His apostles. Through the Spirit, they preached the good news of Jesus' death and resurrection, which won salvation for all who believe in Him and freely accept the gift of faith.

That's the story of Jesus' mission, as taught by the apostles and the evangelists and handed down as the Sacred Tradition of the Church consistently and completely from the very beginning.

But is it a true story? What does it mean? How is it relevant to us today? How does it relate to the Catholic Church?

All fair questions. We will look at them in detail, and see if these matters are consistent with reason and science, common sense and common conscience, revelation and Scripture. And we will see whether the Church's answers to these questions have remained the same since its inception.

Let's begin by considering the accusations of the religious leaders. Their primary problem was Jesus' "blasphemy," His insistence that He was the Son of God, the foretold Messiah. That's an understandable concern, given the magnitude of Jesus' claim. That's why we've been dealing with this claim for the last few chapters. After the question of God's existence, the question of Jesus' divinity is the single greatest, most crucial question there is, despite the fact that nowadays we are all too cavalier about these two questions.

The people of Israel were more religious than we are today. As such, they took Jesus' claim very seriously, whereas we might dismiss it as some kind of delusion or symptom of mental illness.

While some of Jesus' contemporaries did see Him as a madman, others believed that His claims and His actions were deliberately false and fake. Here we see the lunatic and liar options surface in the mouths of the dissenters, as recorded in the Gospels, for those are two of the three possible options. Either Jesus lied about who He was and died for this lie, or He was out of His mind, though the nature and content of His teaching belies this possibility; he was too insightful and wise in His teaching to be delusional on such a foundational level and in such a grandiose way. The third option, remote as it may seem, is that Jesus' claim was true: that He was, in fact, God with us, the Messiah long promised to redeem mankind. That makes Him Lord, the God of the universe—the actual, real, true God here on the planet in space and time. It makes His presence purposeful. Jesus was here for a reason. And it would have to be a really important reason. If true, the suffering and death and resurrection of God is no small matter.

Purpose and Divinity

The purpose of Jesus' presence here on earth is wrapped up in the question of His divinity. If He was indeed God, then this is a profound and penetrating question. If not, the question really doesn't matter all that much. A man may atone for his sins in a worldly sense of justice and repentance; he may even atone for the sins of others, to some degree. But to atone for the sins of all the men and women who have lived and who will ever live is another matter altogether, particularly when it comes to obtaining eternal forgiveness.

So let's delve into the real foundational question about Jesus' nature first; then we will be equipped to examine the question of the purpose for which God came to earth as a man and suffered, died, and rose for us. Once we have answered these questions, we can look into the importance and purpose of Christ's Church, from its beginning until today. (But we'll save that for the next chapter.)

Our first clue is the witness of history as we see in the Gospel accounts, the Tradition of the Church, other historical documents from the early centuries of the Church, and the teaching authority of the Church. It is clear from these sources that Jesus, from the instant His resurrection was discovered, was always seen as the God-man, as Immanuel, which means "God with us."

Lest there be any confusion about this, just consult the opening verses in the Gospel of John. The apostle John writes, "And the Word became flesh and made his dwelling among us, and we saw his glory, the glory of the Father's only Son, full of grace and truth" (John 1:14). Right there, and in many other places in the New Testament, the same claim is made either explicitly, as the passage of John states, or implicitly, throughout the rest of the New Testament books.

It is an absolute fact that the earliest witnesses and Christians down through the centuries all believed that Jesus was the Christ of God, the Messiah, the Son of God who became man and lived among us, just as John writes.

But is this true? Well, Jesus' apostles and disciples, who had accompanied Him for three years, believed it to be true. And many of them were so convinced that they died for this fact: the fact that Jesus was the Son of God, the Savior of the world. Many were tortured or shunned. Many were abandoned by their families. Others were beaten and scorned for this belief.

So many of Jesus' closest followers were abused, beaten, and even killed for their faith in Christ. Just imagine this. Would you endure suffering and death if you thought Jesus was a blasphemer or a liar? Would you endure such trials if Jesus was a lunatic, a delusional man with a messianic complex? Not likely, no matter how much you may have liked Him or wanted this to be true.

You would have to be pretty convinced about the authenticity and truth of Jesus' claim to divinity, as well as the facts of His death and resurrection, in order to suffer and give your life for this fact. I mean, this isn't the type of cultic death we see in modern life.

The Catholic martyrs were people living in many separate parts of the Mediterranean world under different teachers. They did not seek martyrdom, as many followers of contemporary cults do. Their martyrdom came at the hands of those who felt threatened by their claim, who did not like their message or moral point of view. This is a far different matter from the self-destructive modern cults, centered on a charismatic leader, whose members withdraw from social life, stress some form of militant transformation of society, or profess the imminent return of some divine being or aliens.

Also, in light of the truth of Jesus' divinity, the apostles would have to have known with virtual certainty the immediate and ultimate purposes for His presence, His activity, His teaching, His sacrifice, and His ultimate vindication. Even a second- or third-generation believer would have to be absolutely certain that Jesus was God.

Not only were Jesus' followers convinced that He was the Messiah, but the Jewish religious leaders of that time were convinced that Jesus thought He was God. It is no small thing that they did not debate the truth of His many miracles. They had to grant that Jesus was a miracle-worker, since some of them may have witnessed these miracles firsthand.

Nor did they take great issue with His teaching. Their real problem was that Jesus acted as if He was God and that He thought He had the authority of God. And at times He insisted that He was the Messiah, the Son of God, the fullness of divinity, the equal of God Himself.

Ultimately, the Jewish religious leaders rejected Jesus' claim of divinity and sought His death through the various legal means they had at their disposal. They feared that Jesus would seduce and persuade the general masses of Jewish believers, who hailed Him as their Messiah and king. They feared that these people would rise up to protect Him. So they arrested Jesus at night and conducted His trial that same night.

Clearly, they knew Jesus' trial was a provocative and divisive issue. That is probably why they sought to conduct the trial when and where they did. And with Roman backing and support for

Jesus' death, they could appear less culpable to their constituency and vindicated in their assessment of Jesus' claims.

A Real Resurrection

As I mentioned earlier, these leaders also petitioned for Roman soldiers to guard Jesus' tomb, for they feared that His followers would make false claims of His resurrection. Despite the fact that Jesus' disciples did not make such an attempt, and in spite of the soldiers' diligence, Jesus rose from the dead. And not only was this resurrection general public knowledge at the time, but over the course of several days, Jesus appeared in the flesh to His disciples in and around Jerusalem and also in Galilee.

Not only did these events occur, but forty days after Jesus' ascension, the apostle Peter preached a sermon in the temple courts in Jerusalem, the city where Jesus was crucified. Peter's sermon recalled all these facts of Jesus' death and resurrection. Despite the improbability of these events, thousands were converted.

It is reasonable to assume that most of these converts witnessed Jesus' crucifixion firsthand. They likely heard the reports of His resurrection, if they didn't witness it for themselves. So it wasn't just Jesus' followers who converted, but many others.

And this claim of resurrection could easily be dismissed at that time by producing the body or the bones of Jesus. But no one did. Even the religious leaders were mute on this, as far as history goes. There is no evidence that anyone ever found Jesus' body or bones in the tomb. Nor is there evidence that they were ever stored in some other Jewish religious site, as critical evidence against Christianity.

But why did some of the Jews and others convert? Was it just Jesus' resurrection that led them to convert? Was it just this that brought them to give up the faith of their fathers and abandon the Jewish faith for this new religion? Was it just this that led many Gentiles to the faith as well?

In short, any resurrection is amazing, the resurrection of God even more so. But what does it mean? What is its purpose? There must be a reason for the death and resurrection of God. This could not be a random event foisted on the Messiah by the irrational ebb and flow of human existence and events. Because it is God who died and rose, there must be a reason. And there is—a most profound and important one.

It goes back to a few critical things. It goes back to the ultimate reason for human existence. It goes back to the moral order of the universe. It goes back to the essence of human free will, our ability to choose. And it goes back to the need for a means to restore the relationship between God and human beings, and, by implication, our relationship with one another.

It goes back to the redemption and salvation of mankind. For it is about a better life and the afterlife. It is about the meaning of life and final purpose to life, the final destination of all life. It is about the end of life—by which I mean both our purpose and our death. And it is to these two "ends" we now turn, as we consider the ideas of redemption and salvation.

Redemption and Salvation

The ultimate reason for human existence: now there's a pretty big topic, perhaps the biggest any of us will ever face. So we might as well begin here, at the most important of all things. For that is why questions of God and Jesus are so critical. And ultimately, it is the only way the ideas of redemption and salvation make any sense beyond the temporal benefits related to moral attitudes and behavior in space and time.

Yet these benefits, like all fully temporal things, can have significance only in the here and now. I mean, if we have no ultimate destination, no supreme being, no plan, no purpose, then nothing in this life has any meaning whatsoever beyond the transitory.

Everything temporal is meaningless in the end. For the only path to real significance and meaning must lead to eternal and transcendent things: things and behaviors and attitudes that have worth in the moment but are also tied to some ultimate significance.

In fact, the ultimate significance of anything is always a function of higher things, moral things, ultimately meaningful things. And the degree to which anything we do or say, anything we think or desire, can acquire any significance is only through its connection to the big things of life and the ultimate things of all existence.

So we must keep this in mind as we try to grasp what redemption and salvation really mean. We must remember that significance and meaning must be transcendent and eternal. That is why God Himself came to give us access to these things. Again, that is why I'm beginning with the big things, the ultimate things, the transcendent things. They are the key to everything.

And when it comes to the ultimate things in life, most of us already have a clue as to what those things might be. Those of us who still sense the intangible things in life feel the intimations of the eternal and the divine. And we know our final end is to be united with the divine personality.

For Christians, God is a conscious being, a personality, a mind. And mankind's ultimate end is to know Him intimately in loving proximity and complete fullness. This relationship is the harmony of extreme joy, peace, goodness, beauty, truth, and love. This relationship with God is also shared with everyone else who has attained this state. In this state of beatitude, all human beings are fully themselves. This is the completion of the self in loving relationship with God and our fellow human beings.

So salvation is the ultimate destination for all human beings, that we might be united in an intimate, personal relationship with God. And redemption is the way this end is available to us, despite our errors, our weaknesses, our selfishness, our pride, our iniquity.

In order to achieve this final end, we must all face the moral order of things: the moral order of our relationship with others, the moral order of how and what we think about God, and the moral order of how we behave. Not only are we all bound by the moral order of life and living, but we are also bound by the highest of all moral orders: the moral and relational demands of true and perfect love.

Now, I don't know about you, but I don't measure up to these standards even on my best days. I'm just not perfect. And on the occasions I do think and act in a truly loving and moral manner, it doesn't last too long.

So all of us recognize the standards of perfection to some degree. And we all know we miss or fall short of those standards, even though we try, and sometimes try very hard. Well, what do we do about all these errors at the end of our lives? Don't we deserve to be judged accordingly for our history of small and large errors and sins?

Well, this is where redemption comes in, where it becomes the most significant thing in anyone's life. For without redemption, we must face judgment for our mistakes and sins. That's just part of morality, no matter how much our modern world claims otherwise.

But with redemption, we have a way to escape the judgment we deserve and receive the mercy we so desperately need. We have a way back into relationship with God, who is perfectly loving and perfectly just, because He is perfection personified: perfect in fullness and in detail, perfect in all parts and in totality.

And just how does a God who is perfect in every way save the children He created? How does He save us from the mess we have made of ourselves and for ourselves? Well, He can't just set aside justice, the moral consequences of bad and immoral attitudes and behavior. He can't just set aside the demands and imperatives of real love. For that would be unjust, unfair, wrong, contradictory, and wicked. That would make God an unjust judge or a God of mere sentiment, rather than a God of perfect love and truth. In short, it would make God less than perfect, and therefore not really God.

A Good Father, the Perfect Father

Yet He loves us and wants us to be with Him so much that He must do the only thing any good father would do. He must bear the consequences Himself, to spare us what we so deserve. The justice and the judgment that all our immoral and sinful behavior and attitudes inherently warrant He must take from us and bear Himself. For that is what true love and loving truth require and demand. That is what a perfect father would do.

And that is exactly what Jesus did. He came down to our earthly plane and became a man, a man who was perfect in every way. He became a sinless, blameless man, through whose perfections true and complete justice could be served without the death of each and every one of us. Jesus the God-man was the one to redeem all of us. He was the perfect sacrifice, the bearer of our sins big and small.

If we think about this for just a second, we can see how a perfectly loving father, whose children were all condemned to die and suffer eternal judgment, would naturally take this suffering on his shoulders and die instead of leaving his children to bear this painful and eternal fate. When we think about this in terms of relationships and fatherhood and love and justice, it makes perfect sense.

For God is a loving God who wants each of us to know and love Him in the fullest sense. He wants us to know and love all His other children. He wants each of us to receive and live in the love God extends to us. This is why He reminds us constantly who He is and what He wants us to experience, to understand, to think, and to do.

Can you see the common sense, the intuitive moral necessity of His sacrifice? Can you feel the imperatives of love and fatherhood? Isn't it clear that God deeply desires to fix our sorry state and secure for us our ultimate destination? And while this is all very profound, it is not obscure or esoteric. Because it is all morally and relationally driven and linked to our commonsensical understanding of love, truth, justice, and fatherhood, it makes perfect sense.

And that is just what redemption is. We are redeemed, so we can be saved. We are redeemed, so we can join God in an intimate relationship that, at the end of life, we experience more fully and more perfectly than we ever did here on this earth. And this perfect relationship with God and His people never ends. It lasts forever.

Free Will

But—and this is a big one—we still have to decide, for we all have free will, the ability to choose. We all have the ability to welcome God, to refuse Him, or to limit His intimacy and activity. We all have the ability to ignore, alter, limit, or shun His offer of redemption and salvation.

If you think about it for a minute, all our problems come from this free will. And this free will is part of God's plan. In order to love anyone, human beings must be free. We must freely choose without compulsion and coercion.

Love must be openly and willingly given. And it must be openly and willingly received and reciprocated. It cannot be managed or manipulated. It cannot be pushed or leveraged or foisted on any of us. So our free and willing choice to accept Jesus' redemption and salvation must be made without compulsion of any variety and form.

And we must remember that this decision isn't a one-time thing. It is a decision that restores a relationship with God; as such, it must be continually renewed in order to be sustained, as any relationship requires. It is a decision that is really a pledge, a vow, a pact.

It's like a marriage vow. When we get married, we make a pledge that will guide all our future decisions. We promise to act lovingly over the course of our wedded lives. But we fulfill these vows with big and small loving decisions throughout our married life until death separates us from our life's love.

So, too, when we accept God's redemption. When we make this decision, we recognize that the path God offers us gives us everything we need, even in this life. For if this life has any significance, it can only be in an eternal sense. If we have only the affairs and issues of this life, we really have a form of transitory significance only. If things are transitory, can they really have anything more than a passing, ephemeral importance? And if things pass away with the falling sands of time, can they really be all that important, even to us in our personal lives?

When it comes to significance, in our commonsensical and intuitive and reasoned ways, most of us know that things are significant. People are significant. Love and truth are significant. Morality and ethics, kindness, patience, compassion, sacrifice, generosity, and all the other virtues are significant. And if people, behaviors, and attitudes are significant, they cannot be completely and truly significant unless they are inherently grounded in time *and* in eternity.

Unavoidable Truth

For we all know more truth than we may think. And we should all try to know the truth even more. When we realize more fully the truths of life and love, of morality and justice, of meaning and mankind, of relationships and intimacy, then eternal salvation and redemption make perfect sense. We know we need salvation. We know we want it. And we know it is true and real, a wonderful hope and an awaited fulfillment.

And we know this because we all speak a language of truth. Despite the doubts of modern life and all its misleading ways of thinking and living, we all know that there is truth. For even when we debate others with different beliefs, we use the language of truth. For we all know someone must be right.

And when we use language in its fullest sense, when we seek to describe and to encompass life in its most integrated sense, the truth is so glaring and so clear as to be almost blindingly simple and practically profound.

And that is what Jesus wanted us to see and to understand, to accept and to live by. This happens all within our freedom to choose, to accept, to embrace. For we must each choose to accept the gift of faith that brings us salvation. We must each choose to live out our faith as we would live out any sacred vow, be it our wedding vows or our unspoken vows of parenthood. We must choose to love, to be good, to believe. And God's redemptive grace will save us, and His sanctifying grace will work to purify us and edify us and sustain us when we struggle or become lax, when we are confused or apathetic, when we fall back or fall down. But we must strive to get up, to endure, and to aspire to love and trust Him all the more. And we must resolve to show this love to the children of God we encounter each day.

But maybe you're still not sure about Jesus, His mission, or His nature. That's all right. It's all right with Him. For He wants you willingly and completely. That is the desire of true love. So continue to ask God for certainty, if that is what you lack. Or continue to ask God for clarity, if that is what you need. If you need intimacy and peace, ask God.

Remember not to hurry. But remember not to wait. If you already know that Jesus is the Son of God and your Redeemer, you shouldn't wait.

But if you are really uncertain, then look to the evidence surrounding you each and every day of your life. For love is real only if it is not just a biochemical phenomenon. And morality is real only if it is more than worldly norms and judgments.

And your relationships—with your spouse, your parents, your children, your friends, your neighbors, your colleagues—matter only if there is something binding and meaningful in their very nature and purpose.

For all this testifies to the existence of God, the divinity of Jesus, the meaning of His mission, and the reality of His redemptive love. The evidence is all around you. Take it in. Look at it carefully and fairly. Think about it clearly. It is right in front of you.

And when you can see, look to the Church. For in the Church, you will see God and His kingdom all the clearer. If you look to the Church, its endurance, its depth of understanding, its teachings, its witness over time, its struggles, its people, its martyrs, its saints, you will see things more clearly still. And you will be drawn even closer to God than you now are.

So let's take some time to look at the Church for these things. And let's look at the Church to settle the Protestant question as well as questions about the Bible. For after all, the Catholic Church compiled the Bible under the unction of God's power and promise.

And, as we discuss the Church, you should sense a further witness to God's character and Jesus' nature and a greater body of evidence for all of these realities.

18

Matters of the Church

Jesus' resurrection was just the sort of unmistakable proof the early disciples needed in order to know that He was indeed who He claimed to be. He was God, just as He said. By the resurrection, in a definitive and powerful way, the disciples knew that Jesus was, in fact, the Chosen One, the Messiah. He is the Lamb of God who takes away the sins of the whole world, without any restriction, once for all time—for every time, every place, every man, every woman, every age; for our world, in our time, or at any time; even for you, no matter what you may have done. It is a gift, the gift of redemption and salvation, a gift each of us must choose to accept or reject. No matter how we choose, it remains a free gift.

Though we cannot see the risen Savior, as the early disciples did, we have evidence of His resurrection. So our belief is true: Jesus was the God-man, the Incarnate God, the Messiah, the Savior. This is our faith. But it is a faith supported by evidence—evidence similar in quantity and quality to our evidence of the existence of God; evidence that is historical, that comes from eyewitness testimony.

As we all know, claims about the truth must be backed up with evidence. This evidence comes in many forms. Sometimes it is the evidence of reason and science. Sometimes it is the evidence of morality or spirituality. Sometimes it is the evidence of our intuitions, our senses, our common sense. Sometimes it is historical; sometimes it is the evidence of eyewitnesses, as we find in newspapers and in courts.

Evidence

Well, in this case, the resurrection of Jesus was proof positive of Jesus' claim to be the Messiah, the Savior, the true Son of God. For He made that claim before His crucifixion, before His death, before His resurrection. That is why the resurrection was the proof that He was the Messiah. It was proof that He was the Way, the Truth and the Life in ways the early disciples could have only imagined, until the resurrection happened and they witnessed Jesus alive again.

Once they were sure the man in front of them was indeed Jesus back from the dead, the disciples knew something they may have hitherto only suspected or hoped for. This man they had known and followed now stood before them in the flesh, after they had seen Him die. Now they knew something that far surpassed their previous understanding of Him and of God.

Until that point, they had known Jesus as a powerful prophet and a wondrous worker of miracles. He was an insightful, incisive teacher and an inspiring, challenging, and loving leader. He was a healer of hearts, minds, and bodies, and the lover of all people, including the despised, the lost, the sinful, the weak, the unclean, the poor, and the criminal. He was the epitome of perfection and love.

But after His resurrection, He was truly the Lamb of God, the sin offering for all mankind. He was the loving sacrifice sent to remove the stain of sin and to heal the separation between God and His human children. This was the restoration of our intimate relationship with God; it was the central redemptive act for all time. It accomplished our ultimate and final salvation.

And this basic message is what the first disciples and apostles shared with each other and with those they encountered in Jerusalem and Galilee, during the time Jesus was still with them in the flesh after the resurrection.

Forty days after the resurrection, the apostles saw Jesus ascend into heaven, and they shared that fact with the disciples. In the days following the ascension, the disciples waited in Jerusalem and prayed daily at the temple until the Holy Spirit came upon them, as Jesus had promised.

At that point, Peter spoke to the crowds who gathered following the commotion of the Holy Spirit's activity in the disciples. There Peter preached the basic gospel, the good news about Jesus' mission and message. He appealed to the facts that most people knew about Jesus, His preaching, His death, and His resurrection. And all the people in the crowd miraculously understood Peter in their various native languages.

The Catholic Church celebrates the descent of the Holy Spirit and the inspired preaching that followed on the feast of Pentecost, which is probably the holiest day of the Church's liturgical year, aside from Easter and Christmas.

Pentecost marks the first real proclamation of the gospel to the world at large. The good news was spoken by Peter, the man Jesus said would be the leader of His Church.[4] For Jesus told Peter he would be the keeper of the keys to the heavenly kingdom, with

[4] The Church is really a shared relational affiliation, more like a family than a civic organization. Because the disciples and the new converts were intimately linked to God by virtue of their conversion and redemption, they belonged to the family of God. So it is best to think of the Church as a freely chosen bond of familial love for God and for others, rather than a contractual association.

power to bind and to loose on earth and in heaven. So Jesus made him the primary apostle, the leader of the new religion.

Now, Peter was to lead Jesus' Church not as an autocrat or a dictator, but as a servant and a father. And that is why the pope, the successor of Peter, is called the "Holy Father," or "Papa."

Jerusalem

So the Church began after the resurrection. Yet the Church was still small and obscure, without a formal public mission or message until Pentecost. On Pentecost, the new faith broke out in remarkable and miraculous fashion in the most unlikely place: Jerusalem, the site of Jesus' public ministry and His triumphal entrance just before His death. This was the city whose leaders silenced and killed Christ. This was where Jesus died, just as He said He would. And here He rose from the dead, just as He had publicly predicted.

Right from the beginning, this new faith was the Catholic faith, though it was initially referred to as "the Way" by the people at that time. For the word "catholic" means "universal." And right from the start, this new faith was universal. Sure, some of the first converts were Jews from Judea, but there were also converts, Jews and Gentiles alike, from other lands and countries. The Church was universal from its inception.

The Church began with Pentecost and Peter's message and miracles. It was led by Peter right from the beginning. Surely, the apostles met, conferred, and worked together. But there was only one Church. That is clear not only in the Scriptures and in Tradition, but also in history. It's a historical fact.

And right from its very beginning, this new community of faith was persecuted, particularly by the very religious leaders who condemned Jesus to death for "blasphemy." But not all of these leaders remained bent on extinguishing the Church. In fact, many converted from the Jewish religion to the new Catholic faith, the faith of the awaited Messiah.

These conversions led the Jewish religious authorities to punish and kill some of the new believers, the followers of Jesus. One of those involved with investigating and punishing these believers was a young scholar named Saul. Saul was a zealous young Jew with a robust education and a passionate commitment to the Jewish faith. He even held the coats of those who stoned to death in Jerusalem a young disciple of Jesus named Stephen.

Later, Saul was dispatched to Damascus to round up some of these new followers of Jesus. On his way there, he had an encounter with Jesus that left him temporarily blind. After recovering his sight, Saul became a Christian believer and used the name by which we know him today: Paul. After a period of discipleship, he traveled to the Gentile cities and lands to spread the good news of Jesus. His letters to the Christians in these lands eventually formed a large portion of the New Testament.

So with this early history clear, we can ask what the Church actually does. What is its purpose, its mission? And what is its real authority? Does it have any? Should it have any? And what is the extent of its authority and the substance of its teaching? Is this new Catholic Church really what God intended from the beginning? And what evidence is there for any of these questions, so we can settle them clearly and quickly?

Well, its purpose is manifold, though its mission is one. The Church's mission is Jesus' mission. Jesus commanded the apostles and their successors, down through the years to the Church today, to share the good news of the Faith, the good news of redemption, the good news of salvation. This is the good news that life has meaning and an end beyond death; that God is near and active, loving and just; that He wants us to know Him intimately, as only true love can; and that we are to love one another. And that is all really good news.

The Church and Its Ministries

Under the broad umbrella of this mission, the Church serves many purposes and performs many functions. A quick look around your town or state uncovers some of these functions, in buildings and in programs, in institutions and in organizations.

The Catholic Church conducts its sacred liturgy, the Holy Mass, in its many parish churches and cathedrals, as well as its many chapels in prisons, in hospitals, in schools, in convalescent homes, and in the armed services.

This sacred liturgy was instituted at the Last Supper, in response to Jesus' command "Do this in memory of me." From the very beginning, the Holy Mass has been at the heart of the Church's activity. Despite some variations in the liturgy, the Mass is always centered on the sacrament of the Eucharist: the Body and Blood, Soul and Divinity of Jesus Christ, the Lamb of God offered for our sins.

Just as in the Old Testament, the children of Israel sacrificed and consumed a lamb to ensure their deliverance from slavery, so, too, do Catholics partake of this perfect lamb, the Lamb of God.

This is why Catholics have always maintained that Holy Communion is not a symbol or a metaphor. In Holy Communion, we literally receive the Body and Blood, Soul and Divinity of Jesus Christ, the sinless offering of God Himself.

When we receive Holy Communion, we renew our covenant with God. We receive an infusion of grace that joins us more closely to God. He empowers us to love more perfectly and live in greater harmony with the moral and spiritual demands of our faith.

The Mass is also centered on instructing and exhorting all those in attendance about the nature of our faith and its demands and promises. This is called the Liturgy of the Word; and the consecration of the bread and wine and the distribution of Holy Communion is called the Liturgy of the Eucharist. Within the church, the six other sacraments are celebrated: baptism, marriage, confirmation, confession, holy orders, and anointing of the sick.

The Catholic Church sponsors a number of hospitals, hospices, homeless shelters, and other types of programs and services too numerous to name. The faithful carry out these ministries, because Jesus commanded the Church to care for the needy, the ill, the ailing, the hurt, the hungry, the dispossessed, the criminal, the wayward, and the weak. Often, religious brothers and sisters oversee these ministries. These religious orders may be devoted to providing social services, to teaching, to praying, and to articulating a deeper and wider understanding of the faith. The Church has performed these ministries down through the centuries. It does so out of love for humanity—the same humanity to which we belong, the same humanity for which Jesus died.

The Church also instructs each of its believers and educates its children and young adults. Catholic schools are just such a visible and common manifestation of this purpose. In these schools and universities, the Catholic Church ensures that students receive both religious and academic instruction. The Church also maintains a number of seminaries to form and train its priests.

The Church administration follows a structure that is as old as the faith itself. In the early days of Christianity, as the number of Christians grew and the faith spread, the apostles were assigned to specific regions. When they died, other faithful men succeeded them, taking the role of bishop. Bishops are viewed as the successors to the apostles even today. Under them, the various parish priests serve smaller groups, the parishioners in their assigned churches.

And since the beginning, the entire Church has been led by the Holy Father, the successor of Peter, whom Jesus charged with guiding and directing His Church.

This has all been the case from the beginning of the Church, though some of its ministries and organizational structures have changed to meet the new challenges and opportunities for service to mankind. Down through the centuries, the Catholic Church has met the human need for truth, comfort, and meaning.

Authority

This is a brief and broad sketch of the Church's many purposes and its overall mission. Now, does the Church have any authority? And what is the basis for its authority? Should it have such authority?

Well, there's a simple answer, but that answer misses the point of the question. Like any organization, the Church has authority to govern itself, to direct its organizational functioning, to manage its many purposes and ministries, to pursue its mission. So in a straightforward, practical sense, it does have authority.

But generally, most people have in mind deeper questions about the Church's authority. In light of the Church's claims, such questions may be well founded. So let's look a little closer at the deeper question of authority.

First of all, the authority the Church claims is not the same inherent organizational authority any business or political entity might claim. The Church makes a more expansive and important claim, which almost borders on the ridiculous—unless, of course, it is true. You probably know where I am going with this.

The Church claims to speak for God and to represent God here on earth. It claims to be God's chosen instrument for the redemption, salvation, education, and formation of mankind. And that's a big claim. Such a claim requires justification that goes beyond the inherent nature of any organization. For the mission of the Church demands more than a simple appeal to organizational life.

And well it should. For claiming to speak for God and to represent God here on earth is as big a claim as you can make. It is a bold claim, an audacious claim. It is the grandest, most comprehensive, most crucial claim that can be made by any religious organization or any government or any institution.

Let's take a look at what really constitutes these kinds of claims. Then we can look at the Church's claims a bit more clearly and fairly. Let's take a couple of examples to illustrate the essence of truth claims.

When any of us says that murder is wrong, we are making a big claim: we are making a truth claim; we are making a claim that murder is wrong, beyond any shadow of doubt. This seems to be common sense. In fact, it is, and that is why we have laws about murder. Because we also know that circumstances can sometimes change the level of severity and guilt, we have degrees of murder reflected in our legal codes. Our juries and judges decide these issues every day. Most of the time, they get it right; they make right and just decisions.

When they get it right, they are implicitly stating that they know the truth—the truth of the law itself, the truth of the moral imperative behind the law, the truth of the circumstances, and the truth of the guilt or innocence of the accused. And they make a decision. And most of the time, their decision is right, true, and just. That is a claim and an application of truth. For the juries and judges apply the truth of the law about murder to a given case, once they know the truth of the motive and circumstances.

To make it more concrete: Was the Holocaust wrong? Absolutely. It goes without saying. Or is slavery wrong? Is it wrong to buy and sell and breed people against their will, as if they were things not human beings? You bet it is. No question.

We have to remember that any claim to truth is a big claim. And we have seen this throughout this book. We have seen that the existence of God is a truth claim. It is supported by evidence and reason, but it is a truth claim nevertheless.

The same goes for Jesus. Was He or was He not the Son of God, God incarnate as a man? He was. And that is the truth. And there is evidence for this claim. It is not a groundless claim, a blind leap of faith. It is a reasoned claim, based on physical evidence, historical evidence, archaeological evidence, reasoned evidence, moral evidence, and even scientific evidence.

Well, the Church stands on that claim and its evidence. It stands on this fundamental fact of the faith: Jesus was God, and He died for our sins to redeem us and to save us. And this same Jesus instructed His apostles to form a church and to structure a liturgy for worship, for formation, and for sacramental and covenantal purposes. He told them to baptize believers; to perform marriages between them; to instruct converts and children; and to reach out to the poor, the sick, the dying, the widowed, and many others who were suffering or lost.

So the Church has the authority given to it by Jesus at its very beginning, as we have seen. And it has the authority intrinsic to truth itself.

The Church's activity across time is also significant in terms of its authority, for the truth of historical fact and historical tradition prove its authority. The Church has endured since its inception, and Jesus promised that even the gates of hell would not prevail against it.

So we have the Church's authority over time from its very beginning. That is the tradition of the Church, which holds and exercises the authority given to it by Jesus. No other religion can make such a claim, not even the other Christian denominations within the Protestant or Eastern traditions. Nowhere were the Protestant churches present until 1517, nor did the Eastern churches appear as separated entities until 1054. Nowhere are these churches named in Scripture.

From the very beginning of the faith, the only church has been the Catholic Church—despite the squabbles over control and governance that led to the Great Schism in 1054, and despite the errors and heresies that led to the Protestant splits in 1517. And the Church still carries that responsibility and that mantle of authority and leadership down to our very day. It does so because Jesus wanted it that way. He prayed that His disciples and His church would be one, "just as my father in heaven and I are one" (see John 10:30).

The Church is one because that is the nature of truth. The Church maintains absolute continuity in the deposit of faith—the core dogmas and teachings of the Church, from its very first day to our time—though the Church has developed and expounded on this core teaching. The Church's teaching authority arises really from three places: its magisterial authority, its Sacred Tradition, and its Holy Scriptures.

First of all, the Church's magisterial authority comes from Jesus, who established the Church, and Peter, the leader Christ chose. The unbroken line of apostolic succession maintains this authority even today.

The Church's authority also comes from its Sacred Tradition. For the Church sees Tradition as more than the mere continuity of past perceptions and beliefs, as we typically think of tradition. The Church holds its Sacred Tradition to be truth.

The appeal to Tradition is really an appeal that cites the continuity of truth over time. For truth is true, always and everywhere. To our modern minds, that is a huge claim, mostly because we have been inoculated by a large dose of relativism, which leads us to believe that there are no truths whatsoever. We embrace this relativism without much scrutiny or any real examination of its evidence. And as we have seen in earlier chapters, relativism makes a weak and contradictory case that breaks the rules of reason and lacks any real evidence.

Thirdly, the Church's authority comes from the Holy Scriptures, which we often call the Holy Bible. The Church has the authority and the duty to interpret the Scriptures carefully. That is, the Church cautions against reading the Scriptures without being mindful of what they really say, what they really mean. It is why the Church links all three sources of authority—the Magisterium, Sacred Tradition, and the Holy Scriptures—so tightly, in order to prevent error and division.

Now, the extent of the Church's authority is limited by a couple of crucial things. First, recall that God endowed each of us with free will, by which we must choose, decide, and direct our lives. Free will allows us to follow or not to follow. It gives each and every one of us, including the leaders and the clergy of the Church, the ability to make up our own minds, to choose what we choose and to think what we think.

But as you know, freedom doesn't mean we have complete abandon. We are still subject to the laws of reason and science, as well as the laws of morality. This is why we can choose, but we can also err. We can decide, but we can get things wrong. We can make bad decisions and do things we shouldn't.

The Church can teach and admonish, pray and hope, love and forgive. And all these actions respect the divine gift and inherent capacity of our free will. The Church can also correct us when our choices are wrong, inappropriate, evil, or misguided. Thus, the Church reminds us that there are truths beyond free will by means of which our behaviors and attitudes may be evaluated. We are judged according to the laws of nature, the laws of reason, and the laws of God's moral order.

It is to correct and forgive our misuse of our free will that the Church offers the sacrament of confession. And it is there for every member of the Church, from the greatest to the smallest. It is there for everyone, from the pope, to the bishops, to the priests, to the laity. All are welcome to take advantage of the healing and forgiveness of confession, and all of us need this sacrament.

In a sense, the authority of the Church is contingent on the free will God gives each of us. But it is also contingent on the level of certainty the Church has about a given subject or issue.

For example, on matters of faith and morals, the Church can speak with the authority of the deposit of faith and the dogmas and doctrines developed over the past twenty centuries. But there are other areas where the Church must reflect and study, before making a decision. And this takes time because the Church, when it speaks with the voice of truth, wants to get things right. And that is why, sometimes, centuries go by before the Church can offer a definitive stance on some issues or questions.

A simple example is certain questions in the field of bioethics, such as stem cell research. Stem cell research has been given general approval, though the Church is still examining many of these new areas. At the same time, the Church has made a definitive stand on embryonic stem cell research, which relies on stem cells harvested from living human embryos. This research results in the death of these babies. So it is a matter of human life and a violation of the divine commandment against killing human beings.

In general, as technology and science have improved, new frontiers of medicine have opened up. This sometimes raises important moral, theological, and practical questions, which the Church must face with caution and care.

The Church is careful, too, to recognize its own uncertainty. By endorsing only what it knows to be true, the Church provides guidance about how we may navigate difficult moral questions. In short, as God's representative on earth, the Church has an immense responsibility. It wants to get things right.

That is why our leaders are so deliberate and cautious. It is why they issue prudent, carefully worded encyclicals, to provide a measure of clarity and guidance to the faithful and the world at large. That is why Jesus told Peter, "Whatever you bind on earth shall be bound in heaven; and whatever you loose on earth shall be loosed in heaven" (Matt. 16:19). That is a weighty duty, one that needs care and reflection.

As we can see, the Church's authority is limited by our free will and our innate human limitedness. And it is limited by the extent of the truth it now possesses. For the Church clearly has some truth—critical truth, sufficient truth for us to navigate life successfully and morally. But it does not have exhaustive, complete, and perfect truth. That is the province of God and God alone. For God is the embodiment and origin of all truth. He Himself is the truth.

So, if the Church is indeed the authority on faith and morals, then you should be doubly certain of its basic beliefs and how it knows them with such certainty. Examining how the Church knows what it knows will show you the Church's real authority and its mission and purpose in a clearer light.

And it will make God and His love and truth all the clearer, as well. For all this clarity is not just to shape our understanding and knowledge. Its real purpose is to draw you more closely to Him, to draw you into a deeper relationship with and experience of Him, so you may love Him all the more and live for Him all the better.

Again, do not rush this process of learning. Do not rush the reasoning. Be deliberate. Think. Reflect. Open not only your mind, but your heart as well. Open your eyes, not just to the otherworldly side of things, the things of eternity, but to the real and the practical things too. For God wants you to know Him in the fullest sense. And in the knowing, He wants you to see Him more clearly, so you may love Him without restrictions, without compromises, without reservations arising from your fear, your doubt, your guilt, your ignorance, your hardness of heart.

He wants you to know and love Him. And He wants to dispel and dismiss anything that impedes or prevents this. That may mean He must discipline you as He reshapes you. You must cooperate freely with this. For this is an act of love—a relentless, righteous, and redemptive love.

So open up to it as much as you can. But bring your mind and your heart to God. Let Him show you who He is through His Church, through reason, through revelation, through common sense, and through all the other human faculties He has given you.

For if you seek, you will find. And if you seek sincerely, you will find He is waiting for you already. And if you seek and keep seeking, you will surely find and keep finding.

19

Matters of Orthodoxy

As is evident from the previous chapters, the idea and the implications of real, objective truth keep coming up. This shouldn't be surprising, but it can be. That is because in our modern world, we have been programmed unconsciously to believe that truth is really a matter of opinion, as we discussed earlier.

But this modern attitude toward and philosophy about truth are wrong, absolutely and certainly. And when we think about truth, the real right answers about life, and apply them in our lives, we can see how these core truths also expand the number of knowable truths. I mean if we know some foundational truths, we also can know dependent truths and derivative truths, truths that build upon the core foundational truths.

For instance, when we know that the existence of God is a factual truth, other truths immediately spring up from that basic truth. We know there is an intangible reality that is beyond the physical universe. We know there is a powerful, intangible being capable of creating all that we see. We know this being has a mind, a will, a nature. Thus, by knowing basic truths, we come to know the higher, more refined truths that are supported, justified, and sustained by this foundation.

Right Thinking

This principle of dependent and derivative truth is critical to understanding life and thinking. And it is important when it comes to the idea of orthodoxy. For the truths of the Catholic faith are often referred to as its "orthodoxy," which means "right belief" or "right thinking"—that is, thinking in accordance with the truth.

"Orthodoxy" is a word that takes seriously the claims of truth in matters typically but not exclusively religious. For in order for something to qualify as Catholic orthodoxy, it must conform to the truth: the truth about life, the truth about God, the truth about the Church, and the truth of the Church. Some of these Catholic orthodox truths are foundational truths. Others are derivative truths that rely on and are inherently linked to the foundational orthodox truths of the faith—its theological truths and its philosophical truths, its moral and its aesthetic truths, its spiritual and its practical truths.

So when we see Catholic orthodoxy used as a way of describing the Catholic belief system, we should understand that Catholic orthodoxy refers to the real, actual, factual truth revealed to the Church by the Holy Spirit and reasoned out by the Church throughout its existence. And orthodoxy is not simply a version of the truth, the Catholic version of the truth. Catholics believe what they believe not because they are Catholics but because it is true. Or at least they should.

As the introductory chapter stated, I am a Catholic because the Catholic faith is true. I can prove it with strong evidence arising from reason, science, history, revelation, morality, love, common sense, and human experience. And because I can prove it to be true, I am a Catholic.

Now, that doesn't mean I don't continue to think and to learn about my Catholic faith. But the deeper and the longer I look, the more convinced I become. And this deepening and development, this expansion and maturity, come from a growing understanding of what the faith teaches, weighed against the rigors of reason, science, revelation, love, and practical human living.

Degrees of Faith and Certainty

Is there still some faith to this? Absolutely. But it is a relatively small amount of faith, much smaller than the faith required of atheists or modernists, as we discussed earlier. And honesty compels informed Catholics to acknowledge the need for faith even in this small amount. Even St. Paul, who wrote most of the New Testament, had to have faith. He admitted this openly. As he said, in this world, "We see indistinctly, as in a mirror, but then face to face. At present I know partially; then I shall know fully" (1 Cor. 13:12). And indeed this is true, for we do not see God face to face—at least, not yet.

But the question is: How "indistinctly" do we see? This term raises the idea of degrees of clarity and certainty. All this points out that faith is a matter of amount, a matter of degree, a matter of significance. For the clarity of a reflection can vary by degree.

And this mirror metaphor means that we see God's presence in our world and our lives as a reflection, a reflection in and through the things of life. St. Paul's mirror metaphor distinguishes between our life in the present world, where we see artifacts and evidence of God and His nature, and the eternal world, where we will behold Him directly.

The matter of degree implicitly raised by the term "indistinctly" and the mirror metaphor also raises the idea of degrees of certainty. It makes us wonder what things we are absolutely certain of and what things we are mostly certain of. Can you see how some things could be absolutely certain, while others may be a bit more ambiguous? The Catholic Church recognizes this. That is why the

Church and the pope can be infallible about some things, but not all things. So the orthodoxy of the faith includes levels of certainty, from absolute certainty to a mix of certainty and ambiguity.

The existence of God is a matter of fact, not a matter of faith. And that is why an atheist is either right or wrong, just as a Christian is right or wrong, when it comes to God's existence.

So the Catholic Church is certain about some things and a little less certain about others.

Still, there are a significant number of core things on which the Church is certain. This is called the deposit of the faith, the core beliefs of absolute certainty, the dogmas and doctrines of the faith. And following this level of infallible certainty are other issues or questions for which there are declining levels of certainty.

These somewhat or more ambiguous degrees of certainty arise from the fact that the Church is still studying the matter, or it is one where there is a degree of discretion, often dependent on the particular circumstances and people involved. This is why the Church communicates its certainty through canon law, the application of certain truths to the practical circumstances and questions of day-to-day living and their application in case law.

All this means that each of us needs to continue to learn the core truths of our faith. More specifically, as questions arise that we feel are significant, we must learn the truth about them too. And, as we learn continually, along the way, we can know that what we are learning is the level of real, objective truth currently available. We can have increased clarity as we seek God. We gain insight as we think, pray, read, and learn from others. We can study the Church's teachings as explicated in the *Catechism* and the various Church documents. And if we persist and learn, we can know as much as can be known about the things that puzzle or trouble us. And that is just another way of saying what happens when we study and meditate on the Church's orthodoxy.

So let's take a deeper look at orthodoxy. Let's see what this term means regarding dogma and doctrine, and let's examine its implications for the ecclesial authority the Church claims and maintains as a result of such truths. And as we dive deeper into these matters of the Church, let's consider the many Protestant denominations, so we can settle these questions once and for all.

Perhaps there is no better place to begin our inquiry than with the Scriptures, with the Holy Bible. Here we can see the historical significance of the Church's authority. We witness its steady but prudent deliberation about questions of interpretation. And we see evidence of the apostolic succession and the papal mandate by which the Church hierarchy is structured. At the same time, looking at Scripture means confronting Protestantism and its significant deviations from orthodoxy, beginning in 1517.

So let's take a close look at what Protestants believe about how we can know truth. It's pretty straightforward: according to Protestants, the Bible is our only means of knowing truths about faith and morality; whatever the Bible says must be true. We Catholics believe the Scriptures are inspired and true. But for Protestants, the Bible is the sole authority, the sole source of truth.

This is the crucial doctrine of Protestantism, not because it spells out other doctrines, such as the divinity of Jesus or the nature of God. It is crucial because it tells us where Protestants derive their answers to questions of faith and morality. This is their epistemological basis, their basic theory of knowing. It is known as *sola scriptura*, which means "only Scripture" or "Scripture alone."

Let's look at this idea of *sola scriptura*, this theory of knowing. We'll do that one word at a time.

First, let's look at *sola*. *Sola* means "only." That means there is no other source of truth about faith and morality. Most Protestants who remain committed to truth about their Christian faith believe this.

The problem for them is that by their own definition of knowing, the Bible would have to say that the Bible is the "only" source of truth. I mean that the idea of *sola scriptura* would have to be present explicitly in the Holy Scriptures. And that is a real problem for Protestants. For nowhere does the Holy Bible say such a thing.

Now, it isn't that the Bible doesn't claim to have the truth about faith and morals. It does, and it does so consistently and repeatedly throughout. But Scripture never claims to be the singular or the definitive source of truth about these things. Instead, explicitly and implicitly, it points to other means of knowing. For instance, the human mind and the human heart are sources of some truths. Scripture says we have "no excuse" (Rom. 1:20) if we claim we don't know God or His basic moral precepts.

And even more directly, when it comes to truth about the faith and morality, Paul states quite clearly that the "church of the living God is the pillar and foundation of the truth" (1 Tim. 3:15). He also reminded the church of Thessalonica that they should "stand firm and hold fast to the traditions that you were taught, either by an oral statement or by a letter of ours" (2 Thess. 2:15). And again, Paul asserts this idea when he exhorts Timothy, "Take as your norm the sound words that you heard from me, in the faith and love that are in Christ Jesus" (2 Tim. 1:13).

Here, it is obvious that Paul knows that the truths he proclaimed were actual truths, even if he didn't write them down. Additionally, this passage legitimizes the oral tradition of the Church as a source of truth.

Can you see the contradictions in the Protestant way of knowing? Can you see how their belief lacks scriptural support, even though Protestants assert that Scripture is the only way to know truth? Nowhere in Scripture does God, through the inspired writers, ever say Scripture is to be the sole, the only, the single source of truth. He does insist that it is an important and crucial source, but not the only one.

Also, the Scriptures themselves point to the Catholic Church as the source of truth by making references to oral tradition and also through the authority given to Peter by Jesus to lead the new faith and to bind and to loose on earth and in heaven. This is called Petrine authority. So the Protestant view of knowledge, the pathway to truth about the faith and about morality, doesn't really support itself. In fact, it contradicts itself on a remarkable and foundational level. And such contradiction is absolutely fatal, not because Catholics offer a better idea of how we can know truth (which they do), but because the Protestant idea does not even fulfill, nor can it ever meet, its own standards for truth. In other words, it is wrong by definition. For the Scriptures don't say what the Protestants claim. And it is just that simple and just that profound. Period.

To put a little icing on the cake, the Bible was not even codified or organized until centuries after Christ. So that would mean there was no source of truth about faith or morality until the Bible was officially established and codified. That is contrary to the facts of history and the facts of Scripture.

But that's not all. The Catholic understanding of faith and morals is much more sophisticated and integrated. And it aligns with history and the Holy Scriptures. For as we saw earlier, Catholics believe that the truth about faith and morality comes from three interrelated sources, which date back to the beginning of Christianity.

First, the authority of the Church comes from the authority given to it and to Peter by Jesus. This is the authority we mean when we speak of magisterial authority. By this authority, Peter and his successors lead the Church and bear the responsibility for communicating, articulating, and developing the truths of faith and morality.

Additionally, the Church derives its authority from its oral Tradition, handed down to this very day. Paul cites this authority when he tells the faithful to remember what he told them and warns them not to deviate from these oral teachings.

Finally, the Church relies on the truth of the Scriptures, which have always been knit tightly to the Magisterium and Tradition. These three components are woven together seamlessly in a mutually informative and supportive manner.

And if we step back and think about this even briefly, we can see how this has been the case from day one. When Peter first proclaimed the good news, he did so orally under the unction of the Holy Spirit, with the full authority God gave him. And this basic message was preached orally by all of the disciples long before anyone wrote down the Gospels or codified the Epistles. In fact, the Scriptures, which were mostly written within forty years of Jesus' resurrection, were not even officially organized until the Councils of Rome (A.D. 382), Hippo (A.D. 393), and Carthage (A.D. 397). And even though there were many informal lists and degrees of authority attributed to such documents before these final rulings during the three centuries following Jesus' resurrection, the real authority arose from historical Church tradition, the authority of the Church, and the inherently inspired writings themselves even before they were codified in the canon of Scripture, the official list of inspired writings.

At those points, the Catholic Church, which as you will recall from the previous chapter, means the universal Church, had been around for over 350 years. And when the canon of Scripture was determined, it was done by the authority of the Church, with the pope's approval.

So clearly, Tradition and the Magisterium predate the writing of the New Testament books, as well as the formal establishment of the scriptural canon. The motive for codifying the official writings was clarity, consistency, and coherence. The Church intended to ensure accuracy and truth, to make certain there were no errors, to codify right thinking. And that is just what orthodoxy is and means and does.

Scriptura

Now, let's look at the other half of *sola scriptura. Scriptura* means "Scripture" or "the Scriptures." When Jesus preached and taught, He often referred to the Hebrew Scripture of His time, which most of us think of as the Old Testament. And when the Catholic Church established the canon of the Old Testament in the fourth century, it used the same Hebrew Scriptures that Jesus, the apostles, and Jewish religious leaders would have used.

But here is another significant problem for the various Protestant denominations that profess *sola scriptura*. For the Holy Scriptures codified by the Catholic Church were the only Scriptures prior to the Protestant Reformation, the only canon of Scripture until the Protestant revolt in 1517 (though it is true that scholars debated the canon from time to time).

Oddly, the Protestants, the champions of biblical inerrancy and *sola scriptura*, changed the Bible. Specifically, they altered the Old Testament, which had existed in its contemporary form for nearly two thousand years before the Reformation. The Old Testament canon was based on the Septuagint, the translation of the Hebrew Scriptures by seventy scholars into Greek in 200 B.C.

The Protestants rejected seven books of the Septuagint and instead adopted the Masoretic text, dating from A.D. 150, because it was written in Hebrew. They did this despite the fact that Jesus Himself and His apostles used the Septuagint and despite the fact that the canon of the Septuagint was recognized by the Church as the Old Testament canon.

And this alteration to the biblical canon had to do with certain disagreements between the Protestant leaders and the Church about purgatory and other doctrines of the Church supported by the Tradition of the Church, its teaching authority, and the Scriptures of the Septuagint. For the books that were removed taught about purgatory, where the dead must atone for their sins before entering heaven. This process of purgation could be expedited by the intercession and penitential acts on the part of the living.

The Protestant reformers didn't believe in purgatory. And so they rejected the established canon of the Old Testament. That is, despite their insistence on Scripture as the only source of truth, they changed the Scriptures to fit their beliefs. Well, that, too, is a contradiction of catastrophic consequence.

Finally, a further foundational problem with *sola scriptura* has to do with the interpretation of the Scriptures. For Protestants, there has never been a definitive interpretation of the Scriptures. That is why, from the very beginning of the Protestant Reformation, there has been disunity. That is why there are over thirty-five thousand Protestant denominations today. There is no consistent way to interpret what the Scriptures actually say. There is no divine interpreter.

In contrast, the Catholic Church does teach definitive interpretations of Scripture. The Church itself has the authority and Tradition to make certain what can be made certain and to leave ambiguous what is ambiguous. And the Church does all this to an appropriate degree, in the proper proportion, because the Church is prudent in its dogmatic and doctrinal decisions and in its scriptural interpretations.

Faith and Works

Like *sola scriptura*, the other doctrinal assertion of Protestantism —*sola fide* (only faith)—is not supported by Holy Scripture. This opens the door to many of the problems we have already enumerated regarding reason and the relativism of personal experience. But I'll save that for the chapter on spirituality.

Suffice it to say that nowhere does the Bible say we are saved by "faith alone." We are saved by our faith, but not by it alone. We are saved by our faith *and* by our works, by what we believe *and* by what we do. As James puts it, "What good is it, my brothers, if someone says he has faith but does not have works?... So also faith of itself, if it does not have works, is dead" (James 2:14, 17). For faith without works is dead.

For we all have a mind and a will and a decision to make about whom we will follow, not just whom we believe in. And that is why it matters what we do, say, and think. That is why Jesus came to teach us and discipline us and encourage us. For what we do matters.

That is why God sends His Holy Spirit to be with us and to lead us, to guide us, to comfort us, to reveal the truth to us. He does so because what we do, think, and say matters now and in eternity. This is why we must choose to accept the gift of redemption, of salvation. For God teaches us what to do. And He invites us to know and love Him, because we have free will, and how we use it matters. And it matters more than in the here and now. It matters eternally too.

Truth and Unity

Now, all this does not mean the Protestants are to be despised or shunned. That is not the Catholic way. For most of them have not really thought this out very carefully. Others may be unable to come to the fullest knowledge of the truth of these claims, which prevents them from coming into the Catholic Church. And there are still others who may agree that Protestantism is self-contradictory but who find Catholic attitudes and behaviors off-putting. While it is true that our actions matter, what matters most is the truth: the truth about God, the truth about Jesus, the truth about history, the truth about the Church's authority, the truth about knowledge.

As Catholics, we must do what we can to help Protestants see all this. We must be patient with them as they use their free will to know God more deeply and to see Him within His Church. Jesus Himself said, "I pray not only for [my followers] but also for those who will believe in me through their word, so that they may all be one, as you, Father are in me and I in you, that they may also be in us, that the world may believe that you sent me" (John 17:20–21).

And that prayer expresses the orthodox truth that God desires that His followers be united. It expresses, too, the truth of how we are to bring about this unity by our prayer and sensitive, patient witness.

So the truths of the Faith are really its orthodoxy. And this may seem a bit foreign or even arrogant. But it's not, if you think about it. Reason dictates that there must be right answers, so why should we find orthodoxy surprising? If there are right answers, as reason and practicality dictate, why would we surprised by the existence of right answers? And why should we assume that these right answers are few in number and unrelated to each other? In fact, because truths are interdependent, because certain truths can be derived from foundational truths, it is very likely that there are many truths available to us. And shouldn't this be a comfort, not a hindrance; a blessing, not a restriction; a light of clarity, not a fog of confusion?

But sometimes, we prefer to do what we want to do and to think what we want to think, instead of looking at the actual content and meaning of our beliefs. Consequently, we often miss the many truths we see all around us.

When we have ambiguity, it is totally up to us to decide what is right and true. There is no truth, no certainty with which we must grapple. And in our modern times, this desire for absolute ambiguity is something we crave, demand, and expect. This is why truth is ridiculous or judgmental, naïve or insulting to most moderns.

This is why many bristle at the insistence that truth exists. This is why many reject the real content of truth and its many moral and practical implications. We no longer see clearly the nature and substance of actual truth. We no longer feel the wonder of real truth. We no longer experience the freedom of truth in its fullest sense.

Freedom and Goodness

The experience of real, actual, and factual truth leads us to God. And it leads us to real freedom. For, as Jesus tells all of us, "If you remain in my word, you will be my disciples, and you will know the truth, and the truth will set you free" (John 8:31–32). Free because there is a purpose. Free because there is a model of perfection. Free because we can do what truth and God demand of us. Free because we know we are understood and forgiven. Free because we know love is real. We are loved so perfectly, we cannot help but be free.

But here, freedom doesn't mean the ability to do whatever we may want or desire. That is not freedom, but license. As Milton says, "None can love freedom heartily, but good men; the rest love not freedom, but license."[5]

So to love freedom is to love goodness. To use freedom is to be good.

To indulge our thoughts and desires and instinctual urges leads us to court license, not freedom. For freedom properly used is found only in goodness. To use freedom other than for good is to indulge ourselves, ignorant of the moral imperatives of truth and the beautiful demands of love. Using freedom wrongly or selfishly is always license and not true freedom.

[5] John Milton, *The Tenure of Kings and Magistrates* (1649), cited in *The Oxford Dictionary of Quotations*, ed. Elisabeth Knowles (Oxford, UK: Oxford University Press, 1999), 520.

This is why Jesus links truth and freedom together so closely, for we are to know the truth, and the truth sets us free. Free from our sinful and selfish nature. Free from the distractions and the dogmas of man, his world, and his culture. Free from the insidious gnawing of our lusts and appetites, our ambitions and our greed, our sensuality and our temper.

We are free to love and to give. We are free to live with the comfort of clarity and a rich and real confidence that originates beyond us and our standards and desires. Our confidence now rests on the firm bedrock of truth, truth that is not ours in its origin, for the origin of all truth must be outside ourselves and our temporal world.

Our confidence and closure rests on truth that is definite and dogmatic. Truth that is rooted in the order of the universe and the mind of God. Truth that is comprehensive and categorical. Truth that is divine, as all truth must be. Truth that does not contradict, nor clash with love, but is harmonious with it. Truth that affirms the content and the obligations, the substance and the expression of love.

Love and Truth

The unity of love and truth is really what constitutes the sum and substance of orthodoxy. For truth without love is shrill, harsh, strident. Or as St. Paul says, "If I speak ... but do not have love, I am a resounding gong and a clashing cymbal" (1 Cor. 13:1).

The organic, inherent interdependence of love and truth is real and essential. They are two sides of the same coin, two facets of the same crystal, two dimensions of God's essential character. For He is both holy and loving, righteous and compassionate, just and merciful. That is what perfection is—a unified, interconnected, holistic reality. For true perfection is real and evident only when it is comprehensive, without exception or dimension.

And with these many truths and the truth of love, the wisdom of Jesus' call to discipleship rings ever truer and clearer. For truth is sometimes a blazing insight for our minds. But it is often a struggle to move that insight from our minds to our hearts and to our core character. But these core truths, with their derivative and dependent truths, are just the substance of what discipleship is.

Discipleship is more than insight or a softness of heart. It is the sum and substance of truth, the very embodiment of truth, without losing any of its insight or its comfort. Discipleship is the embodiment of truth and the manifestation of love as they both permeate our character and personality, our attitude and our behavior, our priorities and our plans.

Orthodoxy is but one way we can see this call to discipleship. Another is through morality. For God calls us to have His mind and His heart, to be like Him, to be like Jesus. He is holy. He is good. He is pure. He is loving. And He is perfect. For Jesus calls us all to be His disciples and to "be perfect, just as your heavenly Father is perfect" (Matt. 5:48).

Seeing Perfection

So let's take a closer look at just what "perfect" looks like. As we do so, we will come to see God much more clearly and desire to know Him all the more intimately. Through our innate and informed understanding of the perfect harmony of truth and love, we will see that He is the source of these very ideas, perceptions, and realities.

And having covered the ideas of truth and Catholic orthodoxy, we can gradually glimpse a more expansive view of life and living and see the divine hand behind and in it all. Along this line of perfection, we'll continue with morality to enhance our perspective of goodness and perfection and, to a lesser extent, truth. Then, we'll cover spirituality, beauty, and love as we explore the more emotional and relational dimensions of knowing God.

If you need to revisit any of the previous chapters, do so. Take your time. Because orthodoxy, morality, spirituality, beauty, and love reveal the nature of God to us, it is important to take your time, so you can not just know *about* Him but truly come to know Him.

All of these things are rooted in the nature of things in our universe and in the universe itself. They are rooted in the nature of us as human beings. We bear the very image of God. Through our nature, we see His reflection. And in the best of us, the saints and the good people we meet every day, we see examples of God's very nature.

This goodness we see in the moral behavior of others, in the wisdom and truth embodied in the personality and attitudes and behaviors of others, in the spiritual insights and attitudes of those around us, in the beauty of the world and the people we encounter and in the love that abounds in the people in our lives. All these are testimonies and artifacts of God's nature, His presence and involvement, His proximity and activity.

When we see instead evil and meanness, selfishness and pride, we see the opposite of goodness and love and truth. Thus, even all these deficiencies and distortions point us to God and reveal His nature.

When we see how dark things are and how far away we are from truth and love, from holiness and beauty, from the shining light of God's intimate presence and transcendent certainty, we see Him. We see Him in the darkness around us, for we know it is darkness. And that means we also know the light: the light of His goodness and love and truth. So we see Him even in sin and sorrow, sensuality and depravity.

And, we see Him in the small transgressions too. That's how we know that the slights and insults, the inconsiderate attitudes and the small selfish actions we see in ourselves and in others all testify to the truth of real goodness, all testify to the truth of love as it is and as it should be. And, by doing so, all these testify to the existence of God and the perfection of God, to His truth and His love.

So pray and think, ponder and watch. Once you understand that God's nature is manifest throughout your daily life, you will see Him all the clearer, and you will rest in the comfort and consolation that He is right beside you, as your Father. Perfect love assures you of this, just as real truth makes it certain. So be still and know that God is God.

20

Matters of Morality

In the modern world, there are many perspectives on morality, and sometimes these many perspectives lead to sharp discussions and to conflict and hostility. You can be certain of the reaction you will receive when you insist on the truth. The idea that morality, with its inherent justice and judgment, is actually true is an inflammatory challenge in our modern world.

If you want conflict nowadays when discussing moral issues and questions, just insist that someone's opinion is wrong in the absolute, objective sense. Just let that person know that not only do you have a different opinion, but that his opinion is actually wrong, not just different—wrong in an objective moral sense, wrong inherently, wrong factually, wrong in an absolute and timeless sense.

At the same time, insist that your opinion is right, true, and factual. Or that the Church's opinion is right and true in the same objective sense, and that the Church's opinion is therefore your opinion. Do that, and let the games begin. Just insist that the other person is wrong in any or all of those senses, and, before you know it, you're off to the races. It happens that fast. But why?

Inevitable Conflict

Well, this is a consequence of the modern mindset. For when it comes to moral questions, problems, or situations, moderns generally hold the idea that morality is defined and decided by each person only or mostly. Or that morality is just a function of social norms, a matter of polling and opinion surveys that tap into general and collective cultural preferences. Either way, morality is a product of personal preference or merely a matter of social convention to many moderns.

Now, this individually determined morality, this "moral relativism," as it is often called, is always lurking about below the surface of any moral discussion or difference of opinion in modern life. If you insist on objective morality or moral truth of almost any kind, this moral relativism will suddenly spring to the surface, showing itself in accusations of arrogance, pride, and judgment. Modern moral relativists quickly and often aggressively become incensed; then they point out the alleged arrogance of such judgment of anyone's personal moral behavior or attitudes.

And hard on the heels of these accusations comes the deeper and more philosophical indictment of such invasive ideas as moral certainty. For modern people, it is invasive to insist on moral standards by which anyone may judge human behaviors and attitudes.

This crucial, core idea of moral relativism, if not a deliberate dogma of modernity, is at the very least implicit in many modern moral opinions. And that core idea holds that morality, like beauty, is in the eye of the beholder.

This implicit assumption is that morality is a function of individual sensitivities and philosophies. And because the very idea of morality is rooted in personal opinions and individual preferences, almost any issue becomes very contentious. Asserting objective moral principles violates any and every moral opinion based on personal preference or collective conventions.

Now, there are personal perspectives on morality and public perspectives, without question. People do have opinions. And there are moral laws and moral attitudes. There are important moral issues and unimportant ones. There are many perspectives. But whose moral perspectives are right, particularly when these perspectives are diametrically opposed, when they are mutually exclusive, when they cannot be reconciled?

The answer lies in looking at the nature of morality and its connections to existence, the cosmos, and the nature of God, for morality is connected to these and many other aspects of life and living.

First of all, most of us don't really reflect much on morality itself. We usually deal with the issues and situations, the attitudes and behaviors, perspectives and opinions we have at hand, without ever really grappling with the idea of morality itself and what it means to the nature of life and the challenges of living. So let's spend some time looking at what morality is. What is it? And where does it comes from? How did it get here? And what is its nature? Once we have a handle on these deeper questions, we can take some time to look at what things are moral and immoral.

And after that, we will take a look at the role that morality plays in our lives in a temporal and an eternal sense. And at the same time, we'll take a quick look at the presence of evil and the relationship between morality and suffering. For these, too, are crucial to looking at and understanding a Catholic perspective on morality.

All of this will help us to understand more clearly and thoroughly why Catholics insist that their view of morality is the absolute moral truth, the only true form of morality in its fullest and most accurate sense.

Perfection and Morality

Let's begin all this by looking at perfection, for morality involves a sense of the perfect. Morality speaks about what should be, what we ought to do, what the right thing is. It is the perfect expression of all goodness and love, all beauty and truth. It is the perfect expression of all justice, all mercy, all righteousness, all compassion, all forgiveness. All things situated in the proper order and priority.

Well, from a commonsensical perspective, most of us know what perfection is and what it looks like. I mean, we know it when we see it. We know it on the grand and global scale and even on the smaller, more insignificant scale.

For example, we know morality through the small daily events and activities of our lives, in the encounters we have with other people each day. That is why we have a sense of common courtesy and respect. Almost instinctively, we know when people behave courteously and respectfully and when they fail to do so.

In much the same way, we know when we encounter someone whose friendliness, kindness, and behavior are beyond the norm, even in the way they greet us and the tone they take and the expression they have. We have all met people who are radiant in their warmth, respect, and courtesy.

So we all have seen these glimpses of perfection in the mundane encounters we have with other people. And we have all been the bearers of such perfection from time to time. Well, all these small, almost insignificant, interactions are glimpses of moral perfection.

Similarly, when people fail to show respect and courtesy, we don't always chalk it up to a moral flaw on their part. Oftentimes, we give them the benefit of the doubt. For their attitude and tone may have arisen from their personal difficulties and troubles, or their mood, or even an illness.

So even in the mistakes of others, we can demonstrate an aspect of moral truth by our understanding and compassion. Even though someone else may have fallen short of average friendliness or perfect courtesy, we know that he deserves the benefit of the doubt and may need our understanding and patience. Well, all these are variations on the moral principles and virtues we all recognize and deal with throughout our day.

On a grander scale, we all recognize instinctively, though more consciously, when we see an act of perfect courage, an act of unselfish sacrifice for others, an act of love in people we know and read about even in our secular publications: the organ donor, the adopting couple, the tireless advocate, the soldier who risks life and limb for country and comrade—all are simple but profound examples of the fixed moral principles we all know with absolute certainty.

I mean, just think about the Christmas season and the attitudes and acts of giving that it fosters. Only those without some innate sense of love, joy, and generosity could miss this. This is why, in Charles Dickens's novella *A Christmas Carol*, the leading character, Scrooge, is redeemed from his hollow and selfish materialism at the conclusion of the story. We even use the name "Scrooge" as a complex and comprehensive term for miserly, selfish, bitter, and empty attitudes, behaviors, or people.

We all recognize that people can sometimes miss the point when the Christmas season degenerates into flagrant materialism and commercialism, or when gift giving gives way to hollow obligation and mere routine. All of us know that these are distortions of what true goodness is. They are examples of what true moral standards look like when twisted or compromised, when we have the wrong attitude, or when we go about things for the wrong reason.

Why, we even see the fixed and factual moral principles at work even in some debates about immorality and the degree to which a given moral transgression is out of line. And this often shows itself when we discuss and determine the link between the crime and the punishment, between the error and the consequence.

For many of these debates about morality aren't always over the presence or absence of fixed moral laws and principles. Sometimes, they are about how right or how wrong a given attitude, action, or behavior is. Was an immoral act very wrong? Or was this same act somehow lessened in severity based on the circumstances leading up to it or the background of a particular person involved?

I mean, think of a simple example. Let's say a teenager is caught shoplifting, and his actions seem to be a clear violation of the moral principle regarding property ownership and the commandment about stealing. It's simple. Stealing is wrong.

But imagine that this teen stole some food to help feed his destitute family. Now imagine a different teen, who lives in a middle-class home and was caught stealing a video game he really wanted. You'll see these are two very different matters.

And other factors, moral factors, play a part in an appropriate assessment and judgment of immoral behavior. For example, if the thief in our second example was only ten years old, his young age might change our moral judgment. We all know he should have known better. But we all should recognize that maturity and age are often mitigating factors when determining the degree to which a person is culpable and responsible. These factors of age and maturity are moral factors as well. Technically and actually, the youngster is guilty of stealing, just as the teen was. But these mitigating factors reduce the degree to which young children are responsible in a temporal, real-life sense.

This is why, most of the time, our legal standards are the same for everyone, though the level of guilt and the extent of the consequences and punishments change based on a number of other factors, moral factors. The most obvious one is the difference between juvenile law and adult law. This is standard moral thinking applied in our system of justice. And this distinction almost goes without serious questioning, except in extreme cases of premeditated murder, for example.

Some legal codes even make a distinction between youthful offenders and adults to establish a different level of culpability based on age and maturity, in order to protect those between the ages of sixteen and twenty-one.

Often, these other implicit moral factors also weigh on those who must exercise some judgment or make decisions about what to do in cases of moral transgressions or legal violations. In the example of shoplifting, sometimes, the store owners ask for restitution or an apology, rather making it a criminal or civil matter. Again, the moral imperative for forgiveness and mercy becomes more crucial for those who have been hurt or otherwise affected by immoral behavior.

But if forgiveness and mercy are pushed too far and the youngster or teen receives no significant consequences from the store or from his parents, we would all recognize that this is not a proper, morally informed decision. For the lesson has not been taught clearly, and justice has been miscarried. An error of degree has been made.

Well, all these examples and the many factors involved illustrate some important things. First, they show that there are actually certain fixed moral principles, moral commandments, if you will. And these principles, these commandments, are meant to be applied in real life.

But there are other moral factors that come to bear on the execution of justice. And there are moral principles that come into play for those who must decide the degree of guilt and the real nature of the offense.

And all of this is pretty straightforward and commonplace. We see an innate morality, a system of right and wrong as we go about our daily lives, whether it shows up when someone cuts in front of you in line at the store or cuts you off when driving, whether someone is curt and dismissive to you or even just slightly rude.

So morality is very familiar to us. It gives a sense of order to our relationships and interactions. It orders our laws and our government, our culture and our customs, our superficial and more serious relationships, and our most intimate personal affairs with our spouses and our children. It orders our relationship with God and His Church. Not only does it order these many relationships, but it gives them purpose and goals. It lets us know what these many aspects should look like, what we should strive to make these relational things mean.

In the end, it is the Golden Rule that virtually everyone recognizes as the summary and definition of morality, for it is the summary of all things moral: to love others as we want to be loved, "to do to others as we would want others to do to us" (Luke 6:31). And all that is true, almost indisputable.

But notice how love and action are linked together in the Golden Rule. Notice how loving others results in action of some sort, whether in behaviors and attitudes or in interactions and observable actions. Notice how the Golden Rule is more than just an ultimate moral principle or law. It is situated in our relationships with other people personally and in our relationships mediated through structures such as government or society at large, through culture and custom, through specific relationships with particular people right down to our most intimate bonds with our friends, our families, our children, our spouses.

And this is crucial for understanding what real morality is. It is not some distant set of decontextualized rules. Moral principles are not merely rules by which we are to be guided and by which we will be judged in a dry, distant manner, in a manner without any compassion or love.

Morality is the order and structure of relationships. It governs all relationships—relationships with society or our intimate friends, the environment or our employees, our countrymen or citizens of other countries. This is why, at the root of things, morality is more like a set of vows than a set of rules, more like a set of covenant promises than a list of contractual obligations and expectations, more like a family cultural code than a dry legal code. And this relational nature is why morality is often misunderstood.

It is relational by nature. That is why the whole religious code of the Jews and later the Catholics could be summarized so well and so clearly, because it spoke the language of relationship, not rules. Moses told the Israelites that love was to be the standard. And when Jesus was asked to summarize the law, He said, "You shall love the Lord, your God, with all your heart, with all your soul, and with all your mind. This is the greatest and first commandment. The second is like it: You shall love your neighbor as yourself. The whole law and the prophets depend on these two commandments" (Matt. 22:37-40).

Also, Jesus gave us a very clear example when it comes to what this love looks like. He gave us Himself as the model. And He told us, "Love one another as I love you" (John 15:12). For He was perfection in all things. He loved perfectly and lived in accordance with the truth, all truth. He showed us what we are to be, to do, to think, and to strive for. He showed the complete and perfect embodiment of truth and of love, and He sent us out to establish the kingdom of God on those two pillars.

God did not give us this moral code as mere information or as a dry, distant set of rules. He gave us morality to guide us to Himself and to help us to live with one another beautifully, rightly, intimately, lovingly. For morality is the only path to real love and truth. As we see and understand this moral structure, we know that this is how life can be lived properly and perfectly. And we know that this is the only way we can live with one another fully and live with God now and eternally.

As our moral vision and ability grow, we can know God more directly, more fully, more intimately. For morality is a direct reflection of God Himself, His very character and being, His very desire and hope.

The Source of Morality

So obviously, morality must have come from somewhere, and its source, its origin, is God. There is no other possibility, though people do have other ideas, particularly modern people. For moderns often attribute morality to customs or individual preferences or even to some form of adaptive process akin to evolution. But that is just not practical, feasible, or possible.

These other views are incapable of explaining the moral phenomenon itself. Nor can they explain its continuity and consistency across time, across culture, across personality. Just think back on earlier chapters, when we discussed the biochemical reality of a godless, wholly physical universe. Think back to a universe that must explain every single human experience as fundamentally a matter-energy phenomenon.

Morality can't be explained this way, just as reason and love, consciousness and intelligence cannot be explained materially. These phenomena have a physical dimension, to some degree, in that they are activities that are evident in our brains and bodies. But their physical presence does not explain their content or the truth of the content itself.

Science and scientific investigation can show us brain activity and its location and speed. But it cannot show us thought or reason or personality, nor can it explain truth and love or goodness and beauty.

So morality, like reason, is a real intangible reality. And this intangible reality must come from some prior cause, as the law of cause and effect and our reason tell us. Morality must come from somewhere, something, some being. And it does. It comes from the intangible being, the creator of everything that is visible to our senses and to our minds. And that being is God.

But if we think we can have morality of any degree or amount, of any breadth or depth without God, we are sadly and deeply mistaken. For if there is no intangible God whose character radiates in us and guides us with His holiness, love, and truth, then all morality is merely some arbitrary attempt to control us or to organize the social order. And as such, it has no hold over any of us whatsoever, because it is all contrived, just a form of social engineering. It is all custom, but no real substance. It is all the product of power plays intended to prevent people from doing precisely and exactly what they want.

But that physically based, culturally conceived, and conformity-driven morality is a moral vision far outside of morality as we know it and experience it. Like the contradictions arising from reason when it is thought of as a wholly physical thing, morality, whether it is physically or culturally conceived, just doesn't sound moral. And that's because it's not. The only real force of such a physical or cultural moral vision is power and coercion. This type of moral vision has no power in and of itself, for it is arbitrary and constructed.

The real power of morality is its inherent truth. Remember that "inherent" refers to something that is there by the very nature of things. And inherent morality is, by its nature, real. It's a real part of the design of life and the design of human beings. It's in us because we are like God. We are not just physical material, not just matter and energy.

And this is the Catholic view of mankind. We are all the image bearers of God. We are like Him because He made us that way and wants us to be like Him. We bear in our very essence a reflection of God's very character and being. This is evident in many ways. It is there in our moral sensitivity, our reason, our talents, our freedom, our love, our desire for truth and justice, our moral ideals, and our practical moral applications, our sense of beauty and order.

And remember the simple examples of morality above. Just the simple clarity of the few basic moral principles illustrated there should tell you just how real this inherent morality is in us, in our very nature. And it is so clear and available to our reason that we cannot help but see, once again, the true intangible reality of the universe and of human beings.

These intangible realities point us inevitably to God—to the God who is personal, moral, reasonable, loving, just, and perfect; the God who is invisible, but who is made visible in these reflections of His character in us.

Morality Matters

Morality gives us the ideal of what life should look like, how life should be lived. It gives us the ideals for what we should be, do, say, and think. And it gives us the goal for others, for society, and for our ultimate end. And because we know what we should be, morality also tells us what we shouldn't be. It tells us what we should not do, what we should not say, what we should not think.

This is why morality matters in life. It tells us what life should be like and what it shouldn't be like. It gives us a goal and a model and even a means for achieving those things, for morality is not only concerned with good ends, good goals. It is also concerned with the means, the way in which we achieve good goals. It is concerned with the "how" of what we do, not just the "what."

And it matters how many of us strive to do this and how often we all do the right thing. This is why Jesus exhorted His disciples to be the leaven of the world. For just as a small amount of leaven permeates large quantities of flour to make it rise, so too can our degree and quantity of moral success affect society as a whole.

It is also why Jesus said we are to be the salt and light of the world. "Salt" here refers to a preservative. The holier and more loving we are, the more we will influence others and preserve the world from moral error. And by being so holy, so loving, we will also shed light on the truth so that others may find their way to a greater moral vision and, in the process, discover God and renew or restore their relationship with Him. The point of these metaphors is to preserve others from mistakes and from wrongheaded ideas about morality, and to point them to God by linking their own moral sensitivities to the source of such sensitivities, to the author and embodiment of all morality.

But all this talk of goodness doesn't tell the whole story. What about evil and immorality? What about suffering?

Well, let's start with evil and immorality. For these are both evidence for the existence of goodness, love, truth, and purity. And they are also indicators of the truth and nature and substance of the objective moral standards we all know, to one degree or another.

Evil and immorality also point us to the legitimacy of our experience of conscience, that intuitive capacity we all possess that lets us know when and how far we have violated the moral standards. It is also our conscience that indicates the right and good things we do, so that we are affirmed and encouraged when we do them.

But our consciences must also be matured by reason and wisdom and made more sophisticated by deep thought about the nature of morality and its content and application. And this process of reflection on the nature of morality must also always include self-examination. We must always evaluate our attitudes and behaviors against an honest, thorough, accurate understanding of these objective moral standards. This serves another crucial purpose. It serves to keep our moral sensitivities supple and perceptive. It makes them ever more sensitive and finely tuned and prevents us from creating tacit blind spots in our conscience, places where we excuse our errors or minimize them, places where we no longer feel the pull of conscience.

This is why habits can be bad. Bad habits are blind spots where we no longer see our moral error, or places where we have capitulated to moral error, or places where our will is so weak that we cease to try. These blind spots and bad habits arise all too easily when it comes to our own weaknesses and tendencies.

Our consciences are what prevent these blind spots and bad habits from forming. Our consciences prevent our errors and proclivities from degenerating into real blind spots, which hinder us from seeing our errors.

This is why moral reflection and the development of a sensitive and informed conscience are so important. As we age, we all have a natural tendency to bend the standards to excuse or minimize our errors or to ignore them altogether, especially when these moral truths are inconvenient or prevent us from doing things we want to do, even if we want to do bad things, corrupting things, hurtful things, perverted things.

So the care and feeding of our conscience is crucial. And the only rational and practical way to do that is with objective standards, factual standards, true standards. We must apply the standards of truth and of love, of goodness and beauty, of purity and virtue. Any other standards, be they personal, cultural, or legal, will lack the breadth and depth and the inherent moral authority to compel us to acknowledge our errors in full and to resolve and to strive to do better.

Inherent Morality

True morality must come from God. Otherwise, morality comes from us. And if we make it, we can change it. If we build it, we can modify it as we choose, according to our whim.

Because morality is inherent in our daily lives, in our reason, and in our conscience, we know that all morality comes from God. For anything inherent must arise from its maker. That is how the inherent thing got there. It was placed there by the maker. Any and all objective and inherent moral standards manifest God's character, His nature, and His plan.

Just as this is true for reason and its laws, for our consciousness and self-awareness, for our emotions and our experience, so, too, is it true for our consciences. For the human conscience tacitly recognizes the intangible reality of human nature, the inherent morality all around us. Our human conscience shows us the need to care for and develop our conscience. And our conscience shows us that its source is and must be God.

This is why the Ten Commandments deal first with God and then with people. The first three commandments tell us to put and keep God first, to respect and love Him, and to set aside time for Him. The remaining commandments give us the standards for loving our parents, being truthful, respecting property, keeping our marriages holy, forsaking envy, and avoiding murder. This is why Jesus said we are to love God with all our mind, soul, and strength, and to love others as He loves us.

Our consciences are inherent. But they must be developed and corrected, preserved from corruption, blindness, and weakening habits. That is one reason Jesus came to teach us. That is why He explained so many things in terms of love and truth. This is why He saved His sharpest rebukes for the religious leaders who had mistakenly distorted these moral truths into a legal code of obligations, rather than a means of inspiring a deeper love for God and His truth, a deeper, more intimate, more immediate relationship with Him. This is why He scolded them for reducing the idea of love to a minutely defined code of behavior.

Evil and Suffering

So what about evil? Well, just look at the headlines, and you'll see all the evidence you need. Corruption, greed, lust, envy, gluttony, anger, pride. They're all there. And if you don't see it, you're not looking close enough. Or your conscience may need to be resurrected. It's all there for even the blind to see.

Our modern evils are many and prolific, and many of them happen on a public scale for all to see. War, greed, misuses of power, and poverty dominate the media as the new manifestations of the seven deadly sins. It is indeed a very bleak state of affairs.

And when we look on a smaller scale, the moral landscape looks bleaker still, for on this level, the more personal sins litter our everyday lives. These are the moral issues that lead to the larger public ones. The more insidious ones arise from a deliberate philosophy, a reasoned justification for moral evil. And this justification is so common, many moderns no longer see the moral truth of such things. Issues such as divorce, sexual promiscuity and perversion, abortion, child abuse, neglect, and assisted suicide are so common and so rampant that many of us no longer see and understand these as immoral acts.

These are all justified by the very idea of "moral relativism," where each individual can determine his own personal morality, particularly when it comes to sexuality and romance. And unlike the sins on public display, these personal sins no longer are thought of as wrong, morally reprehensible, or sinful. Many of the large-scale sins are still seen as such, but the small-scale, private sins are no longer seen as really sinful. These sins now are just a matter of personal choice.

If the headlines and the many personal sins aren't enough to convince you, then pick up any history book. The fact of evil across time and circumstance, across geography and culture, is there for all to see, with serious certainty. And these historical accounts are just the big things, on the scale of societies, cultures, or nations.

Imagine all the other small evils committed each and every day since the beginning of mankind. Surely, the evidence is overwhelming. And the evidence of such pervasive evil tells us that objective, inherent morality is real, for the evidence of evil is also evidence of the good, the right, the true. It is just that simple. It is just that profound. It is just that sure.

In light of such certainty, some questions come naturally to mind for some, perhaps for you. You may wonder about evil's presence and its widespread occurrence and, at times, even its dominance in a universe created by a good God. Well, that is a fair question. And the answer comes in two ways.

First, for love to be possible, it must be freely chosen. Love cannot be compelled or forced. That is the nature of any relationship. Relationships between people require a choice. A relationship with God requires a choice too. But God is also perfect, and He cannot be in relationship when people do things that are deliberately wrong or evil. This is why the Church teaches us about two levels of sin: mortal sin and venial sin.

Mortal sin is not only serious. It is, well, mortal. It kills our relationship with God, thereby killing us spiritually and severely damaging our conscience. Mortal sin is clearly defined by the Church. Three components are required for a sin to be mortal. First, the sin must be a serious sin, not a small error. Second, the person committing this serious sin must have full knowledge of the sin, its seriousness, its import, its meaning. And lastly, this sin must be committed willingly and willfully. Serious matter, full knowledge, a deliberate act of will. That is what mortal sin is.

Makes sense, doesn't it? If it is a big thing, and you know full well it is, and you still do it intentionally, then it's a big deal.

In contrast, all other sins are venial, including serious sins that you do not freely choose to commit and serious sins about which you are invincibly ignorant. Venial sins damage our relationship with God, but they don't kill it.

Like mortal sins, repeated venial sins can destroy our consciences. This is why regular self-examination of our consciences is important. Such self-examination recognizes the existence and nature of moral standards and our need to keep them ever before our mind, so we may avoid sin and fix our mistakes fast, before they become habitual or overlooked.

Another significant moral question is the problem or question of suffering. This can trip people up, for they fault God for its presence. Some suffering comes from the misuse of free will, which can affect innocent people. Just think about a traffic jam caused by a bad judgment on the part of one driver. Many people are inconvenienced in such circumstances, even if there are no fatalities, even if it is a minor accident.

This is why Jesus exhorted His disciples to be the leaven, the salt, the light of the world. He recognized, as we all do, that human relationships and community can be for good or for ill. And our lives touch those of many others. Sometimes suffering comes from that human interrelatedness, that human proximity.

But not all suffering is of that type. Some suffering comes from following God. Jesus tells us that the world will treat us just as it treated Him. That's not always good news, for Jesus was mocked, scourged, and crucified. So, too, will we suffer as we try to live the life He invites us to live; so, too, will we be mocked as we try to be the leaven, the light, the salt of the earth.

Some suffering is necessary for our growth and development in the faith. Most growth requires some discomfort, some pain. "No pain, no gain" is a familiar adage; so, too, with our growth spiritually, personally.

And as we grow in our faith, we learn to surrender more of our will to God's plan and purpose. And that sometimes means disappointment, pain, suffering. Just look at the martyrs and think about the suffering they endured willingly to follow God's call. Or think about your parish priest. All priests must accept, endure, and invite the obligations of their vows of chastity and obedience (and often poverty); so, too, for women who become nuns.

And then there are the inherent parts of life that involve suffering. Death is the most obvious one. Losing a loved one or witnessing the deaths of strangers can challenge moral absolutes.

But death has no victory for the followers of Jesus, for the lovers of God. Jesus has triumphed over death for us, and though we will die in this world, we will live on eternally with Him, in God's very presence. For Jesus' triumph over death repairs the consequences of Original Sin—the sin Adam and Eve committed when they chose to disobey God willfully and deliberately.

So while death is a loss, it is a vast gain. Through death come eternal life, personal sanctification, the completion and perfection of our personality and character, and the restoration of a perfect loving relationship with God. So sometimes loss is gain. Sometimes pain is the path to fulfillment. Sometimes suffering is the stairway to the next level of development.

"Development," "maturity," "improvement," "sanctification," and "growth" are all words that recognize some inherent goal or model, some ideal or perfection. And that's no real news to us, though it is good news, because this movement toward the ideal, toward moral perfection, is the handiwork of God. It is a reflection, in us and in our daily lives, of His goodness, love, and perfection. That is a glimpse of God we all share.

We all know and share this vision to one degree or another. And where we may differ, we have the Church to inform or remind us of what the real truth is and what the real ideal looks like. For our distortions and understandings, whether they come from ignorance or willful disobedience, whether they come from error or acquired moral blindness, may all be corrected by the Church's clarity and morality, its truth and its love, its judgment and its mercy.

This is where we must turn to inform our moral vision and understanding. This is where we all must turn to remove the modern mists of moral relativism. This is where we all must turn to sharpen our focus and to steel our resolve. This is where the ideal and the model of moral righteousness burns the brightest, for this is where the radiant light of perfect love and perfect truth resides—not in the people who run the Church or in those who belong to it.

For this vision, this light is divine, not human. This vision of love and truth that Jesus gave us and embodied for us all to see in the practical daily struggle of human life and existence—this shows us what we are to do and how we are to act, who we are to be and for what we are to strive, what we are to think and what we must value.

This vision of perfection is brought to us with a clarity that would be searing, were it not so loving; that would be harsh, were it not so merciful; and that would be discouraging and depressing, were it not so kind and compassionate. This moral perfection combines the unmitigated clarity of truth and the unearned mercy and undeserved love of our Father in a way that can only be perfect and divine. And we can all see the essence of this, if not the details. That is why morality is not only evidence of God's existence and nature. It is also evidence of Jesus' nature and the nature and role of His Church.

Think about this. Think about the truth of morality, what it is and what it means. Think about the content of morality. Think about the judgment it requires. And think about this from the standpoint of perfection, of moral perfection and perfect judgment. Think about how moral truth and true love blend and blend perfectly; how judgment and mercy come together; how love does not change the truth and the truth does not ignore love. Think about all this, all these perfections. Think about how God has given us factual moral truth and perfect love as moral ideals, as ideals by which He wants us to live every day.

And pray. Ask God to help you grasp this moral vision and to accept it as evidence of His existence and character. Ask Him to use this to draw you nearer to Him. Ask Him for forgiveness for your sins. Ask Him to help you to understand and to live better.

For it is often through prayer that God draws nearest. In our silent adoration, in quiet moments of intimacy, and in liturgical celebrations, God speaks to us and embraces us as only a father could. But the only way to have this experience is to seek Him, to wait for Him, to listen for Him, to respond to Him. He wants to reveal Himself to you. For He is perfect love, and that is what perfect love does.

21

Matters of Spirituality

When it comes to religion, spirituality can sometimes appear a bit fuzzy next to the precision of philosophy and theology and the clarity and utility of doctrine and dogma. Spirituality often conjures up impressions of sentimentality, emotionality, and ecstasy. It usually entails a more poetic or literary description rather than the analysis and precision of these other disciplines. And some of those observations are certainly true, but only up to a point.

Just because spirituality does not lend itself so easily or directly to analysis and precision, it is no less significant to our human religious experience. It does not take a lesser place in religion, particularly in the sum and substance of the Catholic Faith.

And all of these elements that we group under the broad term "spirituality" may require a more descriptive approach, but this does not mean that analysis and concepts are not operative here. They are. And this descriptive, experiential, and emotional nature of spiritual things does not deprive them of any real content or substance. It is just that spirituality is a different, more personal part of our human nature, through which we come to learn about God, to know God, and to experience Him more directly and more personally.

And you will find that the Church and its spiritual masters have always offered many extensive, rigorous means and methods for deepening our spirituality, so that we may experience and know God personally.

This should not surprise us, even in our modern times. For the essence of theism, the fundamental and most crucial component that separates it from deistic notions, is that God is a being, a person. He is a knowable being, a near and active being. And the divine person of God, whose image we bear, consists not merely of a mind and truth, but of emotions and love.

This softer, more poetic, more descriptive, more emotional, more romantic side is what we will explore next as we look at spirituality. Along the way, we will touch on prayer and the spiritual disciplines, the proper understanding of spirituality within the Church, and how we can cultivate a better understanding of spirituality and its role in our lives, as we come to know, to follow, and to love God.

If we are called to love God, this call is more than a rational idea or a philosophical proposition. It is more than a structure of belief or a form of worship. For us, the created image-bearers of God, it is just as much a matter of our hearts as of our heads. It involves our emotions and our being, just as it involves our mind and our reason.

Knowledge

But let's use an example to bring these two aspects, these two approaches, together. For part of the problem with understanding and describing spirituality comes from some unspoken ideas about knowledge and being that the following example will clarify, though in an odd and counterintuitive way. This example will clarify the difference, not by making the distinction between spirituality and philosophy clearer but by blurring this distinction, by bringing these aspects together in their proper manner, by removing the differences and boundaries, by stressing the interplay and amalgamation of these dimensions in our typical human experience. Such is the nature of human beings, and such is the nature of truth and of love.

When I was a Protestant divinity student, I had to take a course in Greek as preparation for biblical study and exegesis. On the first day of class, the professor introduced the course and then began to teach us the Greek alphabet. On the second day of class, he opened his lecture with an odd question, given the course's content. After writing the word "knowledge" on the board in big letters, he asked us what the opposite of "knowledge" was.

Well, it didn't take long for the class to come to a quick and clear consensus. To a person, we pretty much all decided that the opposite of "knowledge" is "ignorance." Our reasoning was simple. If "knowledge" was to know something, then the opposite of that would be not knowing something, being ignorant. And so we concluded the opposite of "knowledge" was "ignorance."

Then the professor said, "Spoken like the children of the Greeks and Romans. But remember, St. Paul was a Hebrew. And he wrote most of the New Testament. And he spoke to a Greco-Roman world of the things of God. So, given that he was a Hebrew, what would be the opposite of knowledge to St. Paul? What would be the opposite of 'knowledge' to a Hebrew?"

We were perplexed, even stunned, that the professor would think to ask such a question. And the more we thought about it, the worse these initial reactions and impressions became. Small conversations broke out around the room as students conferred about this question and the ideas it raised. And the good professor let us discuss it a bit.

Then he began to prod us for an answer. And with less confidence and with a sense of exasperation, we told him we would give the same answer. We told him the opposite of "knowledge" to a Hebrew was "ignorance," just as it was to us, the children of the Greeks and the Romans.

Having heard our answer and noticed our tentative tone, he replied that we were wrong. He told us that the opposite of "knowledge" to a Hebrew wasn't "ignorance." It was "estrangement," "interpersonal distance," "rebellion." He even made reference to the sexual meaning of "knowledge": to "know" a woman, as we often see in the Bible, was to be sexually intimate with her.

Now, all this was riveting, for it raised many crucial questions and elicited many challenging yet enlightening ideas about knowledge, theology, philosophy, and spirituality, to say nothing of the divine nature and human nature, the presuppositions of our culture or any other culture.

Ten years later, in a study group in my doctoral program, I was using this example to illustrate a point to the group. As luck would have it, there was a rabbi in the group, who was also the principal of a Hebrew school. And when I came to the punchline about the opposite of "knowledge" in Hebrew culture, I didn't give the answer myself. I turned to the rabbi and said to him, "And the opposite of knowledge to a Hebrew is …" And this young rabbi said, "Estrangement, rebellion," just as my divinity professor had said ten years earlier.

So what's the point of all this? Well, there are many points, and they are all pretty profound. Let's take one that is fairly obvious. "Knowledge" to a Hebrew is never just about information or even ideas, particularly when it comes to God. Knowing God is knowing Him, not just knowing information *about* Him. Theology and philosophy are important sources of information about God, just as Scripture and doctrine are. But they are all incomplete, unless we come to know God through these fields of study. And knowing God as a person and in a personal way is just what loving God is all about. For that is the nature of love. And it is the nature of beings, both human and divine.

Think about it for a moment. When we send in a resume to apply for a job, we provide information about ourselves: what we do, what we know, our expertise and experience, our interests and our accomplishments. But all that is just an informational summary of our history and expertise. And if all our education and experience meet the demands of the job, we are summoned to an interview. Why? Because information is not enough to know a person. For this reason, most people are not offered jobs until they have an interview. People want to know potential employees in a fuller, more personal way before they hire them. The same thing applies to dating or friendship. Knowing *about* someone is not the same as *knowing* them. It is just that simple. And, particularly when it comes to God, it is just that profound.

All this applies even more so to knowing God. That is where spirituality comes in and where spirituality merges with philosophy and theology. For the Hebrew way of knowing never loses sight of the fuller context, of the holism inherent in relationships between beings, even between divine beings and human beings. And the Hebrew way never loses sight of the real essence of love.

In love, information and ideas have a place, but they are not the whole thing, the whole person. They are important things, but not everything.

We covered some of this in the previous chapter on morality and how God reveals Himself through morality in its fullness, in its justice and in its mercy, in its principles and in its complexities, in its order and in its essence. For to know Catholic morality is to know God, His mind and His heart and His very nature. And there is something very spiritual about this type of morality. There is something very personal and relational about morality of this type, about the very nature of Catholic morality.

As you may recall, mortal sins involve serious wrongs about serious things. But the end result of mortal sins is the breaking of the sinner's relationship with God, the loss of intimacy and personal connection with Him. And that loss leads to death, spiritual death, through our separation from God. And it even eventually leads to eternal separation after death, unless these sins are confessed and the relationship restored through our contrition and the sacrament of reconciliation.

One important implication of this holistic, interpersonal perspective is that it makes spirituality and even mysticism much more natural. For if we can only truly know God as God, this type of knowing must include more than just information about God. Knowing God must include a more direct, emotional, relational component that does not defy our minds, but informs our minds and fills our hearts. And that is just what Catholic spirituality is in its anticipated and expected form. That is just what it should be in its common form.

For even in the spiritual dimensions of human experience, we receive information. That is why spirituality is sometimes called a form of revelation. But it comes in a different way, through a different medium, and we experience it in a different way. Consider our different senses. We hear things. We see things. We smell them, we taste them, we touch them. And all the while, we may be applying our senses to the same thing. This happens every time we eat a sandwich (even though taste tends to dominate).

And integrating these various senses is such a common experience every day of our lives. We do not usually notice the operation and integration of our senses, unless there is some kind of imbalance that is not part of our common, everyday experience.

All our spiritual experience and the emphasis on relational knowing indicate that we may all expect a fairly rich spiritual life. And so we should, for the personal nature of God and His exhortation for us to love Him surely create not just a heightened expectation for regular and rich communion with God in our spiritual lives. It also makes such experience commonplace—or at least it should.

The Church has instituted the sacraments to provide regular avenues for spiritual experience. And the Church constantly reminds and exhorts all Catholics to pray regularly and to meditate, to listen to God and to contemplate His revealed nature and His particular revelation. It seems that the Church knows we can have a very rich daily experience of God's presence and nature if we but make ourselves available to Him and eagerly seek to be with Him.

This is why the Church, through its various ministries and publications, provides many forms of spiritual aids to assist us in our daily walk and in our daily relationship with God. For these many spiritual disciplines and aids help us to make God and our relationship with Him an inherent part of each of our waking hours.

And these same disciplines, though they order and structure our time and character, really are undertaken for the sole purpose of drawing nearer to God, learning more about Him, and living more intimately with Him.

Spiritual Error

Now, despite everything I've just said about knowing God spiritually, error and heresy can come through our spiritual senses, just as they can infiltrate our minds and our reason. So can deception, for the devil, the "opposer" of all things good and godly, often masquerades as an angel of light (see 2 Cor. 11:14). Such deception, however slight, can lead any of us into error. And when we discover these errors in discernment, they can lead us to blame God.

This is why Scripture warns us to be discerning and wise, and why it counts wisdom and the discernment of spirits as spiritual gifts (1 Cor. 12:4–11), particularly when it comes to the special particularities of our individual lives. This is why the Church requires that candidates for the priesthood and religious life spend many years in discernment, guided by a mentor, a spiritual director. The Church asks these men and women to ensure that religious life is really where God wants them to be.

This is why, if spirituality is taken up on its own, without the necessary integration we have heard so much about from the beginning of this book, personal spiritual experience can lead us all into forms of error or even heresy. And if individual spirituality is left without any form of spiritual direction or accountability to the dogma and doctrines of the Church, the possibility of mistakes becomes much more likely.

Why? Well, because without the safeguards of reason and doctrine, as well as Scripture and the authority of the Church, we are often prone to think our sensory experience is our primary source of truth. Without the help of a competent spiritual director, we are left to discern for ourselves the particular paths our lives will take. And we can come to think our personal spiritual experience is right, accurate, and true, despite what Church dogma tells us.

For some of us, it can get even worse. For in our modern world, some of us are even more prone to such error because of how we devalue reason and limit objective truth to the domain of physical science.

The modern tendency to lend undue credence to personal experience has an even greater effect when spiritual things are discussed, examined, and applied. Real, genuine spiritual things are experiences of profound metaphysical facts. But when people have intense personal experiences, they can sometimes interpret these personal experiences as facts in and of themselves. And that makes a big difference. For it tacitly leaves out the mental and reasoned senses and the essential necessity of integrating these aspects of life into our walk of faith. Excessively emphasizing spirituality makes truth a matter more of spiritual experience and less of logic and reason. This overemphasis on personal spiritual experience undermines the Church's dogma and doctrine by denying reason, Tradition, Scripture, and the Magisterium as the basis for truth. And this is sometimes evident in Catholics who have some form of intense spiritual experience or who have overemphasized the personal, relational, emotional, and spiritual aspects of the faith at the expense of its more rational and dogmatic dimensions.

All too often, people who have poorly integrated the many dimensions of the faith, or who have found their spiritual experiences so compelling, are reluctant to listen to and to learn from philosophical, theological, moral, and ecclesial truth. Many are not easily taught or disciplined, because their personal spiritual experience has become the final bottom line of truth and morality and faith for them. Inadvertently, even unconsciously, they become their own best authority on things religious or spiritual. Left unchecked, that tendency makes error and even heresy almost unavoidable, even for the disciplined and the strong-willed.

So be open to God and a spiritual experience of Him, but remember that the Hebrew way of knowing is an integrated one. It does not say that all knowledge is spiritual. It is not, just as God tells us, for God asks that we love Him with all our mind, all our strength, all our soul. He reminds us to know Him, to love Him, to learn from Him, and to live for Him using all the many faculties and senses He has provided for just those purposes. Just as Jesus said, knowing God and loving God takes all facets of our being—the same being God created.

Summary Exhortations

Have you noticed that I have closed every chapter with some encouragement to think and to pray, to reflect on the preceding material and to talk with God about it? To seek the truth and to seek to know God, to ask Him to show Himself to you?

Well, all these exhortations were designed to break down the barriers between our minds and our senses, between our emotions and our reason, between our intuitions and our analyses. These barriers were not to be broken down because I wanted you to lessen your experience of each. I wanted and still want you to integrate these human aspects and facets, not blend them such that they become unrecognizable.

They are to be brought together harmoniously, just as our various senses are integrated into a seamless, natural flow. Now, that does not mean that we may not have to concentrate intensely on some aspect or dimension from time to time in order to grow and to grasp part of God and His teaching. But the final goal is always more than just a better mental picture. The goal is for integration to become natural. We seek a rich, harmonious fusion of all our human dimensions, so we may love God with all our mind, all our soul, and all our strength in the fullest, most synergistic sense.

Loving God is the most comprehensive goal. It is more than a goal. It is the sum and substance of what life is all about, why we are here in the first place. Loving God means knowing Him, intimately and in detail. And this is why the truth and love are really one and the same. They may differ in emphasis, but this difference is more a function of our human limitedness than a function of the nature of God. It is a function of what happens when our human limitedness and finite nature try to comprehend God's perfection and nature. This is why the Church often encourages us to incorporate contemplation into our spiritual lives.

Contemplation invites us to dwell on particular aspects of the faith, and it also stresses the integration of our insights. Here, you can see how contemplative thought is a critical aspect of spirituality and a spiritual discipline in itself. And you can see how contemplation is focused on getting into the depths of things, as well as getting things back together, once a new insight or sense of God is discovered and explored.

And when we bring them together, the first, last, and continual goal is to know God in the Hebrew sense and to live as He has ordained: in a loving, relational obedience, permeated by love and truth with each and every person we know and encounter. This is a tall order, a vision whose fulfillment lies far beyond our flawed and imperfect human nature. But we become much more capable when we know the truth and when we know God personally, intimately, spiritually. And this is what the Hebrew understanding of knowledge reminds us of, in a most incisive and integrating way.

Spirituality is not a personality trait, a goal in and of itself. We are not to strive to be spiritual. We are not seeking to have ecstatic events of deep emotional significance. Rather, we are regularly and relentlessly seeking God, just as Jesus encouraged us to do two thousand years ago.

Remember, Jesus prayed regularly. And He bids us to pray too. He tells us to share our troubles and concerns with God, to petition Him, to thank Him, and to praise Him for His many blessings, including life itself. He encourages us to bring our shortcomings and sins to Him with contrite, humble hearts in times of prayer as well as in the sacrament of reconciliation.

And when such wondrous experiences come, they are not the end in themselves. For God is the end, the goal, the sum, and the substance. He is the beginning and the end, the alpha and the omega, the first and the last. For He is our Father, our Daddy. We will find home only when we find the Father. We will live in His embrace only when we take steps to be with Him.

That is why we are to use the spiritual disciplines to know God in a detailed, comprehensive sense. We are to become spiritually sensitive by spending time with God, by praying to Him, by worshipping Him through the sacraments, by performing acts of love and mercy and kindness, by loving our fellow image bearers. We are to learn our faith and live our faith.

This is why we use metaphors to communicate this comprehensive perspective. This why we are to use our heads, our hearts, our hands, our bodies, our souls, our spirits. This is why no facet or feature of the human experience escapes the concern and care of God. This is why He loves us as His children and His heirs.

And His legacy to us is meant to be experienced and lived in the here and now, not just in eternity. Our inheritance is more than eternal life. It is eternal life in our temporal lives. It is the eternal kingdom of our Father in the here and now. God promises this to us. And His promise, when He gives it, is not a human promise. It is a fact. You can take it to your heart, to your mind, to your soul, with serene certainty. We can know that because He loves us perfectly and completely. And it is to love we now turn. For this is where all things reach their true perfection—where truth is situated in its proper relational context, where the comprehensive and integrated Hebrew idea of knowledge-as-relationship finds its truest expression.

So let's turn to love and explore it in its fullness, for this is the end of our calling and the hope of our Father. And out of love Jesus came and suffered so we "might have life and have it more abundantly" (John 10:10).

Love is the one virtue we take into eternity. Faith is necessary only here on earth, in this temporal life we lead. And hope has meaning only before we reach heaven, for it is an attitude of anticipation of our eternal life and our intimate relationship with God face-to-face. But love endures from here to eternity. That is why it is the greatest of all virtues. So let's see what love really is, what love truly does, what love's very nature is.

22

The Heart of All Matters

There is an internal and inherent coherence to the Catholic Faith. Things hang together in an organic unity, in a synergistic flow. Our minds and our hearts, our intentions and our actions, our morality and our spirituality, our philosophy and our theology all are knit together in a seamless, functional unity, in a harmonic complementarity, in a symphony of truth and love—at least in those moments when we get it right.

Our minds, our spirits, and our bodies work together to know, to love, and to serve God in the Hebrew sense, which reminds us that knowing God is never about mere information, and serving God is never about dutiful compliance. This foundational and relational reality means that knowing and serving God are always about love: our love for the God whom we know about, the God whom we care for, the God whom we live for. And that is the ideal, the template, the goal, and the hope for all of us.

We serve God out of our love for Him and through His love for us; for our love for God is really but a dim reflection, a faint echo of His love for us, and love is His gift to us. When we experience love as God intends and when we pursue it in the right ways, we all recognize the wonder and thrill of love. Whether it is romantic or altruistic, parental or familial, or any of the many kinds of love we experience every day, love is amazing, wonderful, and touching, though sometimes it can seem in short supply. Whether it is the exhilaration and warmth of love's emotion, the security and certainty of its promise, the generosity and beauty of its actions, love is amazing, even when it comes from and with and through people who are imperfect and inconsistent.

Yet in these experiences of love, we know and experience a significant artifact of God's existence, a direct reflection of God's nature, the essence of God's plan, for love is more than our biochemical activity, despite what the scientific materialists implicitly or explicitly insist. It is more than some ancient adaptive mechanism acquired through the mindless mechanics of survival, as the evolutionary biologists and anthropologists tell us. It is more than mere emotion or mental sensation, as the psychologists seem to say it is.

It is a sensation, for sure, because we are experiencing it. But it is so much more than mere sensation, because our sensations of love all have content, substance, and significance. And as anyone who has ever experienced love will tell you, this is the promise of love, the purpose of love, the plan of love. And these things all give us a strong sense of love's inherent beauty, order, purpose, and perfection. For real and true love, no matter how transitory its manifestations and sensations are, is perfection in its essence.

Love and Divine Perfection

This perfection is a piercing look at the very nature of God, for God is love. And love speaks loudly about what perfection is, just as reason speaks about truth. These impressions of perfection show us love's source, for God is the source of everything, the source of every perfection.

God's love is perfect, as perfect as He is. His love is founded on and grounded in His perfection. Love, when it is right, is always a glimpse, a hint, an echo of perfection. And in those moments of love's high emotion, we experience love's promise. In those times of love's deep insight, we know love's profundity. In those moments of love's action, we live the life love shows us.

God's perfection is really the only perfection there is. Even when we do act perfectly, this is a fleeting thing, a passing moment, a narrow event. These actions are remarkable, because they are so unique and solitary in the broader context of our all-too-typical human frailty and failure.

When God requites our feeble and flawed love with His, the divine love we receive is perfect in all its facets and features, for God is perfect in the only way perfection may be realized. He is perfect in a consummate, complete, and holistic manner. He is perfect everywhere, in every form and dimension, all at once and without end or beginning, for true perfection is really perfection in all things at once and at all times. And our Father loves each of us with a perfect love, the only truly perfect love there is: His perfect love.

Because we are flawed and imperfect, not only do we love Him imperfectly, but our imperfections sometimes get in the way of our knowing and experiencing His love. His love is always what true and perfect love is: indefatigable, incomprehensible, immeasurable in its depth and its breadth. His love is not the love we have for one another. He loves us as love is meant to be, as love promises to be, as love can only truly be—without end or degree, perfect in all its ways.

And all we have to do is to accept His love, willingly and freely. And having made this pledge of faith to love God, we must strive to renew this promise and to let God guide us and help us to become the salt and light of the world, the disciples and saints of the ages, His sons and daughters. But we must choose, and choose regularly, to be the followers of Christ, for love is always a decision for us.

We must decide daily to love God and to follow Him. Through our regular choices, our daily decisions, we build our relationship with God. By requiting His love, we respond to His invitation to follow Him and to love Him in return. And as we respond to Him lovingly and passionately, willingly and joyfully, we let Him shape us. We let Him use us. We let Him love us as a Father.

Our Walk of Love

God is preparing us and molding us to redeem us from our flawed state and our worldly nature, and to save us from our iniquity, so that we may walk through this world in communion with Him in an intimate, personal, objectively factual way, just as a son or a daughter would.

For the walk of faith is a walk of enlightenment, of exhilaration, of transformation. It is not a death march of denial and deferred gratification, as many of the world's religions believe and as many opponents of the Catholic faith misunderstand. We should walk with a gentle, jaunty step through our life, as though we were truly walking with God. For we are. Our metaphoric faith walk through life should therefore not be the plodding gait of drudgery or the mindless and mirthless march of the driven.

At its core, the Catholic faith is a faith of exhilarating and irresistible love: love for God and love for others, no matter how sinful or flawed, no matter how things are or seem. Love, in its perfection and its true manifestations, is not only an emotion, a motivation, a truth. It is not just a state of mind. Our love is a love of action just as much as it is a love of attitude and emotion. For love feels and does; it empathizes and acts. It hopes, it heals, it helps. It desires and it disciplines; it sacrifices and it gives; it pleases and it rebukes. Love does what is right and good and true.

Love and truth are not opposed to one another, but are in harmony, for the Catholic faith is the truth about life and living. But it is not the cold, sterile truth of academic philosophy and raw fact, for at the very depth of truth, we do not find a universe of mere facts and principles, as secular science would lead us to believe. At the very core and center of the universe, there is the person, the being of God. He is there. Just as the Scriptures tell us, "God is love" (1 John 4:16). That is the truth—not *a* truth, not *one* truth. That is the summary and comprehensive truth.

But that does not mean that love is God. For that idea is an inversion that distorts love and tends to deny God. God is God, and His nature is love, love in its fullest sense. God is love, and that means love is God's very nature: a love that is emotion, but more than emotion; a love that is the truth and is, by its very nature, the expression of all truth and all beauty, all moral perfection and all righteousness, all justice and mercy.

The love that is God's nature is a holistic, integrated, harmonious whole. Here we find love in its fullness and perfection. Here the distinctions we make between love and truth exist as a unified oneness, for the love that is God's nature is perfect and does not entail the apparent differentiation we so often struggle with when we think about truth and love. Truth and love are one in the nature of God.

Jesus

And it is to this comprehensive and perfect love that we now turn. For God showed us the manifestation of true and perfect love in the life and death of Jesus, as taught by the Church from its very beginning and as recounted in the Gospels. Jesus said to His followers then, as He says to us now, "This is how all will know that you are my disciples, if you have love for one another" (John 13:35). He instructed us, "Love one another as I love you" (John 15:12).

Jesus' presence on earth with us and His mission to mankind are proof positive of God's love. Before the beginning of time, God knew that the men and women He created would fall into error and sin, would lose their way and corrupt themselves. And their willful deviance from moral goodness and purity necessitated justice, for mistakes need correction and consequences, as any three-year-old can tell you.

But the justice we deserve for our deliberate mistakes and for our habitual sins would leave each of us beaten, broken, dead. When we are judged according to the standards of perfection, our just punishment would be more than even the best of us could bear: our complete estrangement from God. Our estrangement comes from our tacit or explicit rejection of God and His laws, which arise from His very being, His very essence. The degree of our estrangement, in light of our error and sin, would be too vast, too great for us to overcome, even if we could muster the will to restore our relationship. Our sins would leave us too distant from God, and our inconsistent nature would prevent us from making much headway in restoring our relationship with Him. The distance and degree of our estrangement from God is beyond our capacity to rectify, unless God moves closer to us.

And that is just what He did, for that is what love does. His love is perfect love, which affirms and balances the obvious moral standards with the moral demands of mercy and forgiveness, compassion and empathy, sacrificial fatherhood and sympathetic brotherhood.

So God made a way for us to come home to Him, just as any father might do, and certainly as a perfect Father would. I mean, what father whose son or daughter was to be sent to jail or to the gallows would not seek through all legal means to have the sentence reduced, especially when that sentence was death? What father wouldn't plead for mercy for his child? Some fathers might even be willing to serve the sentence, if such an option was open to them.

Well, that is just what God did. He willingly paid the price for us, so we might be forgiven for our sins and so we might learn to do better. He did so for all of us. Our sins are forgiven—forgiven, not set aside. For perfect justice tells us that our sins deserve some punishment in proportion to our sin, its gravity and frequency, and our knowledge and intent; and the necessary punishment for the sins of mankind has been paid already by the very Son of God, Jesus of Nazareth, as we explained earlier. He came here for this purpose, to fulfill the demands of perfect justice by offering the perfect sacrifice in an act of perfect love. As Jesus said, "No one has greater love than this, to lay down one's life for one's friends" (John 15:13). Well, if Jesus' self-sacrifice isn't perfect love, I don't know what is. To give one's life in a single act of mortal self-sacrifice is the consummation of love and courage. It is the height of human goodness.

And similarly, sacrificing our lives in small ways, in daily self-denial for the good of others, is also a loving devotion we all can recognize. Mother (now St.) Teresa of Calcutta comes to mind here. Maybe you can think of another saint, an exemplary parish priest, or a holy member of your family whose love is remarkable for its consistency and the depth and range of the person's actions.

Well, Jesus offered Himself in big and small ways. He came to live among us by taking on our humanity. And He shared in every struggle and pain of human life, even unto death. As if that weren't enough, He patiently taught us, so we all might understand better and live better. He instructed us so we all might draw closer to God and to each other in a bond of real love, not merely a cordial and polite relationship of mutual self-interest.

Having lived as one of us and having taught us during His public life, He died so all our sins would be removed and our relationship with God restored. And because He knew we would not be able to remain pure before God, He gave us the means by which we can continually restore and maintain our intimacy with Him: the sacraments and the Body of Christ, the Church He founded.

Because Christ performed this consummate act of love, He allowed us to live with a level of truth, founded in complete perfection, without becoming discouraged or desperate. For the level of truth God holds before us could break us, were it not for the perfection of love. The warm light of perfect love makes the clear light of truth all the clearer and all the sharper, for love is truth and truth is love. They are the two sides of one reality.

This is why we often misunderstand Jesus and distort His teachings. By skewing things out of proportion, we undermine the unity of truth and love.

Perhaps an example will clarify. We know Jesus spoke about forgiveness and compassion and cautioned us about some types of judgment. Yet He died for our sins, which was necessary for perfect justice, by which our sins were judged rightly and completely, without prejudice and without bias. Or another example: sometimes, we think of Jesus as the Prince of Peace. Indeed He is. Yet He tells us directly, "Do not think that I have come to bring peace upon the earth. I have come to bring not peace but the sword. For I have come to set a man against his father and a daughter against her mother, a daughter-in-law against her mother-in-law; and one's enemies will be those of his household" (Matt. 10:34–36). He tells us He wants everyone to come to Him, while also saying that "no one comes to the Father except through me" (John 14:6).

So here we see the potential for fractures in the harmony of truth and love. Jesus' behavior and His teaching, however, always affirm a harmonic unity, a perfect blend between truth and what we call love. But love is never love without actual content, without moral purity, without truth. For God's idea of love is love in its fullest sense, in its harmonic sense, where truth and love are merged in a manner that defies any separation. Yet they do not lose their distinctiveness.

For real love is like the Trinity, three persons in one God. They are different, but they are one. Marriage is much the same. It is a oneness, a unity without any loss of individuality. The same goes for truth and love. There is a oneness but a distinction. And understanding this prevents most of us from getting things skewed or distorted to any great degree.

This is why we struggle to understand what love is, for we think and hear this word in a narrower sense than Jesus and the Church intend. Love does not come at the expense of truth or justice or judgment. This is why we can hate the sin, yet love the sinner. This is why Jesus says some startling and remarkable things. They startle us because we do not have a full understanding of what love is, what love means. And that is one of the major things Jesus came to teach us and to show us. And it is also His hope for us.

Jesus calls us all to perfection. Even today, He says to us, "So be perfect, just as your heavenly Father is perfect" (Matt. 5:48). But in the Lord's Prayer, the Our Father, He taught us to ask God to "forgive us our trespasses as we forgive those who trespass against us." St. Paul reminds us to "be kind to one another, compassionate, forgiving one another as God has forgiven you in Christ" (Eph. 4:32).

Jesus also tells the people of His time that they are an "evil and unfaithful generation" (Matt. 16:4). By "unfaithful" He means they are morally corrupt and follow other gods, including themselves. Following other gods is against the commandments. But in the Hebrew sense of knowing and in a Catholic sense of love, following false gods is a breach of intimate relationship. So He uses the language of love and commitment by calling their religious error "unfaithful." Other translations translate this as "adulterous" to convey the relational sense of being unfaithful.

In Jesus' teachings, there are words of encouragement and comfort and also words of rebuke and discipline. There are words of compassion and words of correction, words of hope and words of threat over the inevitability of God's judgment.

All of these apparent opposites are not really opposites. They are different dimensions of love, for truth is love, just as perfection is. Judgment, when it is righteous, is also love, just as mercy is. Compassion and kindness are love, just as discipline and correction are. What parent does not correct his child, threaten his child, forewarn his child, embrace his child, forgive his child, encourage his child, inspire his child? In much the same way, what husband or wife does not correct as well as comfort his or her spouse? And what true friend does not do the same?

Well, as Jesus said, "If you then, who are wicked, know how to give good gifts to your children, how much more will your heavenly Father, give good things to those who ask him" (Luke 7:11).

So don't stumble over this distinction between truth and love. This is the truth: love is always truth, and truth is always love. God's nature is clear, though not always easy to grasp or comprehend fully. But we can get it well enough to live by, and we can get it better the longer we persevere.

Know that love does not come at the expense of truth, and truth does not come at the expense of love. They are a oneness, a unity, a harmony of God's nature and part of His plan.

Love Is . . .

Let's look at one final example to illustrate this oneness. In his first letter to the Corinthian Church, Paul offered the following description of love:

> Love is patient, love is kind. It is not jealous, it is not pompous, it is not inflated, it is not rude, it does not seek its own interests, it is not quick-tempered, it does not brood over injury, it does not rejoice over wrongdoing but rejoices with

> the truth. It bears all things, believes all things, hopes all things, endures all things. Love never fails. (1 Cor. 13:4–8).

Inspiring and resonant words, but let's look a bit closer. If we are impatient, are we wrong? Yes. If we are jealous, inflated, rude, selfish, and quick-tempered, have we done something wrong? Yes. If we brood about injury and rejoice over wrongdoing, is that love? If we don't rejoice with the truth, is that love? No. Failing the standards of love is wrong. And we know this for certain as we think about our failings and our loved ones' failings, despite the fact that they do love us. They love us, but they get things wrong, sometimes even intentionally.

And so when we get love wrong, even by degree, we have done something wrong. And love is the standard, a moral standard, a transcendent standard for all times and all places and people. Can you see the oneness here that does not pit love against the truth? They are a unified whole, working together in an inherent, natural way.

The apparent conflict between them is just that: an apparent conflict, not a real one—apparent because our modern idea of love is distorted and limited compared with God's and the Church's understanding of love.

St. Paul also makes this point in the passages just before and just after his definition of love. He reminds the Corinthians how they can distort the harmonic idea of love by pitting knowledge and spirituality against a narrow definition of love. He says to the Corinthians:

> Strive eagerly for the greatest spiritual gifts. But I shall show you a more excellent way. If I speak in human and angelic tongues, but do not have love, I am a resounding gong and a clashing cymbal. And if I have the gift of prophecy and comprehend all mysteries and all knowledge; if I have all

> faith so as to move mountains, but do not have love, I am nothing. If I give away everything I own, and if I hand my body over so that I may boast but do not have love, I gain nothing. (1 Cor. 12:31—13:4)

St. Paul adds, "If there are prophecies, they will be brought to nothing; if tongues, they will cease; if knowledge, it will be brought to nothing. For we know partially and we prophesy partially, but when the perfect comes the partial will pass away" (1 Cor. 13:8–10).

Here we see the distortions of love arising from those who have taken an undue interest in spiritual gifts and thus missed the abiding reality of love. Here knowledge and faith, generosity and self-sacrifice are also labeled as nothing, if love is not their abiding reason, mission, and purpose. For love is the means by which these aspects and experiences are knit together in a proper and godly way. Emphases and distortions lead away from love and eventuate in "nothing." So St. Paul lovingly but clearly corrects them as only he can do, as only love should.

If you think about it, love is the only path to perfection or even improvement, for love hopes and encourages just as much as it makes clear the goal and corrects us when we deviate or miss the mark. Love hopes, and hope is a function of improvement. It points to the ideal, the perfect, the true, the truly good, and it recognizes that we are not there yet. Our hope is realized when we get better, when we meet perfection in the moment and in degree.

The Consummate Proof of God

This is why love is the heart of all matters, the consummation of all things, the very essence of God. God's love is a love that harmonizes all virtue without denying it and without diminishing virtuous perfection to even the minutest degree. The heart of all matters is love, for it is, perhaps, the most visible and visceral of all the evidence for God. It proves that He exists and shows His nature, His character, His heart, His mind. Love, in its holistic and harmonic perfection, is outside the merely physical explanations that materialists offer. Love is knowable and experienced even by agnostics.

And the nature of love itself defies other religious claims of truth and morality, for the love evident in the presence and purpose, the character and the content, of Christ goes far beyond other religious ideas and theologies, beyond pantheism and polytheism, beyond other theistic faiths. No other God came to earth and died for us as an act of pure love, as an act of pure justice, so that we, too, might love Him.

This purity of love we know well. It is familiar, not obscure. It is not some form of private spirituality or ancient revelation. It is proof positive of God's existence. Proof of His nature. Proof of Christ's claim and the covenant He established on the cross. It is also love's vindication, for Jesus' resurrection is the triumph of love in the fullest sense of love and triumph. Love has won the battle with evil in the only way love can. Love's victory leaves us a free choice and creates a way to restore our intimacy with God. Love's victory affirms the truth and the beauty of perfection and invites us to follow this path. But love does not impose its hope, for love must be chosen, entered willingly and joyfully. In this, the claims of Christianity are unique, and our choice clear.

Questions of God's existence and His will cease when we enter eternity, and love will remain. It is all we will take with us. That is just as it should be, for as anyone with even half a heart knows, the greatest thing about life is love.

Love is the essence and substance of life. It is the height and depth of living. It is the thing we most need and desire. And this, the best thing in life, comes with us. And the best thing in life shows us God is there—that He is, that He loves. Our reason and our science, our intuitions and our common sense all confirm that God is there and that He is not silent. He is not passive, distant, disinterested; He is active and involved, intimate and immanent.

Because of love, we can know that all these other ways of knowing about God are just further evidence and greater confirmation of His existence and His nature. We know that He is there and can be known intimately, personally, passionately, joyfully, lovingly. We know that He is there and He wants to be known by us through all of our human faculties. We know that He is there and that He wants us to love everyone else in just the same way He loves us. We know He wants us to be and to do all these loving, virtuous things for Him, for others, and for ourselves. And He wants us to know that He is standing right with us each and every moment, each and every day, until we join Him and the rest of the redeemed in the kingdom of God: a kingdom of love, joy, peace, and perfection for the rest of time.

So think long and hard. And not just in a reasoned or logical manner. Look to your intuitions and common sense. Look at the practicalities of life closely and clearly. And look to the heart of all things. Look within your heart and ponder the evidence and reality of love. Ponder the perfections of love and its intimate and inherent link to moral perfection and truth.

See how everything goes together in an ideal, perfect sense. And think about how this sense of perfection must come from God and be God. See how all this interrelated evidence and all the practical, personal human experiences of our love, our mind, our perfection, our justice, our mercy, our vices, and our errors show us God to one degree or another. And see how God became one of us because He loves us. See how God died for us because He loves us. See how God rose from the dead to ensure and to show us that our hope is real and our triumph and reward certain.

See how all this is not a myth, a fiction, a fantasy, a delusion. See how this is all grounded in reason and science, in history and in the practical experience of living in this fallen and flawed world. See how love and truth are ours for the asking, for the choosing, for the taking. See all this and pray.

Pray in your own words. Talk to God as your Father, your Daddy. Ask Him to help you to see Him. Ask Him to show Himself to you. Ask Him to help you know in your mind. And ask Him to soften your heart, so you can know and see love more clearly and Him more certainly, more nearly, more actively.

This is what God wants. He wants to love you. And He wants you to know this. He doesn't want robotic obedience or disgruntled denial. He wants to show His love to you. For you are His son or daughter, His heir, His offspring. And He wants you to come home to Him, no matter how bad you've been, no matter how bruised and beaten you feel.

He calls you in the fullest sense of love: "Come to me, all you who labor and are burdened, and I will give you rest. Take my yoke upon you and learn from me, for I am meek and humble of heart, and you will find rest for yourselves. For my yoke is easy, and my burden light" (Matt. 11:28–30).

He wants you to come to find this love and truth in the company of others, in the Church Jesus started. For here is where the fullness of truth resides, where the fullest love is taught. Here is where the divinely ordained sacraments are brought to the faithful, even though they are administered by fallen people, just like you and me.

Come home to God as His prodigal child. Do not hesitate for fear or shame. That is why Jesus taught the parable of the prodigal son.[6] He wanted us to know the heart of the Father. He wanted us

[6] The parable of the prodigal son is third in a series of three parables: the lost sheep (Luke 15:1–7), the lost coin (Luke 15:8–10), and the

to know how God's heart responds when we come home to Him because we were lost or confused, because we didn't know Him, because we were wayward in our thinking and our living.

In the parable of the prodigal son, the father is watching for his son, hoping for his return. And when the father sees his son in the distance, he runs to him and embraces him and kisses him, for the son who was lost is found; the son who left home has returned; the son who disobeyed the moral laws and severed his relational ties has come back to the father and the family. And despite all these moral and relational errors, the father's love for the son has been constant and hopeful. That is why the father, overjoyed by his son's return, does not wait or hesitate; he does not want an explanation or even an apology. The father's love for the lost son is all that matters. This is the love of our Father for each and every one of us. For we have all been prodigal children.

And remember, when you return to the Catholic Church, it doesn't mean you'll find perfection. The Church is full of fallen and flawed people just like you and me. But God, the perfect one, is there to comfort and to care for us all, to teach and to encourage us, to love and watch over each and every one of us, each and every day. He wants us to return to Him and His Church with a conscious and deliberate decision, with an informed choice. Most importantly, He wants us to return with a sincere heart and with commitment, which you will work out and work on each and every day of the life God grants you.

So come. Come home to our Father, our Daddy. Don't delay, for the future is upon you. And the Father, the maker of all things, the pure and perfect embodiment of love, is waiting and watching

---

lost son (Luke 15:11–32). These parables serve to illustrate the heart of our Father, who ceaselessly searches for us and rejoices when we return.

for you. He hopes that you will come home to Him. For He has prepared a place just for you, a place in the family, a place for now, and a place forever.

About the Author

As a reverted Roman Catholic, F. X. Cronin thought and lived as an existential atheist, a deist, and an evangelical Protestant before returning to the one true Church in 2007. While his faith in Jesus Christ is thirty years old, his return to the Catholic Church completed his search for the God of the Scriptures and of history and gave him a new and vast treasury of knowledge and spirituality to explore and to share.

As a Protestant, Cronin spoke locally and regionally on many topics, including apologetics, parenting, marriage, media, culture, and the educational imperatives for Christian children. He also conducted Bible studies, Sunday school classes, and lectures on philosophy and modern Christian apologists.

He has studied on a graduate level in philosophy and education at Harvard University; in educational psychology at the University of Connecticut; in organization and leadership at Columbia University's doctoral program in New York City and the University of Connecticut; and in theology at Regent University and Holy Apostles College and Seminary.

He has published articles for the *National Catholic Register* and appeared on an hour-long interview on EWTN's *The Journey Home* with Marcus Grodi.

Professionally, he has worked as an educational administrator, an educational consultant, a teacher, and a counselor for thirty five years. He has taught at all levels, including as a graduate adjunct professor at the University of Connecticut and at Aquinas College in Nashville, Tennessee. He also taught as an elementary homeschooling father for two years.

He is the proud husband of his wife, Annie, who is a speech pathologist and the main reason he is a Christian today. He is also the proud father of three daughters and the grandfather of four granddaughters.

At a crucial point in his life, he decided to find out firsthand how God could direct his life. He discovered that the more enthusiastically and seriously he sought God, the more God was willing to show him what to do.

Since this pivotal time, God put him on a steep learning curve of graduate education and an exhilarating and challenging walk of faith. He gave him a calling to awaken the slumbering to an intimate relationship with God and the breadth and depth of real discipleship. And He called him to teach the imperative for Catholic education for every Catholic child; the necessity of a godly home and marriage; the truth of a sound, sophisticated, and certain worldview; and the joy and challenge of a rich, faith-filled life as a disciple of Christ and a child of God.

Sophia Institute

Sophia Institute is a nonprofit institution that seeks to nurture the spiritual, moral, and cultural life of souls and to spread the Gospel of Christ in conformity with the authentic teachings of the Roman Catholic Church.

Sophia Institute Press fulfills this mission by offering translations, reprints, and new publications that afford readers a rich source of the enduring wisdom of mankind.

Sophia Institute also operates the popular online resource CatholicExchange.com. *Catholic Exchange* provides world news from a Catholic perspective as well as daily devotionals and articles that will help readers to grow in holiness and live a life consistent with the teachings of the Church.

In 2013, Sophia Institute launched Sophia Institute for Teachers to renew and rebuild Catholic culture through service to Catholic education. With the goal of nurturing the spiritual, moral, and cultural life of souls, and an abiding respect for the role and work of teachers, we strive to provide materials and programs that are at once enlightening to the mind and ennobling to the heart; faithful and complete, as well as useful and practical.

Sophia Institute gratefully recognizes the Solidarity Association for preserving and encouraging the growth of our apostolate over the course of many years. Without their generous and timely support, this book would not be in your hands.

www.SophiaInstitute.com
www.CatholicExchange.com
www.SophiaInstituteforTeachers.org

Sophia Institute Press® is a registered trademark of Sophia Institute.
Sophia Institute is a tax-exempt institution as defined by the
Internal Revenue Code, Section 501(c)(3). Tax ID 22-2548708.